URBAN UTOPIAS
IN
THE TWENTIETH
CENTURY

URBAN UTOPIAS IN THE TWENTIETH CENTURY

Ebenezer Howard, Frank Lloyd Wright, and Le Corbusier

ROBERT FISHMAN

The MIT Press
Cambridge, Massachusetts
London, England

Fifth printing, 1994

First MIT Press paperback edition, 1982

The plans, drawings, and writings of Frank Lloyd Wright are reprinted by permission of the Frank Lloyd Wright Foundation and Horizon Press, Inc. Copyright © by the Frank Lloyd Wright Foundation.

The plans and drawings of Le Corbusier are reproduced by permission of La Fondation Le Corbusier, André Wogenscky, President, Paris, France.

Portions of this book have appeared in Russell Walden, ed., *The Open Hand: Essays on Le Corbusier* (Cambridge, Mass.: MIT Press, 1977).

Library of Congress Cataloging in Publication Data

Fishman, Robert, 1946–
   Urban utopias in the twentieth century.

   Bibliography: p.
   Includes index.
   1. Cities and towns. 2. City planning. 3. Howard, Ebenezer, Sir, 1850–1928. 4. Wright, Frank Lloyd, 1867–1959. 5. Le Corbusier, 1887–1965.
I. Title.
HT161.F57 1982   307.7'6   82-15254
ISBN 0-262-56023-2 (pbk.)   AACR2

To My Parents

CONTENTS

Contents

III

Le Corbusier

PREFACE

IN the seven years since I began this book, my imagination has been inspired by beautiful details of utopian cities while the real cities where I lived have steadily deteriorated. Inside the archives and libraries I found magnificent plans for new forms of housing, business centers, parks, and transportation systems. Outside I could not ignore the growing physical blight, social conflict, economic bankruptcy, and—what is perhaps worse than all these—the fear that we lack the knowledge and resources to find a solution. I often felt as superfluous as the man in Bertolt Brecht's parable who painstakingly adorned the walls of his stateroom with beautiful murals while the ship was going down.

Brecht's sardonic image might also seem to apply to the three planners who are the subjects of this book. Ebenezer Howard, Frank Lloyd Wright, and Le Corbusier responded to social conditions which were, in many respects, worse than our own by detaching themselves from immediate action to devote thousands of hours to their urban utopias. But detachment is not necessarily escapism; for the three planners believed that before they could take effective action they had to stage a strategic withdrawal into their own minds. They wanted to escape from the inevitable limitations of short-term solutions devised for particular cities. Instead, they tried to consider the urban problem as a whole. They wanted to comprehend the logic of the twentieth-century city, its inherent structure, and its most efficient form. They attempted to look beyond the distortions that an inhumane social order had imposed upon the cities of their time, and to envision a city based on social justice and equality. They sought, finally, to discover what Le Corbusier called the "rules of the game": the interrelated revolutionary changes in urban design, politics, and economics which must take place if real solutions were ever to be found.

Howard, Wright, and Le Corbusier chose to present their theories not in dry formulas but through three-dimensional models of their total approach—the ideal city for the twentieth century. Planned with both urban reconstruction and social revolution in mind, the three ideal cities were certainly "utopias," but not in the pejorative sense of being vague, impossible dreams. Rather, they come under Karl Mannheim's classic definition of utopia as a coherent program for action arising out of thought that "transcends the immediate situation," a program whose realization would "break the bonds" of the established society.

After decades of controversy, experimentation, and partial realization, the three ideal cities have found a place in the practice (and the collective unconscious) of the planning profession. The utopian aims that originally inspired them, however, have been either forgotten or discarded. My aim in this book is not to argue for one (or all three) of the plans. I have tried instead to recapture the historical context—the political movements and the climate of ideas—from which the three ideal cities first emerged; to connect the three planners' innovations in urban design with the revolutionary goals these innovations were intended to achieve; and thus to restore to the ideal cities the unity of architectural form and social content they once possessed. I have also attempted to understand the personalities and motivations of the three planners. What were the sources of the imagination, will, and energy that led Howard, Wright, and Le Corbusier on life-long quests for the ideal city?

In recalling the utopian origins of the three ideal cities, I have necessarily associated their planners with outmoded methods, long-defeated movements, and great expectations that we can hardly comprehend in our modern era. To the professional planner of today who must patiently shepherd even the smallest project through the bureaucratic maze, the three planners' sweeping programs will appear almost indecently grandiose. Nevertheless, I have tried not to overemphasize the remoteness of Howard, Wright, and Le Corbusier from current ideas because I believe there is much we can still learn from them.

Our present urban crisis is, in part, a crisis of confidence. The decay of our central cities and the wasteful, ever-expanding sprawl that threatens to replace them are national problems whose magnitude would seem to make some form of large-scale urban planning and reconstruction a national imperative. The tools for such a reconstruction exist, but we seem to lack the will to use them. For many contemporary planners (whose theories I shall discuss in the conclusion), any action on the scale advocated by Howard, Wright, and Le Corbusier is a dangerous delusion. They argue that the cities are too complex for us to comprehend, and that their problems are too deep-seated to yield to our limited understanding and even more limited resources. The best we can hope for are small-scale renovation projects which might keep pace with the decay.

Howard, Wright, and Le Corbusier had a different outlook. They were not afraid to ask basic questions about the structure of cities and of societies; or to consider large-scale solutions to large-scale problems; or to envision and work for the social changes that might be necessary to carry them out. They still believed that human efforts could solve human problems. They had the confidence to think that an advanced industrial society could create an urban environment worthy of its highest values. Inevitably, they were disappointed, but I hope that their ideals are not irrelevant to our present tasks.

This book underwent several academic metamorphoses before emerging in its present form. While a graduate student at Harvard University in Professor Stanley Hoffmann's seminar on French political thought, I unexpectedly encountered some of Le Corbusier's early designs for his "Radiant City" in the pages of the obscure syndicalist journals I was then studying. Seeing those famous drawings in that context aroused my interest in the twentieth-century form of utopian thought they represented. As I searched for a dissertation topic, I tried to discover among the literally hundreds of "cities of tomorrow" from the period of 1890 to 1930 those that shared Le Corbusier's combination of (1) radically original urban design; (2) a revolutionary program for social change; and (3) a sustained personal commitment by their creators to make the plan a reality.

After reading more "utopian romances" than I care to remember, I concluded that their rapturous portrayals of cities of the future were too vague (and usually too derivative) to serve my purposes. I regretfully omitted several urban designs, especially Antonio Sant'Elia's *Città nuova*, Arturo Soria y Mata's linear city, and Buckminster Fuller's early work, which were planned as technical exercises without explicit social content. One large category which I also decided to exclude consisted of what might be called "urban ideologies." Mannheim has defined "ideology" as thought which seeks to advance the interests of a class or group within the context of an established social order. The "urban ideologies" were plans for large-scale reconstruction which sought to preserve and to glorify an already powerful class. The most representative urban ideologies were the totalitarian "ideal cities": Mussolini's plans for Rome; Stalinist city-planning in the Soviet Union; and, most notoriously, Hitler's and Speer's megalomaniac designs for rebuilding Berlin and Linz. The General Motors "autopia" exhibited at the 1939 World's Fair might also be included in this category.

Another far higher and more creative form of "urban ideology" which also fell outside the scope of my study was that practiced by the Bauhaus designers of the 1920s. They were ideologists rather than utopians because they focused their imaginations and their social ideals on plans that could be carried out without revolutionary social change (or so they believed). Their basic concept was not the ideal city but *Existenzminimum*—establishing the minimal standards of housing and urban life at a time when attaining even the minimum was an ambitious ideal.

I concluded, finally, that Le Corbusier's approach was fully shared by only two other planners, Ebenezer Howard and Frank Lloyd Wright. There was, as always, one borderline case, the *Cité Industrielle* of Tony Garnier. This detailed and ambitious plan for an industrial city of 35,000 was first exhibited in 1904 when Garnier, who later became municipal architect of Lyons, was still a student. Garnier's utopian designs influenced Le Corbusier, but, as I learned from the Garnier papers in the municipal archives of Lyons, he never attempted to build more than isolated fragments of his ideal city. The *Cité Industrielle* itself was almost forgotten; and in any case, it never attained the complex development (over a period of time) that distinguished the works of Howard, Wright, and Le Corbusier.

I resolved, therefore, to make my Ph.D. thesis a comparison of the ideal cities of the three planners. Ordinarily, such a topic would have been viewed with misgivings by thesis advisors. Not only did it cross the boundaries of academic disciplines, it even transgressed the great divide (which runs somewhere over the Azores) that separates "Americanists" from "Europeanists." Fortunately, my advisor was Professor H. Stuart Hughes, a distinguished champion of interdisciplinary and trans-Atlantic studies. He gave me the encouragement, and above all, the freedom I needed to pursue my work.

To Dr. Paul Neuthaler, senior editor at Basic Books, Inc., I owe the support and advice which enabled me to accomplish the last and most difficult metamorphosis of the thesis into a book. In addition, I am pleased to acknowledge the assistance I received from scholars and archivists. Sir Frederic Osborn gave me the benefit of his reflections on, and reminiscences of, the Garden City movement he led, reshaped, and revived. The staff of the Hertfordshire County Archives, holder of the Ebenezer Howard Papers, was unfailingly helpful. Bruce Brooks Pfeiffer, curator of the Frank Lloyd Wright Foundation, made available to me documents from the Foundation's archives. The Fondation Le Corbusier in Paris, holder of the Le Corbusier Papers and drawings, gave me both access to their collections and a unique environment in which to study them. Sequestered in a quiet cul-de-sac near the Bois du Boulogne, the Fondation occupies Le Corbusier's classic La Roche-Jeanneret houses, now lovingly and accurately restored. The small but dedicated staff somehow found room for an American graduate student who arrived unannounced one fall morning and stayed until spring.

This research was supported by two sources of financial aid, the first a Graduate Prize Fellowship from Harvard University and the second a grant from the Rutgers University Research Council.

My greatest debt, however, is to those friends, Carl Brauer, Steven Kotz, Jerome Nashorn, Susan and Marc Shell, Angela and Daniel Yergin, who took time from their own work to give me the frank and careful criticism which is every writer's greatest need.

URBAN UTOPIAS
IN
THE TWENTIETH
CENTURY

INTRODUCTION

W<small>HAT IS</small> the ideal city for the twentieth century, the city that best expresses the power and beauty of modern technology and the most enlightened ideas of social justice? Between 1890 and 1930 three planners, Ebenezer Howard, Frank Lloyd Wright, and Le Corbusier, tried to answer that question. Each began his work alone, devoting long hours to preparing literally hundreds of models and drawings specifying every aspect of the new city, from its general ground plan to the layout of the typical living room. There were detailed plans for factories, office buildings, schools, parks, transportation systems—all innovative designs in themselves and all integrated into a revolutionary restructuring of urban form. The economic and political organization of the city, which could not be easily shown in drawings, was worked out in the voluminous writings which each planner appended to his designs. Finally, each man devoted himself to passionate and unremitting efforts to make his ideal city a reality.

Many people dream of a better world; Howard, Wright, and Le Corbusier each went a step further and planned one. Their social consciences took this rare and remarkable step because they believed that, more than any other goal, their societies needed new kinds of cities. They were deeply fearful of the consequences for civilization if the old cities, with all the social conflicts and miseries they embodied, were allowed to persist.

They were also inspired by the prospect that a radical reconstruction of the cities would solve not only the urban crisis of their time, but the social crisis as well. The very completeness of their ideal cities expressed their convictions that the moment had come for comprehensive programs, and for a total rethinking of the principles of urban planning. They rejected the possibility of gradual improvement. They did not seek the amelioration of the old cities, but a wholly transformed urban environment.

This transformation meant the extensive rebuilding and even partial abandonment of the cities of their time. Howard, Wright, and Le Corbusier did not shrink from this prospect; they welcomed it. As Howard put it, the old cities had "done their work." They were the best that the old economic and social order could have been expected to produce, but they had to be superseded if mankind were to attain a higher level of civilization. The three ideal cities were put forward to establish the basic theoretical framework for this radical reconstruction. They were the manifestoes for an urban revolution.

These ideal cities are perhaps the most ambitious and complex statements of the belief that reforming the physical environment can revolutionize the total life of a society. Howard, Wright, and Le Corbusier saw design as an active force, distributing the benefits of the Machine Age to all and directing the community onto the paths of social harmony. Yet they never subscribed to the narrow simplicities of the "doctrine of salvation by bricks alone"—the idea that physical facilities could *by themselves* solve social problems. To be sure, they believed— and who can doubt this?—that the values of family life could be better maintained in a house or apartment that gave each member the light and air and room he needed, rather than in the cramped and fetid slums that were still the fate of too many families. They thought that social solidarity would be better promoted in cities that brought people together, rather than in those whose layout segregated the inhabitants by race or class.

At the same time the three planners understood that these and other well-intended designs would be worse than useless if their benevolent humanitarianism merely covered up basic inequities in the social system. The most magnificent and innovative housing project would fail if its inhabitants were too poor and oppressed to lead decent lives. There was little point in constructing new centers of community life if the economics of exploitation and class conflict kept the citizens as divided as they had been in their old environment. Good planning was indeed efficacious in creating social harmony, but only if it embodied a genuine rationality and justice in the structure of society. It was impossible in a society still immured in what Le Corbusier called "the Age of Greed." The three planners realized that they had to join their programs of urban reconstruction with programs of political and economic reconstruction. They concluded (to paraphrase one of Marx's famous *Theses on Feuerbach*) that designers had hitherto merely *ornamented* the world in various ways; the point was to *change* it.

The ideal cities were therefore accompanied by detailed programs for radical changes in the distribution of wealth and power, changes which Howard, Wright, and Le Corbusier regarded as the necessary complements to their revolutions in design. The planners also played prominent roles in the movements which shared their aims. Howard was an ardent cooperative socialist who utilized planning as part of his search for the cooperative commonwealth; Wright, a Jeffersonian democrat and an admirer of Henry George, was a spokesman for the American decentrist movement; and Le Corbusier had many of his most famous designs published for the first time in the pages of the revolutionary syndicalist journals he edited. All three brought a revolutionary fervor to the practice of urban design.

And, while the old order endured, Howard, Wright, and Le Corbusier refused to adapt themselves to what planning commissions, bankers, politicians, and all the other authorities of their time believed to be desirable and attainable. They consistently rejected the idea that a planner's imagination must work within the system. Instead, they regarded the physical structure of the cities in which they lived, and the economic structure of the society in which they worked, as temporary aberrations which mankind would soon overcome. The three planners looked beyond their own troubled time to a new age each believed was imminent, a new age each labored to define and to build.

Their concerns thus ranged widely over architecture, urbanism, economics, and politics, but their thinking found a focus and an adequate means of expression only in their plans for ideal cities. The cities were never conceived of as blueprints for any actual project. They were "ideal types" of cities for the future, elaborate models rigorously designed to illustrate the general principles that each man advocated. They were convenient and attractive intellectual tools that enabled each planner to bring together his many innovations in design, and to show them as part of a coherent whole, a total redefinition of the idea of the city. The setting of these ideal cities was never any actual location, but an empty, abstract plain where no contingencies existed. The time was the present, not any calendar day or year, but that revolutionary "here and now" when the hopes of the present are finally realized.

These hopes, moreover, were both architectural and social. In the three ideal cities, the transformation of the physical environment is the outward sign of an inner transformation in the social structure. Howard, Wright, and Le Corbusier used their ideal cities to depict a world in which their political and economic goals had already been achieved. Each planner wanted to show that the urban designs he advocated were not only rational and beautiful in themselves, but that they embodied the social goals he believed in. In the context of the ideal city, each proposal for new housing, new factories, and other structures could be seen to further the broader aims. And, in general, the ideal cities enabled the three planners to show modern design in what they believed was its true context —as an integral part of a culture from which poverty and exploitation had disappeared. These cities, therefore, were complete alternative societies, intended as a revolution in politics and economics as well as in architecture. They were utopian visions of a total environment in which man would live in peace with his fellow man and in harmony with nature. They were social thought in three dimensions.

As theorists of urbanism, Howard, Wright, and Le Corbusier attempted to define the ideal form of any industrial society. They shared a common assumption that this form could be both defined and attained, but each viewed the ideal through the perspective of his own social theory, his own national tradition, and his own personality. Their plans, when compared, disagree profoundly, and the divergences are often just as significant as the agreements. They offer us not a single blueprint for the future, but three sets of choices—the great metropolis, moderate decentralization, or extreme decentralization—each with its corresponding political and social implications. Like the classical political triad of monarchy–aristocracy–democracy, the three ideal cities represent a vocabulary of basic forms which can be used to define the whole range of choices available to the planner.

Seventeen years older than Wright and thirty-seven years older than Le Corbusier, Ebenezer Howard started first. His life resembles a story by Horatio Alger, except that Alger never conceived a hero at once so ambitious and so self-effacing. He began his career as a stenographer and ended as the elder statesman of a worldwide planning movement, yet he remained throughout his life the embodiment of the "little man." He was wholly without pretension, an earnest man with a round, bald head, spectacles, and a bushy mustache, unselfconscious in his baggy pants and worn jackets, beloved by neighbors and children.

Yet Howard, like the inventors, enlighteners, self-taught

theorists, and self-proclaimed prophets of the "age of improvement" in which he lived, was one of those little men with munificent hopes. His contribution was "the Garden City," a plan for moderate decentralization and cooperative socialism. He wanted to build wholly new cities in the midst of unspoiled countryside on land which would remain the property of the community as a whole. Limited in size to 30,000 inhabitants and surrounded by a perpetual "greenbelt," the Garden City would be compact, efficient, healthful, and beautiful. It would lure people away from swollen cities like London with their dangerous concentrations of wealth and power; at the same time, the countryside would be dotted with hundreds of new communities where small scale cooperation and direct democracy could flourish.

Howard never met either Frank Lloyd Wright or Le Corbusier. One suspects those two architects of genius and forceful personalities would have considered themselves worlds apart from the modest stenographer. Yet it is notable that Wright and Le Corbusier, like Howard, began their work in urban planning as outsiders, learning their profession not in architectural schools but through apprenticeships with older architects and through their own studies. This self-education was the source of their initiation into both urban design and social theory, and it continued even after Wright and Le Corbusier had become masters of their own profession. Their interests and readings flowed naturally from architecture and design to city planning, economics, politics, and the widest questions of social thought. No one ever told them they could not know everything.

Frank Lloyd Wright stands between Howard and Le Corbusier, at least in age. If Howard's dominant value was cooperation, Wright's was individualism. And no one can deny that he practiced what he preached. With the handsome profile and proud bearing of a frontier patriarch, carefully brushed long hair, well-tailored suits and flowing cape, Wright was his own special creation. His character was an inextricable mix of arrogance and honesty, vanity and genius. He was autocratic, impolitic, and spendthrift; yet he maintained a magnificent faith in his own ideal of "organic" architecture.

Wright wanted the whole United States to become a nation of individuals. His planned city, which he called "Broadacres," took decentralization beyond the small community (Howard's ideal) to the individual family home. In Broadacres all cities larger than a county seat have disappeared. The center of society has moved to the thousands of homesteads which cover the countryside. Everyone has the right to as much land as he can use, a minimum of an acre per person. Most people work part-time on their farms and part-time in the small factories, offices, or shops that are nestled among the farms. A network of superhighways joins together the scattered elements of society. Wright believed that individuality must be founded on individual ownership. Decentralization would make it possible for everyone to live his chosen life style on his own land.

Le Corbusier, our third planner, could claim with perhaps even more justification than Wright to be his own creation. He was born Charles-Édouard Jeanneret and grew up in the Swiss city of La Chaux-de-Fonds, where he was apprenticed to be a watchcase engraver. He was saved from that dying trade by a sympathetic teacher and by his own determination. Settling in Paris in 1916, he won for himself a place at the head of the avant-garde, first with his painting, then with his brilliant architectural criticism, and most profoundly with his own contributions to architecture. The Swiss artisan Jeanneret no longer existed. He had recreated himself as "Le Corbusier," the Parisian leader of the revolution in modern architecture.

Like other "men from the provinces" who settled in Paris, Le Corbusier identified himself completely with the capital and its values. Wright had hoped that decentralization would preserve the social value he prized most highly—individuality. Le Corbusier placed a corresponding faith in organization, and he foresaw a very different fate for modern society. For him, industrialization meant great cities where large bureaucracies could coordinate production. Whereas Wright thought that existing cities were at least a hundred times too dense, Le Corbusier thought they were not dense enough. He proposed that large tracts in the center of Paris and other major cities be leveled. In place of the old buildings, geometrically arrayed skyscrapers of glass and steel would rise out of parks, gardens, and superhighways. These towers would be the command posts for their region. They would house a technocratic elite of planners, engineers, and intellectuals who would bring beauty and prosperity to the whole society. In his first version of the ideal city, Le Corbusier had the elite live in luxurious high-rise apartments close to the center; their subordinates were relegated to satellite cities at the outskirts. (In a later version everyone was to live in the high-rises.) Le Corbusier called his plan " 'the Radiant City,' a city worthy of our time."

The plans of Howard, Wright and Le Corbusier can be summarized briefly, but the energy and resources necessary to carry them out can hardly be conceived. One might expect that the three ideal cities were destined to remain on paper. Yet, as we shall see, their proposals have already reshaped many of the cities we now live in, and may prove to be even more influential in the future.

The plans were effective because they spoke directly to hopes and fears that were widely shared. In particular, they reflected (1) the pervasive fear of and revulsion from the nineteenth-century metropolis; (2) the sense that modern technology had made possible exciting new urban forms; and (3) the great expectation that a revolutionary age of brotherhood and freedom was at hand.

Caught in our own urban crisis, we tend to romanticize the teeming cities of the turn of the century. To many of their inhabitants, however, they were frightening and unnatural phenomena. Their unprecedented size and vast, uprooted populations seemed to suggest the uncontrollable forces unleashed by the Industrial Revolution, and the chaos that occupied the center of modern life. Joseph Conrad eloquently expressed this feeling when he confessed to being haunted by the vision of a "monstrous town more populous than some continents and in its man-made might as if indifferent to heaven's frowns and smiles; a cruel devourer of the world's light. There was room enough there to place any story, depth enough there for any passion, variety enough for any setting, darkness enough to bury five millions of lives."[1]

The monstrous proportions of the big city were relatively new, and thus all the more unsettling. In the first half of the nineteenth century the great European cities had overflowed their historic walls and fortifications. (The American cities, of course, never knew such limits.) Now boundless, the great cities expanded into the surrounding countryside with reckless speed, losing the coherent structure of a healthy organism. London grew in the nineteenth century from 900,000 to 4.5 million inhabitants; Paris in the same period quintupled its population, from 500,000 to 2.5 million residents. Berlin went from 190,000 to over 2 million, New York from 60,000 to 3.4 million. Chicago, a village in 1840 reached 1.7 million by the turn of the century.[2]

This explosive growth, which would have been difficult to accommodate under any circumstances, took place in an era of laissez-faire and feverish speculation. The cities lost the power to control their own growth. Instead, speculation—the blind force of chance and profit—determined urban structure. The cities were segregated by class, their traditional unifying centers first overwhelmed by the increase in population, and then abandoned. Toward the end of the nineteenth century the residential balance between urban and rural areas began tipping, in an unprecedented degree, toward the great cities. When Howard, Wright, and Le Corbusier began their work they saw around them stagnation in the countryside, the depopulation of rural villages, and a crisis in even the old regional centers. First trade and then the most skilled and ambitious young people moved to the metropolis.

Some of these newcomers found the good life they had been
seeking in attractive new middle-class neighborhoods, but
most were caught in the endless rows of tenements that
stretched for miles, interrupted only by factories or railroad
yards. Whole families were crowded into one or two airless
rooms fronting on narrow streets or filthy courtyards where
sunlight never penetrated. In Berlin in 1900, for example,
almost 50 percent of all families lived in tenement dwellings
with only one small room and an even smaller kitchen. Most
of the rest lived in apartments with two tiny rooms and a
kitchen, but to pay their rent, some of these had to take in
boarders who slept in the corners.[3] "Look at the cities of the
nineteenth century," wrote Le Corbusier, "at the vast stretches
covered with the crust of houses without heart and furrowed
with streets without soul. Look, judge. These are the signs of a
tragic denaturalization of human labor."[4]

Howard, Wright, and Le Corbusier hated the cities of their
time with an overwhelming passion. The metropolis was the
counter-image of their ideal cities, the hell that inspired their
heavens. They saw precious resources, material and human,
squandered in the urban disorder. They were especially fearful
that the metropolis would attract and then consume all the
healthful forces in society. All three visualized the great city
as a cancer, an uncontrolled, malignant growth that was
poisoning the modern world. Wright remarked that the plan
of a large city resembled "the cross-section of a fibrous
tumor"; Howard compared it to an enlarged ulcer. Le Corbusier was fond of picturing Paris as a body in the last stages
of a fatal disease—its circulation clogged, its tissues dying of
their own noxious wastes.

The three planners, moreover, used their insight into technology to go beyond a merely negative critique of the
nineteenth-century metropolis. They showed how modern
techniques of construction had created a new mastery of
space from which innovative urban forms could be built. The
great city, they argued, was no longer modern. Its chaotic

concentration was not only inefficient and inhumane, it was unnecessary as well.

Howard, Wright, and Le Corbusier based their ideas on the technological innovations that inspired their age: the express train, the automobile, the telephone and radio, and the sky-scraper. Howard realized that the railroad system that had contributed to the growth of the great cities could serve the planned decentralization of society equally well. Wright understood that the personal automobile and an elaborate network of roads could create the conditions for an even more radical decentralization. Le Corbusier looked to technology to promote an opposite trend. He made use of the skyscraper as a kind of vertical street, a "street in the air" as he called it, which would permit intensive urban densities while eliminating the "soulless streets" of the old city.

The three planners' fascination with technology was deep but highly selective. They acknowledged only what served their own social values. Modern technology, they believed, had outstripped the antiquated social order, and the result was chaos and strife. In their ideal cities, however, technology would fulfill its proper role. Howard, Wright, and Le Corbusier believed that industrial society was inherently harmonious. It had an inherent structure, an ideal form which, when achieved, would banish conflict and bring order and freedom, prosperity and beauty.

This belief went far beyond what could be deduced from the order and power of technology itself. It reflected instead the revolutionary hopes of the nineteenth century. For the three planners, as for so many of their contemporaries, the conflicts of the early Industrial Revolution were only a time of troubles which would lead inevitably to the new era of harmony. History for them was still the history of progress; indeed, as Howard put it, there was a "grand purpose behind nature." These great expectations, so difficult for us to comprehend, pervaded nineteenth-century radical and even liberal thought. There were many prophets of progress who contributed to creating the optimistic climate of opinion in which Howard, Wright, and Le Corbusier formed their own beliefs. Perhaps the most relevant for our purposes were the "utopian socialists" of the early nineteenth century.

These reformers, most notably Charles Fourier, Robert Owen, and Henri de Saint-Simon, drew upon the tradition of Thomas More's *Utopia* and Plato's *Republic* to create detailed depictions of communities untainted by the class struggles of the Industrial Revolution. Unlike More or Plato, however, the utopian socialists looked forward to the immediate realization of their ideal commonwealths. Owen and Fourier produced detailed plans for building utopian communities, plans for social and architectural revolution which anticipated some of the work of Howard, Wright, and Le Corbusier. Two themes dominated utopian socialist planning: first, a desire to overcome the distinction between city and country; and second, a desire to overcome the physical isolation of individuals and families by grouping the community into one large "family" structure. Most of the designs envisioned not ideal cities but ideal communes, small rural establishments for less than 2,000 people. Owen put forward a plan for brick quadrangles which he called "moral quadrilaterals." One side was a model factory, while the other three were taken up with a communal dining room, meeting rooms for recreation, and apartments.[5] His French rival Fourier advanced a far more elaborate design for a communal palace or "phalanstery" which boasted theaters, fashionable promenades, gardens, and gourmet cuisine for everyone.[6]

The utopian socialists were largely forgotten by the time Howard, Wright, and Le Corbusier began their own work, so there was little direct influence from them. As we shall see, however, the search of each planner for a city whose design expressed the ideals of cooperation and social justice led him to revive many of the themes of his utopian socialist (and even earlier) predecessors. But one crucial element sharply separates the three planners' designs from all previous efforts. Even the most fantastic inventions of an Owen or a Fourier could not anticipate the new forms that twentieth-century technology would bring to urban design. The utopian socialists' prophecies of the future had to be expressed in the traditional architectural vocabulary. Fourier, for example, housed his cooperative community in a "phalanstery" that looked like the château of Versailles. Howard, Wright, and Le Corbusier were able to incorporate the scale and pace of the modern world into their designs. They worked at the dawn of the twentieth-century industrial era, but before the coming of twentieth-century disillusionment. Their imaginations were wholly modern; yet the coming era of cooperation was as real to them as it had been for Robert Owen. Their ideal cities thus stand at the intersection of nineteenth-century hopes and twentieth-century technology.

The three ideal cities, therefore, possessed a unique scope and fervor, but this uniqueness had its dangers. It effectively isolated the three planners from almost all the social movements and institutions of their time. In particular, it separated them from the members of two groups who might have been their natural allies, the Marxian socialists and the professional planners. The three ideal cities were at once too technical for the Marxists and too revolutionary for the growing corps of professional planners. The latter was especially intent on discouraging any suggestion that urban planning might serve the cause of social change. These architect–administrators confined themselves to "technical" problems, which meant, in practice, serving the needs of society—as society's rulers defined them. Baron Haussmann, that model of an administrative planner, had ignored and sometimes worsened the plight of the poor in his massive reconstructions of Paris undertaken for Louis Napoleon. But the plight of the poor was not his administrative responsibility. He wanted to unite the isolated sectors of the city and thus quicken the pace of commerce. The wide avenues he cut through Paris were also designed to contribute to the prestige of the regime and, if necessary, to serve as efficient conduits for troops to put down urban disorders. Haussmann's physically impressive and socially reactionary plans inspired worldwide imitation and further increased the gap between urban design and social purpose.[7]

Even the middle-class reformers who specifically dedicated themselves to housing and urban improvement were unable to close this gap. Men like Sir Edwin Chadwick in London bravely faced official indifference and corruption to bring clean air, adequate sanitation, and minimal standards of housing to the industrial cities. Yet these philanthropists were also deeply conservative in their social beliefs. Their rare attempts at innovation almost always assumed the continued poverty of the poor and the privileges of the rich. The model tenements, "cheap cottages," and factory towns that were commissioned in the second half of the nineteenth century were filled with good intentions and sound planning, but they never failed to reflect the inequities of the society that built them. When, for example, the English housing reformer Octavia Hill built her model tenements, she kept accommodations to a minimum so that her indigent tenants could pay rents sufficient not only to cover the complete cost of construction, but also to yield her wealthy backers 5 percent annual interest on the money they had advanced her.[8] (This kind of charitable enterprise was known as "philanthropy at 5 percent.") Not surprisingly, designs put forward under these conditions were almost as bleak as the slums they replaced.

Howard, Wright, and Le Corbusier were not interested in making exisiting cities more profitable or in building "model" tenements to replace the old ones. These views might have been expected to have attracted the sympathetic attention of the Marxian socialists who then controlled the most powerful European movements for social change. Indeed, the *Communist Manifesto* had already recognized the necessity for radical structural change in the industrial cities by putting the "gradual abolition of the distinction between town and country" among its demands. Nevertheless, the socialist movement in the second half of the nineteenth century turned away from what its leaders regarded as unprofitable speculation. In an important series of articles collected under the title *The Housing Question* (1872), Friedrich Engels maintained that urban design was part of the "superstructure" of capitalist society and would necessarily reflect that society's inhumanities, at least until after the socialist revolution had succeeded in transforming the economic base. He concluded that any attempt to envision an ideal city without waiting for the revolution was futile and, indeed, that any attempt to improve the cities significantly was doomed so long as capitalism endured. The working class must forget attractive visions of the future and concentrate on immediate revolution after which the dictatorship of the proletariat would redistribute housing in the old industrial cities according to need. Then and only then could planners begin to think about a better kind of city.[9]

Howard, Wright, and Le Corbusier could therefore look neither to the socialists nor to the professional planners for support. Initially, at least, they were forced back upon themselves. Instead of developing their ideas through collaboration with others and through practical experience, they worked in isolation on more and more elaborate models of their basic ideas. Their ideal cities thus acquired a wealth of brilliant detail and a single-minded theoretical rigor that made them unique. This isolation was no doubt the necessary precondition for the three planners' highly individual styles of social thought. Certainly their mercurial and independent careers showed a very different pattern from the solid institutional connections of, for example, Ludwig Mies van der Rohe or Walter Gropius. Mies, Gropius, and the other Bauhaus architects were also deeply concerned with the question of design and society; yet none of them produced an ideal city. They had more practical but also more limited projects to occupy them.[10] The ideal city is the genre of the outsider who travels at one leap from complete powerlessness to imaginary omnipotence.

This isolation encouraged Howard, Wright, and Le Corbusier to extend their intellectual and imaginative capacities to their limits, but it also burdened their plans with almost insurmountable problems of both thought and action. They had created plans that were works of art, but the city, in Claude Lévi-Strauss' phrase, is a *"social* work of art." Its densely interwoven structure is the product of thousands of minds and thousands of individual decisions. Its variety derives from the unexpected juxtapositions and the unpredictable interactions. How can a single individual, even a man of genius, hope to comprehend this structure? And how can he devise a new plan with the same satisfying complexities? For his design, whatever its logic and merits, is necessarily his alone. In imposing a single point of view, he inevitably simplifies the parts which make up the whole. Howard, Wright, and Le Corbusier each filled his ideal city with *his* buildings; *his* sense of proportion and color; and, most profoundly, with *his* social values. Would there ever be room for anyone else? The three ideal cities raise what is perhaps the most perplexing question for any planner: in attempting to create a new urban order, must he repress precisely that complexity, diversity, and individuality which are the city's highest achievements?

The problem of action was equally obvious and pressing. Deprived of outside support, the three planners came to believe that their ideas were inherently powerful. As technical solutions to urban problems and as embodiments of justice and beauty, the three ideal cities could properly claim everyone's support. By holding up a ready-made plan for a new order, Howard, Wright and Le Corbusier hoped to create their own movements. This strategy, however, led directly to the classic utopian dilemma. To appeal to everyone on the basis of universal principles is to appeal to no one in particular. The more glorious the plans are in theory, the more remote they are from the concrete issues that actually motivate action. With each elaboration and clarification, the ideal cities move closer to pure fantasy. Can imagination alone change the world? Or, as Friedrich Engels phrased the question: how can the isolated individual hope to *impose his idea* on history?

These two related problems of thought and action confronted Howard, Wright, and Le Corbusier throughout their careers; yet they never doubted that ultimately they could solve both. Each believed that if a planner based his work on the structure inherent in industrial society and on the deepest values of his culture, there could be no real conflict between his plan and individual liberty. Patiently, each searched for that harmonious balance between control and freedom: the order which does not repress but liberates the individual.

With equal determination, they sought a valid strategy for action. Their ideal cities, they knew, could never be constructed all at once. But at least a "working model" could be begun, even in the midst of the old society. This model would demonstrate both the superiority of their architectural principles and also serve as a symbol of the new society about to be born. Its success would inspire emulation. A movement of reconstruction would take on momentum and become a revolutionary force in itself. Rebuilding the cities could thus become, in a metaphor all three favored, the "Master Key" that would unlock the way to a just society.

The three planners, therefore, looked to the new century with confidence and hope. Against the overwhelming power of the great cities and the old order that built them, Howard, Wright, and Le Corbusier advanced their designs for planned growth, for the reassertion of the common interest and higher values, for a healthy balance between man's creation and the natural environment. It would seem to be an uneven contest. Nevertheless, the three planners still believed that an individual and his imagination could change history. The revolution they were seeking was precisely an assertion of human rationality over vast impersonal forces. They resolved that in the coming era of reconciliation and construction, the man of imagination must play a crucial role. He would embody the values of his society in a workable plan, and thus direct social change with his prophetic leadership. For Howard, Wright, and Le Corbusier, this next revolution would finally bring imagination to power. "What gives our dreams their daring," Le Corbusier proclaimed, "is that they can be achieved."[11]

I

Ebenezer Howard

1

The Ideal City Made Practicable

Town and country *must be married*,
and out of this joyous union will
spring a new hope, a new life, a new
civilization.

EBENEZER HOWARD (1898)

OF THE THREE planners discussed here, Ebenezer
Howard is the least known and the most influential. His
To-morrow: a Peaceful Path to Real Reform (1898, now known
under the title of the 1902 edition, *Garden Cities of To-morrow*) has, as Lewis Mumford acknowledged, "done more than
any other single book to guide the modern town planning
movement and to alter its objectives."[1] And Howard was more
than a theoretician. He and his supporters founded two English
cities, Letchworth (1903) and Welwyn (1920), which still
serve as models for his ideas. More importantly, he was able
to organize a city planning movement which continues to keep
his theories alive. The postwar program of New Towns in
Great Britain, perhaps the most ambitious of all attempts at
national planning, was inspired by his works and planned by
his followers.

In the United States the "Greenbelt Cities" undertaken by
the Resettlement Administration in the 1930s owed their

form to the example of the Garden City. The best recent example of an American New Town is Columbia, Maryland, built in the 1960s as a wholly independent community with houses and industry. In 1969 the National Committee on Urban Growth Policy urged that the United States undertake to build 110 New Towns to accommodate 20 million citizens.[2] The following year, Congress created a New Town Corporation in the Department of Housing and Urban Development to begin this vast task.[3] So far, sixteen American New Towns have either been planned or are under construction. The most fruitful period of Ebenezer Howard's influence is perhaps only beginning.

If Howard's achievements continue to grow in importance, Howard the man remains virtually unknown. The present-day New Town planners are perhaps a little embarrassed by him. They are highly skilled professional bureaucrats or architects; Howard's formal education ended at fourteen, and he had no special training in architecture or urban design. The modern planners are self-proclaimed "technicians" who have attempted to adapt the New Town concept to any established social order. Howard was, in his quiet way, a revolutionary who originally conceived the Garden City as a means of superseding capitalism and creating a civilization based on cooperation. Howard's successors have neglected this aspect of his thought, and without it the founder of the Garden City movement becomes an elusive figure indeed. He shrank from the personal publicity which Frank Lloyd Wright and Le Corbusier so eagerly and so skillfully sought. Throughout his life he maintained the habits and the appearance of a minor clerk. He once said that he enjoyed his chosen profession, stenography, because it enabled him to be an almost invisible observer at the notable events he recorded. Even at the meetings of the association he headed, he preferred to sit in an inconspicuous position behind the podium where he could take down the exact words of the other speakers. Frederic J. Osborn, one of his closest associates, remembered him as "the sort of man who could easily pass unnoticed in a crowd."[4] He was, Osborn added, "the mildest and most unassuming of men . . . universally liked, and notably by children."[5]

Nonetheless, Howard succeeded where more charismatic figures failed. In 1898 he had to borrow £50 to print *To-mor-row* at his own expense. Five years later his supporters were advancing more than £100,000 to begin the construction of the first Garden City. The rapidity of this turn of events surprised Howard and is still difficult to explain. The root of the mystery is Howard himself. He had reached middle age before beginning his work on city planning and had never given any indication that he was capable of originality or leadership. His book, however, was a remarkable intellectual achievement. He concisely and rigorously outlined a new direction for the development of cities and advanced practical solutions which covered the whole range of city planning problems: land use, design, transportation, housing, and finance. At the same time, he incorporated these ideas into a larger synthesis: a plan for a complete alternative society and a program for attaining it.

Howard, moreover, proved to be a surprisingly effective organizer. He was an indefatigable worker who bent with slavelike devotion to the task of promoting his own ideas. At cooperative societies, Labour Churches, settlement houses, temperance unions, debating clubs—at any group that would pay his railroad fares and provide a night's hospitality—he preached the "Gospel of the Garden City" under the title "The Ideal City Made Practicable, A Lecture Illustrated with Lantern Slides." He possessed a powerful speaking voice, and, more importantly, he was able to communicate an overwhelming sense of earnestness, an absolute conviction that he had discovered "the peaceful path to real reform." Mankind, he proclaimed, was moving inevitably toward a new era of brotherhood, and the Garden City would be the only fitting environment for the humanity of the future. His original supporters were not planners or architects but social reformers whose own dreams he promised would be realized in the Garden City. Patiently, he assembled a broad coalition of backers that ranged from "Back to the Land" agrarians to George Bernard Shaw. Working constantly himself, he felt free to draw upon the resources and talents of others. He thus made his ideas the basis of a movement which, fifty years after his death, continues to grow. As one of Shaw's characters in *Major Barbara* observes, absolute unselfishness is capable of anything.

2

Inventing the Garden City

HOWARD never called himself a planner. His activities can be described in many words—theorist, organizer, publicist, city founder—and yet he always preferred to describe himself as an inventor. He was, he proudly proclaimed, the "inventor of the Garden City idea." The term is both appropriate and significant. In an image dear to the nineteenth century, Howard saw himself as one of those dreamers and backyard tinkerers who emerge from obscurity with one great idea, brave neglect and ridicule from the "practical" world, and finally see the skeptics confounded and the invention become an integral part of a better world. Howard in his moments of triumph was fond of comparing himself with George Stephenson, the self-taught engineer who built the first practical locomotive. The Garden City, he hoped, would be an equally significant innovation, revolutionary in itself and, like the early locomotive, capable of great improvement. It would be an engine of progress with the ability to unlock social energy and move society toward beneficent ends which even its inventor could not forsee.

The term "inventor" had one other meaning for him. As a devoted admirer of the great inventors and an occasional practitioner himself, he knew that the most important inventions were rarely the most original. They were, rather, uniquely serviceable applications of ideas which were already well known. This was precisely what Howard claimed for his innovation. In language borrowed from patent office applications he described the Garden City as a "unique combination of Proposals" which were already before the public. Howard was being truthful as well as modest. One can easily demonstrate that almost every aspect of the Garden City was borrowed from other schemes which were in existence at the time Howard began his work, some for the decentralization of cities, some for the democratization of wealth and power. This, however, would be to miss the point of Howard's achievement, for he alone saw the connection between the diverse ideas that went into his plan. With the ingenuity and patience of an inventor putting together a useful new machine out of parts forged for other purposes, Howard created a coherent design for a new environment and a new society.

Howard was able to assemble the disparate elements of the Garden City so successfully because he had a firm set of unquestioned beliefs that guided his actions. Unlike Wright and Le Corbusier, who were always emphasizing their own uniqueness, Howard was a remarkably typical product of his milieu. This prophet of decentralization was born in the center of London in 1850; his parents ran a small shop in the city. He left school at fourteen to become a junior clerk in a stockbroker's office. To better his prospects he taught himself the new Pitman system of shorthand and set up shop on his own.[1] He thus raised himself from the bottom of the hierarchy of clerkdom and joined that group of "little men"—petty entrepreneurs, commission salesmen, shopkeepers—who struggled to maintain a proud independence in the era before large organizations absorbed the white-collar class.

This success, however, never satisfied him. For Howard was touched by the great expectations of the nineteenth century. He wanted to contribute to the "unexampled rate of progress and invention" which he believed characterized his times. He started to tinker with gadgets: a keyless watch, a breech-loading gun, a typewriter that automatically allotted to each letter the space it occupied in print typography.[2] These projects, never successful, absorbed his attention and his ready cash. In his most unusual attempt to make his fortune he emigrated briefly to the United States, where a year spent as a homesteader in Nebraska convinced him of the virtues of stenography. He returned to London in 1876.[3]

After this episode his ambitions took a less material turn. While struggling to build up his stenography practice he grew preoccupied with what was then called "the Social Question" —the origins and causes of all the poverty that daily surrounded him. Perhaps his own failure and temporary poverty in the United States had awakened his sympathy for the poor in his own country. The principles of moral duty he had learned in Sunday school and his own innate kindliness surely also played their part. In any case, he soon joined a series of reading and discussion groups with names like the "Zetetical Society." For him and the other members, these groups represented an opportunity to educate themselves in the great political and economic questions of the day. Together they taught themselves John Stuart Mill on political economy, Herbert Spencer on social science, Darwin and Huxley on evolution. There he met high-minded men and women with concerns similar to his own and was initiated into the world of middle-class London Radicalism.

These genteel revolutionaries have rarely been appreciated or even understood in our time. They were amateurs and idealists in a field that has come to be dominated by professionals and politicians. Their plans for reconstructing society survive only in the pages of old pamphlets with titles in ornate type: *Brotherhood, Cooperation*. Photographs in these pamphlets show us their faces, which have no elegance and little humor but much hope and integrity; the men are in stiff white collars, the women in severely buttoned dresses. Under each picture is an identifying caption: "Secretary, Temperance Union and Cooperative Society" or "Spiritualist and Social Reformer." The Radicals had more than their share of cranks, but their movement was the home of much that was most humane in nineteenth-century British society, as well as the source of much that would prove most fruitful for the twentieth century. When Howard designed the Garden City in the 1890s, he followed unhesitatingly the social ideals he had learned as an obscure Radical of the 1870s and 1880s.

The Radicals believed that Victorian England was not the best of all possible worlds; that the economic life of the nation was corrupt, inhumane, inefficient, and immoral; and that political power, despite the appearance of democracy, was unjustly concentrated in the hands of a few. This concentration, they feared, would ruin the nation if allowed to continue. In the countryside the near-monopoly of landholding by large owners was bankrupting agriculture. The farm worker, deprived of any hope of owning his own land, was fleeing the land and swelling the urban slums. There he and his fellows were easily exploited by "sweating" employers whose sharp practices and monopolistic tactics were driving the honest "little man" out of business. If these trends were to continue, the result would be a society polarized between capital and labor. The Radicals were not Marxists, so they saw in this last prospect only violent conflict which would destroy both sides.

Their remedies for this dismal situation were democracy and cooperation. They wanted first to break the power of the landed gentry who controlled Parliament and to institute a thoroughgoing land reform. This would draw farm workers back from the slums and create a new class of yeoman smallholders, prosperous and independent. For the urban industrialized areas the Radicals called for cooperation to replace large-scale capitalism. Profit-sharing in production would gradually erase the distinction between worker and employer, thus ending class conflict. At the same time, cooperative stores would end profiteering and wasteful anarchy in distribution.

The Radicals devoutly believed in Progress, and they held that mankind was evolving toward a higher stage of social organization—the cooperative commonwealth—in which brotherhood would become the basis of daily life. But while they were sure that mankind was capable of creating this better world, they had no definite strategy for achieving their goal. They rejected what were to be the two great engines of social change, government intervention and the labor movement. They rejected big government as a dangerous concentration of power, even if it were on their side. For the Radicals, independence and voluntary action were both means and ends. Nor did they support organizing the working class. As we have seen, they regarded class struggle as one of the evils of modern society.

Without a plan of action, the Radical movement alternated between long periods of discussion and short bursts of activity when the true path seemed to be found. One such burst accompanied the arrival in London in 1884 of Henry George, the American reformer whose proposal for a "single tax" of 100 percent of all rental income would, in effect, accomplish the Radical program of land reform in a stroke. George's ideas left their imprint on the Radical movement in general and, as we shall see, on Howard in particular, but they failed to win over the British electorate and the enthusiasm subsided. Sometimes individuals or small groups would abandon their homes and businesses to form utopian colonies like Topolobampo in Mexico. There they hoped to create a "working model" of true cooperation to win over a skeptical world.

More frequently, the Radicals allowed themselves to hope that their small-scale cooperative enterprises might, through voluntary action alone, supplant their profit-making competitors. If the Trusts had grown great on the force of selfishness, why should not brotherhood prove even more powerful? Cooperative socialism could then prevail without any legislation. A good example of these hopes—and illusions—was a scheme propounded by two friends of Howard's, J. Bruce Wallace and the Reverend Bruce Campbell, to bring cooperative workshops and stores to the slum dwellers of London's East End. At the beginning of 1894 the co-ops, aptly named the Brotherhood Trust, had enrolled over 100 customers. "Suppose," Wallace urged his supporters on February 1, 1894, "suppose one fresh customer gained monthly for every old customer." After some rapid calculations he was able to announce that by February 1, 1896, they would have over 100 million enrolled. "In the third year the trade of the whole world would be in the hands of the Trust, for fraternal purposes."[4]

Wallace was quick to add: "I am not so sanguine as to believe that our little movement will actually spread with such rapidity."[5] Nevertheless, it was a revealing fantasy, the dream of a "little man" that his modest enterprise might one day change the world—without coercion. Slightly transposed, it was the same as an inventor's dream of worldwide success by virtue of his superior product. As we shall see, Howard's conception of the Garden City as "the peaceful path to real reform" combined elements of both dreams.

Throughout the 1880s, Howard continued to absorb both the principles and the problems of the Radical movement. He remained a follower, emerging from anonymity only once to deliver a speech on spiritualism at the Zetetical Society. His cogitations on interplanetary ether waves as the possible physical basis of spiritualist communication gave no hint of his coming concerns.[6] His period of quiesence ended suddenly, however, in 1888 with a single event which made him an activist for the rest of his life: he read Edward Bellamy's *Looking Backward*. Published in Boston in 1888, *Looking*

Backward had won immediate popularity in the United States and exercised a profound influence over such men as Thorstein Veblen and John Dewey.[7] Written against the background of the industrial depression and growing labor unrest that engulfed both America and Europe in the third quarter of the nineteenth century, the book presented a graphic depiction of a society in which these problems had been overcome. The hero of the novel is a prosperous Bostonian who has the good fortune to sleep soundly from 1887 to 2000 and wake in a society organized on moral principles. Industry has been efficiently grouped into one government-owned cooperative Trust. Distribution has also been concentrated into one great Department Store whose branches in every city and village sell everything the nation has produced. Competition has been replaced by centralized planning; poverty and unemployment are unknown; all citizens between twenty-one and forty five occupy ranks in the "industrial army," and everyone receives an equal salary.

Although Bellamy's novel was only one of the genre of "utopian romances" that seemed as ubiquitous in their time as murder mysteries are in ours, it was by far the most effective in its critique of industrial capitalism and its imaginative demonstration that a better alternative could exist. *Looking Backward* was sent to Howard by an American friend. He read it at one sitting and was "fairly carried away." The next morning

> I went into some of the crowded parts of London, and as I passed through the narrow dark streets, saw the wretched dwellings in which the majority of the people lived, observed on every hand the manifestations of a self-seeking order of society and reflected on the absolute unsoundness of our economic system, there came to me an overpowering sense of the temporary nature of all I saw, and of its entire unsuitability for the working life of the new order—the order of justice, unity and friendliness.[8]

Howard was sufficiently enthusiastic to believe that many others would share his revelation. He was especially impressed with Bellamy's use of an imaginative portrayal of an alternative to demonstrate the "absolute unsoundness and quite transitory nature" of existing society. In the absence of any other viable movement for change, Bellamy's vision of a better future could become the standard around which men of goodwill would unite. Howard claimed that he was responsible for persuading an English firm to publish *Looking Backward* in London in 1889.[9] In imitation of the Bellamy Clubs then forming in the United States, Howard soon began meeting with small groups to discuss Bellamy's ideas. In 1890 he participated in the formation of the English Nationalisation of Labour Society, the counterpart of Bellamy's Nationalization Party in the United States.[10]

As *Looking Backward* won an enthusiastic readership in English Radical circles, Howard allowed himself the belief that the Nationalization movement was the plan for action the Radicals had been seeking. Even at the time of his greatest hope, however, he could not believe that the movement would have the power to take over the industry of Great Britain very soon. "This perception, naturally, led me to put forward proposals for testing Mr. Bellamy's principles, though on a much smaller scale."[11] Howard began to devise a model community of a few thousand people in which—as in *Looking Backward*—everyone would be employed by the community, whose directors would run every enterprise. If successful, this project would prove the efficacy of Bellamy's ideas to those who would not be moved by purely literary arguments, and thus speed the day when nationalization could occur on a national scale.

Characteristically, Howard's maiden attempt at planning was not an attempt to advance his own ideas but to adapt those of another. Nonetheless, as Howard began to work on the scheme, he came to realize that Bellamy's novelistic gifts had blinded him to the differences between his own goals and those advanced in *Looking Backward*. For Howard shared the Radical mistrust of all concentrations of power, whereas Bellamy made centralization the key to his reforms. Howard saw more clearly than many other readers that behind Bellamy's faith in control from above there was a strong authoritarian bias. Bellamy proudly compared his "industrial army" to the Prussian army. As for its leaders, he spoke grandly and vaguely of a small corps of managers who could plan the economy of the United States or any other nation in the year 2000. In his system, he claimed, the management of all American industry would be "so simple, and depending on principles so obvious and easily applied, that the functionaries at Washington to whom it is trusted require to be nothing more than men of fair ability."[12] Although Bellamy was realistic about the likely intelligence of the bureaucrats of the future, he had unlimited faith in their efficacy, a faith which Howard could not share. Bellamy had seized upon all the forces of concentration and centralization in late nineteenth-century society and saw in them the possibility for a more humane order. Not only did Howard doubt the practicality of extreme centralization, but he also denied its desirability even if it could work.

Howard continued to work out the plan of a model community; now, however, it was designed to put forward and test his own ideas. The Garden City was not the simple result of Bellamy's influence on Howard. Rather, it grew out of Howard's attempt to correct Bellamy's authoritarian bias and to devise a community in which social order and individual initiative would be properly balanced.

He began with Bellamy's plan for "nationalization," the concept that the entire productive capacity of a nation could be managed as if it were one huge Trust, and all its stores and shops controlled as if they were branches of one great Department Store. In thinking about his own model community, Howard was particularly aware of the problems connected with farming. His own failure as a farmer had sufficiently sensitized him to the difficulties in that area, and he doubted that even a small community could successfully manage all its farms. He had, moreover, followed the decline of the Radical utopian colony in Mexico, Topolobampo, whose directors had controlled all productive activity. Their attempts at management had merely focused all the dissatisfactions of the colony on themselves and destroyed the experiment. Howard proposed, therefore, what would become the policy of the Garden City: that the community include both privately and collectively owned enterprise and leave to the citizens the choice of how they wished to work.

From this, Howard proceeded to an even more significant transformation: a critique of Bellamy's ideal of centralization. Bellamy believed that the industrial society of the future ought to be controlled by bureaucrats working from their command posts in the great cities. In opposing nationalization, Howard also began questioning the inevitability of centralization. Specifically, he began to modify his original view that the community he was designing was only a scale model of the centralized society of the future. Was the balance of individual and society he was seeking possible in the metropolis? Or did the small decentralized community have an inherent value of its own?

In wrestling with this question, Howard was no doubt influenced by Peter Kropotkin, a Russian anarchist whose articles appeared in the widely read London journal *The Nineteenth Century* between 1888 and 1890.[13] These articles, later collected as *Fields, Factories, and Workshops* (1899), argued that while steam energy and the railroads had brought large factories and great cities, the dawning age of electricity would make possible a rapid decentralization. He saw the future in what he called "industrial villages," twentieth-century versions of the old craftsmen's villages of the pre-industrial era. There electrically powered, cooperatively owned cottage industries would turn out goods more efficiently than the old urban factories, while the workers' homes and gardens would be nestled in unspoiled countryside.

Kropotkin's views found a deep response in English Radical circles, especially his prediction that all the great urban concentrations of people and power were destined to disappear; his conviction that the future belonged to small-scale cooperators; and his belief that decentralization would make possible a society based on liberty and brotherhood. Howard, who called Kropotkin "the greatest democrat ever born to wealth and power,"[14] decisively abandoned his temporay infatuation with the centralized schemes of Edward Bellamy. Kropotkin had called his attention to the crucial importance of *scale* as a factor in social theory. "On a small scale," Howard proposed, "society may readily become more individualistic than now and more socialistic."[15] Conversely, he came to realize that the great city could never become the home of the cooperative civilization he was seeking. He was now ready to formulate the fundamental principle of the Garden City: *Radical hopes for a cooperative civilization could be fulfilled only in small communities embedded in a decentralized society.*

Howard thus turned to decentralization as a means of action, a way of voting with one's feet against the concentration of power and wealth that the cities represented. His antiurbanism had nothing in common with the vague longings for a more natural life propagated by the "Back to the Land" movement, which was then enjoying one of its periodic revivals. He loved the excitement of London and deeply valued the social qualities of the great cities.[16] It was their economic and political role that disturbed him. "Palatial edifices and fearful slums are the strange, complementary features of modern cities."[17] Howard's identification of the metropolis with the extremes of wealth and power was the starting point of his analysis of the modern city and the real source of his antagonism toward it. He realized that the concentration of wealth and misery in the city would require an equally vast concentration of power to combat it. His favorite example of this was slum clearance. In a large city the inflated price of urban land and the vast numbers of slum dwellers meant that an effective program required a government with powers of taxation and confiscation that Howard, as a good Radical, shrank from even seeking. To accept the nineteenth-century metropolis as the inevitable context for modern life meant that either the force of vested interest would continue to prevail or an equally monstrous force based on class conflict would be raised to topple it.

Both alternatives affronted Howard's belief that mankind was moving to a higher stage of brotherhood. He drew the necessary conclusion: large cities had no place in the society of the future. Surveying the "ill-ventilated, unplanned, unwieldy, and unhealthy cities—ulcers on the very face of our beautiful island,"[18] he proclaimed: "These crowded cities have done their work; they were the best which a society largely based on selfishness and rapacity could construct, but they are in the nature of things entirely unadapted for a society in which the social side of our nature is demanding a larger share of recognition."[19] Everything genuinely valuable in the social life of the city could and must be preserved in new communities designed so that the advantages of the town could be "married" to those of the country. "Human society and the beauty of nature are meant to be enjoyed together."[20] In communities of about 30,000 people based on small business and agriculture, everyone could enjoy the benefits of a healthy environment. Reduced to the scale of a Garden City, the gulf between capital and labor would be narrowed, social problems would become amenable to cooperative solutions, and the proper balance of order and freedom could be achieved.

How could this great social transformation be achieved? Howard summed up his response in his diagram of the "Three Magnets." Town and country were compared to magnets, each with its particular drawing power, its particular combination of attraction and repulsion. The town, with its excitement, high wages, and employment opportunities, suffered from high prices and poor living conditions. The beauty of the countryside was vitiated by its economic backwardness and "lack of amusement." The task for the planner would be to create a third magnet, the Town-Country magnet, the new community which would have high wages and low rents; beauty of nature but "plenty to do"; "bright homes and gardens" along with freedom and cooperation.

In the diagram, "The People" are poised like iron filings between the magnets. This aspect of the metaphor is unfortunate, for Howard's point is that people will respond freely and rationally to the environment that gives them the most advantages. No one had been drafted into the cities. The great migration from the countryside which in Howard's lifetime had brought 7 million rural residents to the British urban centers occurred without legislative compulsion. Similarly, the great exodus from the city to which Howard looked would require no coercive power.

What it required was planning. The Town-Country magnet had to be created consciously to yield that combination of physical and social benefits which were promised. This task Howard took upon himself. Although he had no training in architecture or city planning, he did have the inventor's confidence that he could find the better way. Working alone in the time he could spare from his stenography practice, he set out to give the Radical movement not only a new goal but the strategy for action it had been lacking. Building new towns, creating a new environment—that was the way to the cooperative commonwealth. Howard strove patiently to design that Third Magnet which he called the Garden City, whose promise of a better life would draw people away from the urban centers into a new civilization.

3

Design for Cooperation

BETWEEN 1889 and 1892 Howard created the basic plan for his ideal community. He envisaged his Garden City as a tightly organized urban center for 30,000 inhabitants, surrounded by a perpetual "green belt" of farms and parks. Within the city there would be both quiet residential neighborhoods and facilities for a full range of commercial, industrial, and cultural activities. For Howard did not conceive the Garden City as a specialized "satellite town" or "bedroom town" perpetually serving some great metropolis. Rather, he foresaw the great cities of his time shrinking to insignificance as their people desert them for a new way of life in a decentralized society. No longer would a single metropolis dominate a whole region or even a whole nation. Nor would the palatial edifices and giant organizations of the big city continue to rule modern society. Instead, the urban population would be distributed among hundreds of Garden Cities whose small scale and diversity of functions embody a world in which the little man has finally won out.

Howard does not seem to have been familiar with the designs for geometric cities that utopian socialists had put forward earlier in the nineteenth century. Nonetheless the perfectly circular, perfectly symmetrical plan he devised for the Garden City bears a distinct resemblance to some of these, notably James Silk Buckingham's cast-iron Victoria (1849).[1] The explanation, however, lies not in direct influence but in shared values. For Howard had inherited that tradition in English utopian thought in which it was assumed that society could be improved just as a machine could—through the appropriate adjustments. A properly functioning society would thus take on the precise and well-calculated look of a good machine.

For Howard, therefore, there was nothing merely "mechanical" in the relentless symmetry of the Garden City. He wanted to make the design the physical embodiment of his ideal of cooperation, and he believed that his perfectly circular plan would best meet the needs of the citizens. He promised that every building would be "so placed to secure maximum utility and convenience."[2] This "unity of design and purpose" had been impossible in old cities formed, in Howard's view, by "an infinite number of small, narrow, and selfish decisions."[3] In the Garden City, however, an active common interest would make possible a uniform, comprehensive plan. With selfish obstructions removed, the city could assume that geometric form which Howard believed was the most efficient and the most beautiful. The symmetry of the Garden City would be the symbol and product of cooperation, the sign of a harmonious society.

The only relevant book he remembered reading was written by a physician, Dr. Benjamin Richardson, and entitled *Hygeia, A City of Health*.[4] It was an imaginative presentation of the principles of public sanitation in which Dr. Richardson depicted a city whose design would be the healthiest for its inhabitants. He prescribed a population density of twenty-five people per acre, a series of wide, tree-shaded avenues, and homes and public gardens surrounded by greenery. "Instead of the gutter the poorest child has the garden; for the foul sight and smell of unwholesome garbage, he has flowers and green sward."[5] Howard was happy to follow this prescription. The public health movement, of which Dr. Richardson was a prominent representative, was a vital force for civic action; it had persuaded the public that there was a strong correlation between the health of a community and its political and moral soundness. Howard maintained that the Garden Cities would be the healthiest in the nation. He incorporated the low population density, the wide avenues, and other features of *Hygeia* into the geometry of his own city.

The problem of health was especially important because Howard planned the Garden City to be a manufacturing center in which the factories would necessarily be close to the homes. In order to separate the residential areas and also to ensure that everyone would be within walking distance of his place of work, Howard put the factories at the periphery of the city, adjacent to the circular railroad that surrounds the town and connects it to the main line. Here one can find the enterprises appropriate to a decentralized society: the small machine shop, or the cooperative printing works, or the jam factory where the rural cooperative processes its members' fruits. As usual in the plan, physical location has a symbolic aspect. Industry has its place and its function, but these are at the outskirts of the community. Howard had little faith in the role of work—even if cooperatively organized—to provide the unifying force in society. This he left to leisure and civic enterprise.

There are two kinds of centers in the Garden City: the neighborhood centers and the (one) civic center. The neighborhoods, or "wards" as Howard called them, are slices in the circular pie. Each ward comprises one-sixth of the town, 5,000 people or about 1,000 families. Each, said Howard, "should in some sense be a complete town by itself" (he imagined the Garden City being built ward by ward).[6] The basic unit in the neighborhood is the family living in its own home surrounded by a garden. Howard hoped to be able to provide houses with gardens to all classes. Most residents would be able to afford a lot 20 by 130 feet; the most substantial homes would be arranged in crescents bordering Grand Avenue, a park and promenade that forms the center of the ward. In the middle of Grand Avenue is the most important neighborhood institution, the school. This, Howard commented, should be the first building constructed in each ward and would serve as a library, a meeting hall, and even as a site for religious worship. Churches, when they are built, also occupy sites in Grand Avenue.[7]

There are two cohesive forces that bring the residents out of their neighborhoods and unite the city. The first is leisure. The center of the town is a Central Park which provides "ample recreation grounds within very easy access of all the people."[8] Surrounding the park is a glassed-in arcade which Howard calls the "Crystal Palace": "Here manufactured goods are exposed for sale, and here most of that class of shopping which requires the joy of deliberation and selection is done."[9]

The Crystal Palace, in addition to providing an attractive setting for consumption, also permits the town, by granting or withholding leases, to exercise some control over distribution. Howard, as always, recommended a balance between individualism and central organization. He rejected the idea of one great cooperative department store run by the community, like the one in *Looking Backward*. Instead, he advocated that there be many small shops, but only one for each category of goods. If customers complain that a merchant is abusing his monopoly, the town rents space in the Crystal Palace to another shopkeeper in the same field, whose competition then restores adequate service. Whatever the merits of this solution, it aptly reflects the Radical ambivalence toward the trades that supported so many of them, the desire for economic independence without the self-destructive competition that accompanied it.

Important as consumption and leisure were in his system, Howard nonetheless reserved the very center of the Central Park to the second cohesive force, "civic spirit." He wanted an impressive and meaningful setting for the "large public buildings": town hall, library, museum, concert and lecture hall, and the hospital. Here the highest values of the community are brought together—culture, philanthropy, health, and mutual cooperation.

We might wonder what kind of cultural life a Garden City of 30,000 could enjoy, but this question did not bother Howard. He never felt the need of that intensification of experience—the extremes of diversity and excellence—which only a metropolis can offer. We must also remember, however, that Howard lived in a milieu that did not look to others to provide entertainment or enlightenment. The English middle class and a sizable part of the working class created its own culture in thousands of voluntary groups: lecture societies, choral groups, drama guilds, chamber symphonies. Here, as elsewhere, Howard disdained the kind of centralization that focused the life of a nation on a few power metropolitan institutions. He looked to small-scale voluntary cooperation not only for the economic base of the community but also for its highest cultural attainments.

The Garden City occupies 1,000 acres in the middle of a tract of 5,000 acres reserved for farms and forests.[10] This "Agricultural Belt" plays an integral role in the economy of the Garden City; the 2,000 farmers who live there supply the town with the bulk of its food. Because transportation costs are almost nonexistent, the farmer receives a good price for his produce, and the consumer gets fresh vegetables and dairy products at a reduced price. The Agricultural Belt, moreover, prevents the town from sprawling out into the countryside and ensures that the citizens enjoy both a compact urban center and ample open countryside. "One of the first essential needs of Society and of the individual," wrote Howard, "is that every man, every woman, every child should have ample space in which to live, to move, and to develop."[11] He added a new element to the rights of man—the right to space.

The Garden City in all its aspects expressed Howard's ideal of a cooperative commonwealth. It was the Zion in which he and his fellow Radicals could be at ease, the environment in which all the Radical hopes could be realized. Yet the Garden City was more than an image of felicity for Howard had carefully wedded his vision of the ideal city to a concrete plan for action. Indeed, he devoted relatively little attention to the details of the new city and a great deal to the means of achieving it. He wanted to show that there was no need to wait for a revolution to build the Garden City: it could be undertaken immediately by a coalition of Radical groups working within the capitalist system. The first successful Garden City would be a working model of a better society, and those that succeeded it would decisively alter English society. Building the Garden City was itself the revolution. The planned transformation of the environment was the nonviolent but effective strategy that the Radical movement had been seeking. The Garden City was, as Howard put it, "the peaceful path to real reform."

Howard wanted the building of the first Garden City to be an example of voluntary cooperation, and he devoted most of his book to outlining and defending his method. The key to Howard's strategy was his contention that building a new city could be *practical*, i.e., that money advanced for its construction could be paid back with interest. Funds could thus be solicited from high-minded and thrifty Radicals with the assurance that they would be both helping the cause and earning a modest return for themselves. The germ of Howard's scheme could be found in an article written in 1884 by the distinguished economist Alfred Marshall.[12] Marshall had pointed out that the rail networks which covered Great Britain rendered the concentration of so many businesses in

London economically irrational. Many businesses could be carried out far more cheaply, efficiently, and pleasantly where land was inexpensive and abundant. Marshall proposed that committees be established to buy up suitable land outside London and coordinate the movement of factories and working people. The value of the land in these new industrial parks would rise sharply, and the committees that owned them would reap a handsome profit.

Howard, who knew both the proposal and its author,[13] took up this suggestion and transformed it to suit his own ends. He began by asking the reader to assume that a group of his supporters—"gentlemen of responsible position and undoubted probity and honor," as he hopefully described them—had banded together to form a nonprofit company. They would raise money by issuing bonds yielding a fixed rate (4 or 5 percent), purchase 6,000 acres of agricultural land, and lay out a city according to Howard's plans. They would build roads, power and water plants, and all other necessities, and then seek to attract industry and residents. The company would continue to own all the land; as the population rose, the rents too would rise from the low rate per acre for agricultural land to the more substantial rate of a city with 30,000 residents. All rent would go to the company and would be used to repay the original investors. Any surplus that remained after the financial obligations had been discharged would provide additional services to the community.[14]

Howard proposed, in other words, that the Garden City be founded and financed by philanthropic land speculation. The scheme was speculative because it was a gamble on the rise in values that would result from attracting 30,000 people to a plot of empty farmland, and philanthropic because the speculators agreed in advance to forgo all but a fixed portion of the expected profits. The concept was not original with Howard. "Philanthropy at 5 percent" was a familiar feature in English reform circles, and activists from the Owenites to the Christian Socialists made use of fixed-dividend corporations to raise money for cooperative stores and workshops. The Reverend Charles Kingsley, a Christian Socialist, aptly illustrated the spirit of this reconciliation of God and Mammon when he exhorted his followers to "seek first the Kingdom of God and his Righteousness with this money of yours and see if all things—profits and suchlike— are not added unto you."[15]

Howard did add a new emphasis to this method. He stipulated that part of the rental income each year be placed in a sinking fund and used to purchase the bonds of the original investors. As the number of bondholders decreased, the amount that the company had to pay each year to the ones remaining would also decrease. Meanwhile, income from rents would be constantly growing as the town grew; the surplus, as we have seen, was earmarked for community services. Eventually the Garden City would buy out all the original investors, and the entire income from rents could be used to benefit the citizens. Taxes would be unnecessary; rents alone would generously support schools, hospitals, cultural institutions, and charities.[16]

The residents of the Garden City would thus continue to pay rent, but landlords would be eliminated. The private ownership of land for the benefit of individuals would be replaced by collective ownership for the benefit of the community. Howard placed tremendous emphasis on this change. He, like almost every other Radical, believed that the "land question"—the concentration of the ownership of land in Great Britain in the hands of a few—was, as he put it, the "root of all our problems."[17] As late as 1873 an official survey had shown that 80 percent of the land in the United Kingdom was owned by less than 7,000 persons.[18] The spread of Garden Cities would transfer land ownership on a large scale from individuals to the community, thus inaugurating an economic and social revolution.

Howard's analysis of the crucial importance of the "land question" derived from the writings of the American reformer Henry George, a hero of English Radicals in the 1880s. George was probably the most influential man of one idea in nine-teenth-century Anglo-American history. His panacea, the Single Tax (the appropriation of all rent by taxation) was based on his view that there was no real conflict between capital and labor. The "antagonism of interests," he argued, "is in reality between labor and capital on the one side and land ownership on the other."[19] The great landowners used their natural monopoly to demand exorbitant rents and thus appropriate without compensation the lion's share of the increased wealth from material progress that ought to go to the workmen and entrepreneurs who actually produced it. This perversion of the economic order impoverished the proletariat, imperiled the manufacturer, and upset the natural balance of supply and demand. It was the real cause of depressions, class conflict, and the spreading poverty that seemed an inevitable companion to progress.

Characteristically, Howard accepted everything in George's theory that pointed toward reconciliation and rejected everything that promised conflict. He rejected the Single Tax because he saw that it meant the expropriation of a whole class. He accepted, however, George's view that the solution to the land question would restore the economy to a healthy balance and create the conditions for a reconciliation of capital and labor. He believed he had found the solution to the land question himself. The Garden City, he wrote, "will, by a purely natural process, make it gradually impossible for any landlord class to exist at all." Private landholding "will die a natural but not too sudden death."[20] Building Garden Cities would accomplish all of George's aims "in a manner which need cause no ill-will, strife or bitterness; is constitutional; requires no revolutionary legislation; and involves no direct attack on vested interest."[21] The Garden City company would, in fact, enjoy all the privileges of a profit-making concern. The legal forms which landlords had designed to protect their own interests would now foster the creation of a higher form of society.

The powers extended to the Garden City company as sole landlord would be greater than the legal authority possessed by any nineteenth-century English municipality. Through its control of all leases it could effectively enforce the ground plan and zone the community without special legal authority. Howard was a firm believer in "gas and water socialism," and he stipulated that the town's board of management should provide all utilities on a nonprofit basis. He also thought the town might well establish municipal bakeries and laundries.[22]

Although the Garden City company would have the legal right to own and operate all the industry in the Garden City, Howard favored a balance of public and private control. The large factories on the periphery were clearly to be established by private industry, though Howard hoped that through profit sharing they would eventually take on a cooperative character. They still would be subject to the authority which the town as sole landlord could impose: no polluters or employers of "sweated" labor would be allowed.[23] The board of management would also share responsibility for public services with private citizens. Howard hoped that individuals would establish a large group of what he called "pro-municipal enterprises." These were public services whose necessity was not yet recognized by the majority of the citizens, but "those who have the welfare of society at heart [would], in the free air of the city, be always able to experiment on their own responsibility, . . . and enlarge the public understanding."[24] In addition to the more conventional charitable and philanthropic activities, "pro-municipal enterprises" included cooperative building and pension societies.

As income from rents grew, the municipality would gradually take over the services that voluntary cooperation had initiated. In industry, too, Howard believed the evolutionary trend was toward greater public ownership and control. The most important principle, however, was that no one have the right to impose a degree of socialism for which the citizens were not ready. The elimination of landlord's rents would remove, in Howard's view, any immediate conflict of capital with labor and permit the peaceful coexistence of capitalist and socialist industry. The balance between the public and private sectors must shift slowly with the increasing capacity of the citizens for cooperation.

Howard had the patience to begin with imperfect forms because he had the capacity to see his ideal society evolving in time. He realized that a single Garden City of 30,000 was too small to provide the full measure of diversity which a genuine city must have. A Garden City could not, however, increase its size or density; that would spoil its plan. He proposed that it grow by establishing a new sister city beyond the Agricultural Belt. Howard believed that the cities should eventually organize themselves into "town clusters, each town in the cluster being of different design from the others, yet the whole forming one large and well-thought-out plan."[25] A diagram which appeared in To-morrow showed six Garden Cities arranged in a circle around a larger Center City. The plan had the cities connected by a circular canal which provided power, water, and transportation. In the 1902 edition the canal was replaced by a more sober rapid-transit system.[26]

The Social City, as Howard called each cluster of towns, represented his most advanced conception of the marriage of town and country; here "each inhabitant of the whole group, though in one sense living in a town of small size, would be in reality living in, and would enjoy all the advantages of, a great and most beautiful city; and yet all the fresh delights of the country . . . would be within a very few minutes' ride or walk."[27] With small communities already established as the basic units in society, these units could be arranged in planned federations to secure the benefits of larger size as well. Rapid communications between the towns meant greater convenience for trade, and, "because the people, in their collective capacity own the land on which this beautiful group of cities is built, the public buildings, the churches, the schools and universities, the libraries, picture galleries, theatres, would be on a scale of magnificence which no city in the world whose land is in pawn to private individuals can afford."[28] Once established, the Social City would become the base for still higher stages of evolution that Howard never ventured to describe.

Howard's reluctance to prescribe every detail or to foresee every contingency is one of the most important aspects of his method. The visionary planner can easily become a despot of the imagination. Working alone, deprived of the checks and balances of other minds, he is tempted to become the *roi soleil* of his realm and to order every detail of life of his ideal society. If Howard's geometric plans resemble a Baroque *Residenzstadt*, Howard himself was singularly free of the pretensions of a Baroque monarch. His plans, as he pointed out, were merely diagrams to be modified when put into practice.

The same may be said for his plans for social organization. In Howard's time the advocates of Socialism and Individualism (both usually capitalized) confronted each other like Matthew Arnold's ignorant armies. Bellamy, as we have seen, believed that the entire economy of the United States could be centrally directed by a few men of "fair ability." Herbert Spencer in his individualist phase held that the use of tax money to support public libraries was a step toward collectivist slavery.[29] Howard did not presume to judge this momentous debate. He made the spatial reorganization of society his fundamental demand because he believed that a new environment would open possibilities for the reconciliation of freedom and order that neither Bellamy nor Spencer could imagine. Howard sought to discover the minimum of organization that would secure the benefits of planning while leaving to individuals the greatest possible control over their own lives. He was a collectivist who hated bureaucratic paternalism and an apostle of organization who realized that planning must stay within self-imposed limits.

4

The Peaceful Path

Whatever its intrinsic merits, the Garden City plan suffered from one overwhelming disadvantage. It was the private creation of an obscure individual, a man without credentials or connections. By 1892 Howard had succeeded in formulating his ideas;[1] but this self-proclaimed prophet of decentralization remained in real life a middle-aged London clerk, tied to his tiny office near the Inns of Court, unknown to political leaders, social reformers, or the general public. Yet Howard, who had shown no special talents in his thirty years in business, soon transformed himself into a surprisingly effective organizer for his own ideas. For the next decade he worked with the perserverance and persuasiveness of the great inventors whom he admired. By 1903 he had succeeded not only in publicizing his ideas but in amassing enough supporters and capital to begin construction of the first Garden City.

His one advantage was that he started with a clear idea of

both the strategy and tactics necessary to achieve his aims. His strategy was to assemble an "earnest and resolute minority" who could recruit the residents for the new city and, more importantly, raise the money to build it. The first community would be the prototype, and Howard believed that he could trust to the "natural growth of sound ideas" to ensure that his invention would then take hold all over England.

Howard's basic tactic was to seek supporters among those Radical groups whose aims the Garden City would further. "The work of organization," he claimed, "is therefore in large measure accomplished. The army is in existence; it has but to be mobilized."[2] Howard, however, looked only to voluntary groups for backers. He resisted the temptation to make the Garden City a matter of party politics and to seek from the state the funds and authority to build the prototype. "Parliament will simply block the path," he predicted. "The government of this country does not try great social experiments: it has first to be taught their value and convinced of their practicality by enterprising individuals and groups of individuals."[3]

Howard was not one of those utopians who are reluctant to face the inevitable modifications of their plans that soliciting allies entails. He had no rigid pattern to impose, and he actively sought to incorporate the aims of others into his schemes. The development of his ideas, therefore, did not cease with their first formulation. As we shall see, the process of winning support exerted an important influence on the meaning of the Garden City.

Howard began, appropriately enough, with the followers of Edward Bellamy whose hopes for a "Home Colony" had started him on his own plans. In 1892, when Howard was finally ready to make public his theories, the Bellamy-inspired Nationalisation of Labour Society was continuing with its scheme for organizing a 500-acre community for 2,000 people based on *Looking Backward*.[4] Despite his fundamental differences with Bellamy, Howard still hoped that the society

would adopt his plans. His first public presentation of the
Garden City idea came at a public meeting organized by the
society in February 1893.[5] As a summary of Howard's
proposals which appeared that month in the newspaper
Nationalisation News makes clear, Howard's idea was contrary to the principles of the society and beyond their capacity
to finance. Nevertheless, it caught the imagination of the members and the plan was tentatively adopted. The society, however, was unable to find the money for even a 500-acre Home
Colony; Howard's Garden City had no hope as a project of
theirs. Howard realized that he must follow Bellamy's example
and not his supporters. His goal became to publish his plan as
a book and then build an association of his own around the
supporters which the book would attract.[6]

The next five years were frustrating ones for Howard. He
collected his manuscripts into a book to be titled "The Master
Key" but was unable to find a publisher. In 1896 he submitted
a shorter version entitled, "A Garden City, or One Solution
to Many Problems," to the *Contemporary Review*.[7] The article
was rejected. Finally, in 1898, an American friend lent Howard
the £50 he needed to publish the book.[8] It appeared that year
under the title *To-morrow: a Peaceful Path to Real Reform*. If
Howard was expecting a spontaneous burst of enthusiasm
similar to that which greeted *Looking Backward*, he was again
disappointed. In its blend of interest and condescension, the
review in the *Times* (London) was typical of the many that
Howard cut out and meticulously pasted in his scrapbook. The
reviewer remarked that "if Mr. Howard could be made town
clerk of such a city he would carry it on to everybody's satisfaction. The only difficulty is to create it; but that is small
matter to Utopians."[9]

Howard was aware of the difficulty and, despite his book's
indifferent reception, he continued undaunted with his
strategy. He turned next to a group vitally interested in the
redistribution of population, the land reformers. These were
people who wished to reverse the exodus of labor from the

countryside to the cities and thus to revitalize English agriculture, which had been suffering a severe depression since the 1870s. An agricultural depression would seem an odd time for a "Back to the Land" movement; in fact, the motives of its leaders were as much social and political as economic. The rural migration to the cities, which between 1851 and 1901 reduced the percentage of the work force employed in agriculture from 21.7 to 8.7 percent, was seen as threatening the health and stability of Great Britain.[10] The former farm workers were prime recruits for the armies of the unemployed that camped in Victorian cities, and middle-class moralists feared that even the gainfully employed were exposed each day to the temptations of drinking, vice, and Marxism.

The land reformers noted that the agricultural depression did not affect all of English farming with equal severity. The largest estates, held by the great landowners, were the hardest hit, wheat, their principal product, was swamped by foreign imports and dropped 50 percent in price between 1876 and 1896. Livestock and dairy farms—which were often family farms—fared much better.[11] The idea arose that the poor of the cities could be profitably returned to their own land and the dangerous imbalance in English society reversed. Proposals ranged from forming cooperative unions of family farms (as in Denmark) to providing labor camps "where the unemployed could be profitably employed in spade labor."[12]

The largest and most influential of the reform groups was the Land Nationalisation Society, founded by Alfred Russel Wallace in 1881. Its enemy was the large landowner, and its program was state ownership of the land. The great estates would be broken up—the owners bought off with pensions—and the landless laborers who had fled to the slums of the great cities would be lured back by the promise of a family homestead held at low rents from the state. England would then reach a healthy and prosperous balance between capitalist industry in the cities and "independent yeomen" in the countryside.[13]

If the middle-class reformers who made up the Land Nationalisation Society were sufficiently radical to envisage the
expropriation of the landlords, they were also sufficiently
bourgeois to fear the social upheaval which alone could make
their program a reality. It was this impasse that Howard exploited. He argued that his plan would achieve all the goals
of the society without threatening property. Large farms in
the Agricultural Belt of the Garden City would be broken up
into small holdings, and every effort would be made to aid
city dwellers who wished to return to the land. Farmers would
have a convenient and growing market for their produce, and
their rents would return to them in the form of community
services.[14]

Wallace agreed. "Such cities," he told the annual meeting
of the Land Nationalisation Society in 1899, "would offer a
practical and very striking illustration of the truth and importance of our fundamental principles."[15] He asserted that the
Garden City was "the only proposal that" went "to the root
of the matter without being of such an alarming nature as to
be for the present out of the sphere of practical politics."[16]

The Garden City thus won its first influential advocates as
a solution to agrarian rather than urban problems. Howard
put the endorsement of the Land Nationalisation Society to
good use; with the society's help he formed his own organization. The Garden City Association was founded on June 10,
1899, in the offices of the treasurer of the LNS, Alex Payne.
A leading member of the society, Alfred Bishop, presided, and
F. W. Steere, the honorary secretary of the older organization,
assumed the same post in the younger. At first, the Garden
City Association seemed little more than an adjunct of the
LNS. A corner in the LNS office was designated as the headquarters of the Garden City Association, and a majority of its
members were prominent in the older body.[17]

Howard, however, considered that he had "mobilized" the
LNS in his own army. He still had to earn his living as a
stenographer, but he could devote most of his energy to lectur-

ing as the representative of an organized body. He traveled tirelessly throughout Great Britain, addressing any group that would listen to him. When Howard was a teenager, the pastor of his church (who was also a phrenologist) had examined his head and stated, "Mr. Howard, I will say to you what many young men have wished me to say to them, but I have not always been able to say it. I think you should become a preacher."[18] As the preacher of the "Gospel of the Garden City," Howard had finally found his calling.

The lectures won over individuals, but they still did not bring him the organized support he needed. The promise of major reinforcements came in 1901, when Howard noticed an unsolicited article endorsing the Garden City written by a prominent London lawyer, Ralph Neville. Howard hurried to Neville's office and soon secured not only his support but also his services as chairman of the Garden City Association.[19] Neville had a reputation for soundness and probity which immediately lent respectability to Howard's cause. If Neville's interest in reform stemmed from a love of humanity, he was careful to hide it. He had the same horror of sentiment that he had of bankruptcy; he supported reform measures only when he believed they followed logically from the laws of biology and economics. When Neville concluded that the Garden City was "based on sound economic principle,"[20] it was the highest accolade he could bestow, and Howard was happy to receive it.

If Howard was a classic Radical, Neville was a classic Liberal, an individualist who believed that inequality and competition were necessary parts of any society. Howard's vision of a cooperative society had no appeal to him, and he denied that radical change was either possible or desirable. Neville was attracted to the Garden City because it appeared to be a workable scheme for decreasing social conflict without government spending or intervention. Like many other Liberals, Neville was intensely afraid of urban class violence, which he attributed in large part to the baneful influence of the city itself. In the metropolis, he wrote, "the multitude of impressions received by the brain and the rapidity of their impressions, tend to induce shallowness of thought and instability of purpose. An increase of emotionalism and a loss of steadfastness are marked characteristics of town dwellers."[21] He believed that if the large city continued to be the home of the working class, "nothing could prevent the ultimate decadence and destruction of the race."[22]

The Garden City would avert this doom while its promoters served the cause of social peace and made a modest profit for themselves. Neville had a lively appreciation of the fundamental practicality of Howard's ideas, as well as of the merits of the city plan itself. He hoped in particular that the improved quality of life in the Garden City would satisfy working-class demands for higher wages, for he believed that it was "impossible to raise wages substantially without endangering the commerce upon which all classes ultimately depend."[23] In this connection he had been especially active in an organization grandiloquently called the Labour Association for Promoting Co-operative Production Based on Co-partnership of the Workers. "Co-partnership" meant that the workers had the right to become shareholders in the factories where they worked. Neville and the other members despaired of any real improvement for the working class unless the workers became capitalists and shared in the profits. As G. D. H. Cole remarked, "the idea of co-partnership appealed to them because it held out the prospect of amending capitalism without doing away with it."[24] Neville believed that the Garden City represented the logical extension of the idea of co-partnership. He was especially impressed with Howard's system of retaining landlord's rent for the community, which he saw as yet another way of raising the standard of living of the working class without endangering the capitalist system.

Under Neville's firm hand the Garden City movement moved up in the world: away from the crowded parlors of English radicalism into the more affluent drawing rooms of English liberalism. Howard and Neville developed a tacit division of labor. Howard continued to preach his Gospel of the Garden City, often to the same Radical organizations, while Neville took charge of organizing and soliciting among the substantial men of affairs who were his political colleagues. The leaders of the Labor Co-partnership Association proved to be as responsive a recruiting ground for Neville as the Land Nationalisation Society had been for Howard. More than half of Neville's associates on the board of the co-partnership group became prominent members of the Garden City Association.[25] He also drew into the movement many Liberals rather different from himself, "those devoted and kind, if rarefied, people," as Sir John Squire termed them, who were the most active element in English philanthropy. One of them, Aneurin Williams, who took a prominent role in the Garden City movement, represents what was best in this group. "His inherited means he regarded as a public trust," Squire wrote of him. "In and out of Parliament, in accordance with the general fluxes in the fortunes of Liberals of his quiet and industrious type, he never showed the slightest trace of personal ambition, merely serving the causes of political and economic reconstruction as he saw them."[26]

Finally, Neville attracted two wealthy adherents whose support brought the Garden City within striking-distance of realization. Alfred Russel Wallace had suggested that the Garden City would be an excellent investment for a philanthropic millionaire. Such men did not seek out Howard, but, through Neville's connections, he was introduced to two of them, George Cadbury and W. H. Lever. Both were self-made industrial magnates: George Cadbury and his brother Richard had built their father's cocoa firm into a great chocolate company, and Lever had attained a similar eminence in soaps. Both men, moreover, had built model towns to house their workers, Cadbury's at Bournville and Lever's at Port Sunlight. The careful planning of these towns, their open layout and ample gardens—often maintained by the team of company gardeners—made them precursors of the Garden City.[27] They were also prime examples of late nineteenth-century industrial paternalism. Cadbury and Lever were uncomfortable in the lofty position of "captains of industry" to which their business success had raised them. Their paternalism was an attempt to reestablish contact with their workers, and the company towns were founded to recreate the closer ties between master and man they remembered from their youth. The result was an environment of superior amenities, but one which invited constant interference in the workers' lives. Cadbury, for example, distributed a set of "Rules of Health" to the Bournville residents in which he cautioned them to let tea brew for more than three minutes and advised them to sleep with their mouths closed.[28] At Port Sunlight the picturesque landscaping for which the town was famous was the result of Lever's insistence on hiring a large corps of gardeners—paid for by the residents. As F. L. Olmsted, Jr. pointed out, the landscaping costs represented a far larger percentage of the workers' incomes than they would have elected to spend themselves.[29]

Howard, of course, did not share Cadbury's or Lever's paternalism. He realized, however, that their financial aid could make the Garden City a reality, and he worked with his usual persistence to win them over. He and Neville convinced them that the Garden City was the continuation of their own efforts and that his plan would spread their ideas throughout Britain. The Garden City Association moved quickly to announce its newfound support as effectively as possible. Thomas Adams, the energetic new secretary of the association, persuaded Cadbury and Lever to sponsor a conference to promote the Garden City. It was held at Bournville in September 1901; over 1,500 officials who were concerned with urban problems attended.[30] City planning as a profession hardly existed at that time. The meeting at Bournville assembled a miscellaneous group of town clerks, counselors, health officers, and aldermen who were charged with improving the cities but did not have the funds, training, or authority to do so. The Housing of the Working Classes Act of 1890 provided limited subsidies for demolishing slums and erecting new buildings, but money was hard to find for knocking down even the most noisome dwellings and even rarer for constructing their replacements.[31] George Bernard Shaw, an early supporter of the Garden City movement who attended the conference in his capacity as vestryman of St. Pancras (London), expressed the frustration of his fellow officials when he remarked that outlawing slums meant "that you turn a great mass of people out into the streets without homes. Do you suppose that that sort of reform is popular with the very class of people you intend to benefit?"[32]

Howard spoke to this problem by emphasizing that his proposals opened the prospect of creating decent and sanitary housing without mass evictions, new legislation, or grant of public funds. The Bournville conference won the Garden City a place in British town planning discussions which it never lost. "As almost every newspaper in the land gave a report of the proceedings," Howard later recalled, "our scheme was, at a bound, as it were, before the whole country."[33] Flanked by Cadbury and Lever on the platform, Howard could allow himself a measure of triumph:

> George Stephenson, when he saw the country should be covered with railroads, did not say: "This is a national matter and Parliament must build the first railway or else the country will come to grief"; he set his hand to the plough himself; and there is in this room sufficient power to start a Garden City.[34]

Howard had the right to be elated. With Neville's help he had come very far in less than a year. The days of lecturing to remote reform societies to gain one or two new adherents were over. He was the leader of a national movement, and one which appeared to command the resources to build a Garden City. All this was apparent at Bournville, and something more. The scene at the conference was richly symbolic of the future direction of the movement. The "little men" to whom Howard had originally addressed the Garden City were nowhere to be found. At his side were millionaires, and in front of him were government officials. Neither group wanted to hear of the cooperative commonwealth or radical social change. They looked to the Garden City as a plausible and thrifty means to relieve urban overcrowding. Already the Garden City design was being separated from its original purpose; the broad Radical coalition that Howard had envisioned was narrowed and refocused to an elite of notables and bureaucrats. The Garden City was succeeding not as a social movement but as a planning movement.

Howard failed to protest against these trends, in part because he had no choice, in part because he believed that once one Garden City was actually built, its example would inspire the broad support he had originally sought. The essential thing was to build the first working model while the enthusiasm generated by the Bournville conference still held. On this point, at least, Howard's associates agreed. In December 1901 the Garden City Association voted that "steps be taken at once to form a preliminary Company for the object of raising sufficient funds to investigate estates, or to secure a site or the option of one."[35] By July 1902 the Garden City Pioneer Company had raised £20,000 for the purpose.[36]

The agricultural depression, which had helped Howard earlier, was once again a factor in the success of the plan. The fall in farm prices had cut rents up to 50 percent.[37] The landed gentry, who had once zealously guarded their real estate, had become anxious to divest themselves of their ancestral heritage and to use their capital to share in the bounty of British commerce and imperialism. The Duke of Marlborough remarked in 1885 that "were there any effective demand for the purchase of land, half the land of England would be on the market tomorrow."[38] The severity of the depression had abated by 1902, but in Hertfordshire County, where the Pioneer Company most seriously pursued its search, it was estimated that 20 percent of the farms were unoccupied.[39] In the spring of 1903 the company's agent located a tract of over 3,800 acres in Hertfordshire, 34 miles northeast of London—sufficiently isolated to provide the tabula rasa for the experiment, yet connected to London by road and mainline railroad. The estate was called Letchworth after the hamlet of twenty persons that was its most densely settled area. In June 1903 the directors of the Pioneer Company resolved to buy the land, and in September the company charged with developing the new community, the First Garden City Ltd., was officially registered.[40] A month later Howard, the Earl of Grey, George Cadbury, W. H. Lever, Ralph Neville, and other Garden City supporters assembled at Letchworth to take possession of the estate and to inaugurate the new era in civilization with a round of speeches.[41]

5

Building the Garden City

HOWARD'S THEORIES were now irrevocably tied to what happened on the more than 3,000 acres in Hertfordshire. The necessity of finding large sums of money to develop the new city made Howard increasingly dependent on the support of a few Liberal magnates like Cadbury and Lever. He never succeeded in building the broad coalition of reformist groups he had hoped to assemble—a fact that inevitably modified the tone and substance of his ideas. One source of working-class support that could have improved the balance was conspicuous in its absence: the cooperative movement. Howard looked to the "cooperators" to provide the leadership and experience for the working class to begin their own enterprises. "The true remedy for capitalist oppression where it exists," he wrote, "is not the strike of no work but the strike of true work. . . . If labor leaders spent half the energy in cooperative organization they now waste in cooperative disorganization, the end of our present unjust system would be at hand."[1]

The cooperative movement, moreover, was probably the only working-class organization which had the resources to contribute significantly to the building of the Garden City. The movement had more than 2 million members organized into 1,600 local societies which sold £92 million of goods in 1903 and distributed £10 million in profits.[2] The cooperative societies had either built or advanced the money for more than 37,000 houses by 1903, and the movement's factories manufactured more than £10 million of goods annually.[3]

Howard's supporters in the movement hoped that cooperators would be the principal builders of the Garden City. At each of the annual Cooperative Congresses from 1900 to 1909 they argued that the next step toward the cooperative commonwealth was to organize the movement's stores, factories, and homes (which were now scattered over Great Britain) into the new environment that Howard promised.[4] Despite influential support among the national leaders—J. C. Grey, chairman of the Cooperative Wholesale Society, was among the founders of the Manchester branch of the Garden City Association[5]—the congresses refused either to support First Garden City Ltd., or to build their own Garden City. The individual distributive societies were more anxious to preserve their independence than they were to create a new civilization. The cooperative counterbalance to capitalist investment and production at Letchworth never developed.

In the absence of any significant working-class support, the values of Neville and his fellow businessmen dominated First Garden City Ltd. For Howard, the Garden City was an environment in which capitalism could be peacefully superseded. Most of his supporters, however, looked to the Garden City as the place where capitalism could be most easily preserved.

Neville, who assumed the post of chairman of the executive of First Garden City Ltd., proposed to raise funds to begin construction by issuing £300,000 in shares with the annual dividend not to exceed 5 percent of their par value. Neville believed that if the shares were to be sold, the company must purge itself of any utopian hopes and present itself at all times as a solid business venture and a good investment. "For mere philanthropy the money would not be forthcoming."[6] When Howard in his speeches mentioned the risks involved in starting a new city, Neville sternly reproached him. "I appreciate your reluctance to ask poor people to invest their savings, but there is all the difference in the world between refraining from enticing and deprecating investment."[7]

Faced with a board of prominent businessmen who were used to getting their own way, Howard was in danger of losing control of his own movement. The first test came over the land question. Howard proposed to retain the rise in land values for the community by disposing of all land in 1,000-year leases which would provide for reassessment by an impartial committee every four years. If the value had increased over the last assessment, the rent would also be increased.[8] Howard hoped, as we have seen, that the rising income from rents would soon far exceed what was necessary to pay the 5 percent return to the stockholders and that the surplus could be used for community services.

Neville believed, however, that potential residents of Letchworth would be confused by the unfamiliar features of such a lease and would be frightened off by the fear of drastic rent increases. He therefore advocated a standard ninety-nine year lease at a fixed rent.[9] The community, in other words, would have to wait 100 years before negotiating a new lease at a higher rent and thus collecting its share of the "unearned increment."

The other businessmen on the board agreed with Neville. Howard, who was still earning his living as a stenographer, was no match for a cocoa millionaire or a soap magnate. He took the defeat in good spirits because he agreed with the businessmen that concern for details must not stand in the way of the speedy completion of the town. The prototype must first exist; it would then inspire others to more perfect efforts.

> The first result [of the building of Letchworth] will be that the number of people who favor the Garden City will be increased a hundredfold; and then a glorious task which an insignificant minority could not compass will be found quite easy by a majority of the nation. A splendid organization will be created and a City will then arise as superior in its beauty and magnificence to our first crude attempt as is the finished canvas of a great artist to the rough and untaught attempts of a schoolboy.[10]

In 1903 the company made perhaps its most important decision: it chose the firm of Parker and Unwin to be the architects of Letchworth. Barry Parker was a young architect from Derbyshire who began his career as a designer of textiles and wallpapers influenced by the arts-and-crafts movement.[11] Raymond Unwin, whose association with the Garden City was the start of a long career in city planning that would make him the leading British authority, was trained as an engineer and came to architecture under the influence of William Morris.[12] Both men were early supporters of Howard; as followers of Morris, they were engaged in a search that paralleled Howard's own. Morris had taught that the artist's efforts to create a beautiful society could not be separated from the activist's attempts to create a just one. "Before there can be a city greatly beautiful," wrote Unwin, "there must be some noble common life to find expression."[13]

But if Parker and Unwin sympathized with Howard's goals, they had no use for his rationalistic, geometric methods of town planning. They gave to the Garden City movement their own vision of the "city greatly beautiful," a vision derived from the medieval village as seen through the eyes of William Morris. They wanted to adapt what they believed were the still-valid principles of traditional English town planning to the decentralized society of the future. Where Howard had expressed the architecture of cooperation in the mechanical symmetry of his original plan, Parker and Unwin sought instead what they called "organic unity."

They followed Howard's lead to the extent of clearly separating the town from the countryside that surrounded it. They placed the new city roughly in the middle of the Letchworth estate, setting aside 1,200 acres for the city proper and 2,800 acres for the Agricultural Belt that would surround it. Within the city, however, they rejected Howard's rigidly symmetrical diagrams and instead sought a more subtle "organic" sense of order suggested by the terrain. They took advantage of the positions of the hills, streams, an old Roman road, and even some of the larger trees to define the plan of the town. The "Crystal Palace" was replaced by a gently curving street of shops. Only the town center remained exactly what Howard intended it to be: a formal arrangement of municipal and cultural buildings.[14]

The contrast between Howard and his two architects was not, however, one simply between Howard's utilitarian bias and Parker and Unwin's aesthetic bent. If anything, Parker and Unwin were more practical than Howard. Industry, instead of forming a uniform periphery to Howard's circle, was grouped into an industrial park adjacent to the power plant and to the railroad. The tracks, in turn, separated industry from the residential area. The plan is effective without calling attention to itself through a calculated prettiness. In their quest for a natural unity Parker and Unwin succeeded—perhaps too well. As Herbert Read has pointed out, it is possible to visit Letchworth and even to live there without being aware that it is a conscious creation.[15]

Parker and Unwin believed that organic unity must extend up from the plan to embrace a common style of architecture. They saw the eclectic architecture of their time—in which a suburban villa tricked out with classical porticoes might be sandwiched between a Gothic extravaganza on the right and a Renaissance palazzo on the left—as a horrible symptom of the chaotic individualism of their time. They held that the victory of cooperation in the Garden City could best be expressed in a consistent style derived from traditional village architecture, the brick and stucco, the gables and tile roofs of Hertfordshire. This was not mere antiquarianism, for Parker and Unwin "democratized" traditional architecture. Where other architects had used the vocabulary of picturesque gables and tiled roofs to glorify the suburban castles of the rich, Parker and Unwin employed traditional designs to express the unity of a cooperatively organized community of equals. In the context of their time, their designs for Letchworth stood for cleanliness, simplicity, and the honest use of materials—qualities the arts-and-crafts movement associated with the fourteenth century and hoped to revive in the twentieth. The fourteenth-century village, they believed, was the truest community that England had ever known, and its beauty was the expression of a unique balance of order and uniformity. This balance they hoped to recapture in that revitalized community of the future, the Garden City.

Parker and Unwin's designs thus bore little resemblance to Howard's plan for geometric boulevards and iron-and-steel Crystal Palaces. Nevertheless, both concepts derived from a common search for an architecture of cooperation. Parker and Unwin's plan was a sort of translation of Howard's original diagrams. It was, however, a loose translation which introduced some themes of its own. Unwin's hope that the Garden City would "give life just that order, that crystalline structure it had in feudal times,"[16] sounds a note of nostalgia for vanished stability not heard in Howard. Unwin's aesthetic glorification of the traditional village was also a glorification of the stable social relations he imagined existed there, and an implicit critique of the modern quest for change. For Unwin, the beautiful old English villages had "the appearance of being an organic whole, the home of a community" because they were "the expression of a corporate life in which all the different units were personally in touch with each other, consciously and frankly accepting their relations, and, on the whole, content with them."[17] Like the villagers themselves, "every building honestly confessed just what it was, and so fell into its place."[18] The Garden City, too, would be a community where everyone has his place and is content with it.

Parker and Unwin's concept of the Garden City thus had its reactionary as well as its forward-looking aspects. The two architects lacked Howard's confident faith in industrialization and the nineteenth-century world of rapid social change. For them, the Garden City was a place in which industrialization could be kept in its proper (subordinate) place and the incessant striving of modern times would yield to order and contentment. In their idealization of the English village, Parker and Unwin brought to prominence an element in the Garden City that had hardly existed in Howard: the fear of the great city and its social turmoil, the desire to discard the burdens of progress and return to the simple life. Their plans embodied the new stage in the Garden City movement, the stage in which Howard's influence was counterbalanced by Liberals like Cadbury, who looked back to an imagined paternalistic order. With their mixture of the enlightened and the medieval, Parker and Unwin reflected this split in the movement between an optimistic endorsement of the future and a nostalgic wish to escape from the modern world.

But Parker and Unwin, like the Garden City movement in general, ought to be judged not only on their realized plans but also on their aspirations. Their most revolutionary idea was never put into practice. In 1901, even before the decision to build a Garden City had been taken, Unwin proposed that the houses in the new city be organized cooperatively. His plan provided for "quadrangles" of homes in which three sides would be devoted to private apartments and the fourth to a common dining room, recreation room, and nursery. Food and coal would be purchased jointly, and the residents would share the cost of hiring cooks and maids. The quadrangle, he hoped, would become the basic unit of Garden City architecture, giving the city a "greater harmony and unity of effect" than would be possible where the land was carved into separate plots.[19]

Howard himself took up the plan in 1906—"I believe the time has now come when [cooperation] can be successfully tried as one of the central ideas in domestic life,"[20] he wrote—but even his efforts resulted in only one quadrangle called Homesgarth.[21] Although Unwin modeled the quadrangle on an Oxford college, Homesgarth was too close in conception and design to communitarian experiments to be entirely respectable. Homesgarth, however, was no utopian scheme. "Its first object," Howard said, was "to provide a house of comparative comfort and beauty for the numerous folks of the middle class who have a hard struggle for existence on a mere budget—for those who require domestic help but can very ill afford it."[22] Homesgarth's small scale—only twenty-four families—and careful balance between family privacy and community functions is characteristic of Howard's pragmatic reinterpretation of the utopian tradition. In Howard's view, it was a piece of the new civilization and an important attempt to make cooperation part of the daily life of the Garden City.

Parker and Unwin hoped that even if First Garden City Ltd. would not support their plans for quadrangles, it would still provide funds to build the houses of Letchworth according to their designs. The company, however, was in serious financial difficulty. The original stock issue sold slowly; the directors bought £40,000, and some £60,000 was sold to the public in the first year, but it took three years to reach £150,000.[23] During those three years the company was forced to spend over £600,000 to provide the roads, gasworks, electrical generators, and other utilities the town needed.[24] The company was able to borrow the funds for these necessities, but it was unwilling to go more deeply in debt. Many of the first houses in Letchworth were built by speculative contractors whose designs introduced precisely those eccentricities that Parker and Unwin had wanted to banish from the town. These homes, however, were well suited to the tastes of Letchworth's first residents, many of whom were men and women of independent means and "advanced" opinions. Their enthusiasms included theosophy, vegetarianism, dress reform, and amateur theatricals; Letchworth was soon reputed to have more committees per person than any other town in England.[25] The company, fearing that Letchworth might soon get the reputation as a colony of cranks, then solemnly informed the press that only one resident habitually wore a toga and sandals.[26] When several men broke with convention by refusing to wear hats (which were then considered as necessary to outdoor attire as trousers), the town staged a public debate between the "Hatters" and the "No-hatters." A company agent who believed that manufacturers would refuse to locate their plants where the norms of society were so openly questioned interrupted the proceedings and roundly denounced the "No-hatters" as unpatriotic citizens who did not have the interests of Letchworth at heart.[27]

Despite the company's apprehensions, manufacturers did come to Letchworth. Only a few, like the cooperatively run Garden City Press Ltd. were attracted to the city for ideological reasons. Most came for precisely the practical reasons that Howard and especially Neville had foreseen. The rise in business activity in the first decade of the twentieth century created a demand for increased space that was hard to satisfy in London. Letchworth offered low rents, minimal taxes, and ample room to grow. When, for example, the publishing firm of J. W. Dent discovered that its London facilities offered no room for expansion, the publisher established a branch plant at Letchworth. The "Everyman" series of inexpensive classics was printed there.[28] Other enterprises began as the project of an amateur inventor and moved from a Letchworth garage to the industrial park. Light engineering and printing were the principle Garden City industries.[29]

The new factories promised to make Letchworth a self-supporting community. As houses and shops began to line the streets that Parker and Unwin had laid out, the social structure of the new town underwent a rapid change. A census taken of the 1,400 Letchworth residents in 1905 showed that almost all of them were from two groups: middle-class men and women of independent means (and their servants) and the skilled artisans who were building the new town.[30] By 1907 the population had more than doubled, and almost all the new residents were factory workers.[31]

Howard was now faced with the challenge to make good his claim that the Garden City would bring to working people health and living standards they could never have obtained in the old cities. Whatever the interests of his associates, he had not forgotten his belief that the Garden City would provide all the benefits which others were seeking from political and economic revolution. In practice, this challenge focused on housing. Could the Garden City accomplish what no other public or private organization in England had been able to do: construct decent dwellings that even the lowest-paid workers could afford? This meant, of course, building under existing social conditions. Howard had to assume that the tenants' wages would remain low, that interest on capital would continue to be paid, and that no government subsidy could be expected. If the Garden City would create good housing for all its citizens under these circumstances, then Howard's claim that it represented "the peaceful path to real reform" would receive powerful support.

Howard was convinced that planning, architectural ingenuity, and voluntary cooperation could solve the housing question. A cooperative building society, Garden City Tenants Ltd., was established in 1904 to raise capital for workers' housing.[32] As a stopgap measure, Thomas Adams persuaded the editor of *Country Life* to hold that magazine's "cheap cottage" competition at Letchworth. After the exhibition, the model cottages were sold very cheaply indeed to Letchworth workers.[33]

Garden City Tenants Ltd. then turned to Raymond Unwin

for the multi-unit dwellings the new town needed. Unwin's designs show the Garden City movement at its best—pragmatic, democratic, responsive to the needs of the people it served.[34] Unwin gave the same attention to these projects that other architects devoted to the rich man's villa. He made sure that every cottage got its share of sunlight, that every window and door were properly placed. That institutional bleakness which afflicts British (and not only British) architects when planning for the "lower orders" was completely absent from Unwin's work. Instead, there was a real sense of individual well-being and community solidarity, precisely the "organic unity" that Unwin had proclaimed.

The individual cottages were not left detached, as in the middle-class villas, but joined into rows of three to ten. These rows were then grouped around a central courtyard or field. This plan used far less land per unit than the villas and gave to each family the privacy of a two-story dwelling with its own garden. At the same time, there was substantial open space which could be shared in common. Within each cottage Unwin decided not to attempt to duplicate middle-class layouts, with their separate parlor, living room, dining room, and kitchen; on the small scale of the cottage this would have made the rooms claustrophobic. Moreover, Unwin wanted to design houses that "honestly confessed just what they were," not scaled-down copies of inappropriate models. He appreciated the fact that working-class family life traditionally centered around the hearth, and he therefore designed a combination living room–kitchen to be as comfortable, spacious, and open as possible.

At its best, Unwin's work represents that fruitful balance of individual and community which the Garden City stood for and which housing projects have seldom achieved since. It had, however, one great deficiency. When the costs of the new houses were added up, only skilled workers could afford them. The wages of the unskilled were simply too close to the subsistence level for them to be able to pay the rent for any home that Unwin or Howard would call decent. As Howard later admitted, it was the bicycle that saved the situation. Workers who could not find housing in the Garden City bicycled each day from their jobs to apartments in the older towns beyond the Agricultural Belt, where cheap but substandard accommodations could be found.[35] One can hardly blame Unwin and Howard for their failure. If they were unable to build decent workers' housing without a subsidy, neither could anyone else.

These efforts in housing illustrate the real strengths and ultimate limitations of the Garden City idea as a social movement. By 1910 the practicality of Howard's basic concept had been proved. The new town of Letchworth was a clean, healthy, and well-planned environment; it had shown its capacity to attract industry and residents; and the First Garden City Ltd., though still financially pressed, was beginning to reap the rewards of its investment and declare its first dividend. The housing question, however, demonstrated that, despite Howard's hopes, the Garden City could not create its own oasis of social justice in an unjust society. Lower costs, better planning, community ownership of land—none of these could fully compensate for the inequities that were inherent in the social system of Howard's time. The path to real reform lay outside the Garden City.

By 1910, however, Howard was still looking to the future with confidence. He realized that Letchworth had its limitations, but Letchworth was only the first working model which would surely inspire dozens and then hundreds of improved successors. But in 1910 the First Garden City was still the only Garden City, and no more were in the works. The problem for Howard was: where were the other Garden Cities that would begin to transform England?

6

Elder Statesman

THROUGHOUT the rest of his life Howard attempted to cope with the implications of his partial success at Letchworth. His hopes for a fundamental change in British society rested on the faith that his experiment would inspire numerous others, but the long and arduous task of building the first Garden City did not encourage anyone to attempt a second. Howard's self-examinations, however, stopped short of questioning his basic strategy. He believed that the chief shortcomings of Letchworth were the lack of cooperative enterprise and the needless duplication of inefficient shops.[1] These, however, were deficiencies that could be corrected. Howard never confronted the inherent shortcomings in his method. Building the prototype of a decentralized civilization had, in fact, centralized the activities of its supporters and concentrated all the available capital and talent on one city. The Garden City Association made the completion of Letchworth its fundamental priority, an inevitable consequence, perhaps, of the sizable sums that the leading members of the Association had invested in First Garden City Ltd. Any new project that threatened to divert scarce resources from Letchworth received faint encouragement from the association. Continual absorption in the specific problems of Letchworth inevitably narrowed the outlook of the movement and diminished its élan; the publicity and interest that Howard and his associates had aroused at the ground-breaking could not be maintained over a decade. Meanwhile, London and the other great English cities continued to grow on a scale that dwarfed Howard's efforts to oppose them. The greater London area alone added 450,000 new residents to its population in the decade 1900–1910, the equivalent of fourteen full-sized Garden Cities.[2]

If Howard still believed that voluntary groups of philanthropic citizens could reverse this trend, many of his younger supporters began to look to the state as the only body which could effect the changes on a national scale that both they and Howard were seeking. The Liberal victory in the general election of 1906 seemed to open the possibility for new legislation that Howard could not have foreseen in the 1890s. Forty-seven MP's in 1906 were members of the Garden City Association or stockholders in First Garden City Ltd.[3] With the encouragement of the association they actively supported a new Town Planning Bill which became law in 1909. Although the provisions of this act gave little help to the towns and none whatsoever to the Garden City, it raised the possibility of more substantial action.[4]

The promise was not fulfilled, however, until World War I, when Lloyd George announced a program of "homes for heroes" to be built when peace returned. In 1917, C. B. Purdom wrote a pamphlet, "The Garden City After the War," in which he argued that the new housing should become the basis for national planning according to Garden City principles.[5] Purdom joined with two other Young Turks, W. C.

Taylor and F. J. Osborn, to issue a manifesto of their program, *New Towns After the War*, which called upon Parliament to provide funds for more than 100 Garden Cities.[6]

There was a fourth signer of the manifesto, Ebenezer Howard. Howard was sufficiently pragmatic to accept support from any source, even the government. He had, in fact, proposed in 1911 that the government found a Garden City as a memorial to Edward VII, but he had little enthusiasm for this method.[7] As his colleagues drafted a memorandum to the Ministry of Reconstruction and sought support from the political parties, Howard wrote privately to a friend that the founding of another Garden City by private efforts would be "the very best form of propaganda."[8] Without informing his friends he began looking for suitable sites for a new city. In the spring of 1919 he learned that 1,000 acres near the Hertfordshire village of Welwyn—midway, roughly, between Letchworth and London—were about to be auctioned off. He hurriedly raised some money from wealthy supporters but not enough to pay even an auctioneer's deposit. Nevertheless he sent an agent to the auction, put in the highest bid for the land, and persuaded his agent to lend him the money for the deposit.[9] He then used the same powers of argument to convince his younger supporters to join him in the arduous task of starting Welwyn Garden City. As Osborn put it, "The four New Townsmen, who set out to persuade Britain to build one hundred new towns, found instead that for a large part of their lives they were to participate in the building of one new town."[10]

The same method of philanthropic land speculation that had been used at Letchworth was now employed to finance Welwyn. Howard had not lost his skill in persuading rich men to back his projects, and his experiences at Letchworth had greatly increased his contacts. Welwyn Garden City Ltd. was headed by Sir Theodore Chambers, and its shares—their dividends limited to 7 percent of par value—were bought by a group of wealthy subscribers.[11] Welwyn had one important advantage that Letchworth lacked: the Housing Act of 1919 provided crucial subsidies for building working-class homes. Another notable source of support came from the New Town Council, a Quaker organization that leased a large tract in the prospective Agricultural Belt to divide up into smallholdings for ex-servicemen.[12] The architect, Louis de Soissons, followed Parker and Unwin's lead at Letchworth, but he took advantage of their experience (and the more ample funds at his disposal) to design a more efficient and consistent layout. The uniform blandness of the neo-Georgian style he adopted for Welwyn, however, makes the second Garden City less interesting architecturally than the first.

Howard had just turned seventy when the construction of Welwyn Garden City began. Although, as at Letchworth, he soon learned to leave the details of management to the company officials, he did devote considerable attention to the arrangements for shopping. At his insistence the company founded a new department store, the Welwyn Stores, and gave it a temporary monopoly. Howard believed that one large store could provide goods for the citizens of Welwyn more cheaply and efficiently than many small ones could; at the same time, it would earn a profit for Welwyn Garden City Ltd. equivalent to the rents the company would have received from a normal shopping district.[13]

The store, a small-town version of the national Department Store in *Looking Backward*, showed that the elderly head of the Garden City movement had not forgotten the radical enthusiasms of his youth and middle age. The movement itself, however, had grown increasingly remote from the social concerns that inspired its founder. Howard's original plan to make the Garden City the basis of a "great and glorious revolution at the end of the nineteenth cenutry"[14] seemed utopian indeed to his followers in the 1920s. Those who still shared his hopes for land reform, social welfare measures, and the reconciliation of capital and labor turned to the political parties in Parliament to fulfill them. The two aims of creating a new environment and creating a just society, which were so closely linked in Howard's mind, were sharply separated in the minds of his supporters. This was especially true of the bureaucrats and professional planners who claimed to be "neutral" and "above politics." They completed the suppression of the radical content of Howard's ideas that Neville and his fellow businessmen had initiated.

The Garden City movement, therefore, gradually lost its commitment to social change and became a city planning movement in the narrow sense. The sponsors of Welwyn Garden City no longer claimed to be initiating a revolutionary transformation in English society: their hope was to create one new community which would be clean, compact, and close to nature. The opponents of the movement no longer accused it of being subversive. Their principal charges were that the Garden City was dull, "anti-urban," and self-consciously provincial.[15]

Howard took little part in this debate. As the construction of Welwyn progressed, he gradually withdrew from an active role in the movement. He took up Esperanto in the belief that this language would help him communicate with potential supporters in other countries.[16] He also returned to his youthful search for an invention that would make his fortune. The Garden City had earned Howard an international reputation but very little money. George Bernard Shaw wrote that the English nation owed Howard a earldom for Letchworth and a dukedom for Welwyn.[17] He actually received a Civil List Pension of £75 per year in 1913 and was knighted in 1927. Neither honor enabled him to rise above the modest standard of living he would have enjoyed as a stenographer. Shortly before his death he had to borrow £50 from Shaw to continue work on an improved stenography machine which he hoped would revolutionize the trade.[18]

Howard revived another enthusiasm of his youth—spiritualism. He attended seances in order to communicate with his first wife, who had died in 1904.[19] When the lighting was adequate, he would use his stenographic skills to preserve an exact record of the messages from the beyond.[20] Aside from this diversion, Howard settled comfortably into an obscure retirement in Welwyn Garden City. He bought a cottage near the center of the city he had founded and devoted himself to gardening, tinkering with new inventions, and entertaining the neighborhood children. He died at his home on May 1, 1928.

Beyond the Grave

AT A SEANCE he attended in 1926, Howard received this message from his first wife: "You have accomplished more than you know." He was not comforted by her assurance; he had been hoping for something more specific.[1] We can now see that his wife's spirit had at least a generalized gift of prophecy. The prospects for building even one more Garden City seemed dim in 1926, but twenty-five years later a series of New Towns inspired by Letchworth and Welwyn were changing the living patterns of Great Britain. Howard's working models had at last stimulated a nationwide transformation. This posthumous achievement was brought about by his former associates, led by Frederic J. Osborn. They pushed forward the process of pragmatic accommodation which Howard had begun, modifying still further the original Garden City idea. The story of Howard's accomplishments and theories does not end with 1928.

The decade that followed Howard's death was a period of ideological reappraisal for the Garden City movement. The building of Welwyn Garden City did not resolve the problem of finding a successful strategy of action. Although the town grew faster than Letchworth—a considerable achievement in the British economy of the 1920s and 1930s—neither the government nor private enterprise was inspired to establish additional Garden Cities. The leaders of the movement were forced to consider the growing disparity between the scale of their efforts and the scale of the problem they intended to solve. F. J. Osborn pointed out that, in the absence of national planning, the government's new housing subsidies merely accelerated urban sprawl.[2] Raymond Unwin despairingly observed in 1932 that "we have worked for thirty years and have only succeeded in accommodating about 24,000 persons in the two garden cities of Letchworth and Welwyn; whereas during the last ten years that number of available persons have settled in the Greater London area every twelve weeks."[3]

Unwin concluded that the only possible answer was government action to plan whole regions. The case for state action soon found a full-time spokesman in Osborn, who resigned from his post at Welwyn Garden City to become honorary secretary of the Garden Cities and Town Planning Association in 1936. Like Howard, Osborn was an "amateur" at city planning. He was an impoverished London clerk and an earnest Fabian until an offer of a job as a rent collector brought him to Letchworth in 1912. His early years as a Fabian are directly relevant to his later career; the strategy of "permeation" which he practiced as chief lobbyist for the Garden City movement owed more to the Fabians than to Howard. Osborn decisively discarded Howard's tactics of appealing to private individuals and relying on voluntary action. He sought instead to win over politicians, civil servants, and professional planners. At the same time, he adapted Howard's ideas to the ideology of the centralized welfare

83

state. Howard, as we have seen, believed that the creation of Garden Cities was an alternative to the growth of state power. Osborn, on the other hand, did not wish to limit centralized government. He held that the only hope for the Garden City was to make it part of the program of a government committed to planning at the national level. The citizen's right to space, he argued, must be guaranteed along with his right to food, clothing, and shelter.[4]

If Osborn's attachment to the welfare state seems to align him exclusively with left, his equally strong attachment to the single-family home won him many supporters among the Conservatives. Osborn believed that only the detached house surrounded by its own garden could prove the proper environment for the English family. (He was especially critical of high-rise apartments as a setting for family life.) New Garden Cities would provide ample sites for family homes with industry nearby; but, as he made clear to the Conservatives, only government planning could create the scores of New Towns necessary to make England a nation of homes. In this approach he maintained the balance between individualism and collectivism that characterized Howard's thought.

Osborn, however, had no illusions that the centralized bureaucracies would plan themselves—and the great cities which were their natural homes—out of existence. He abandoned Howard's hopes for a genuinely multicentered society. The new cities he hoped to construct were explicitly conceived as "satellite towns," necessarily peripheral to the large cities, which would remain the real centers of English society.

Osborn's attempts to persuade the British government to build Garden Cities were a remarkable example of successful permeation. He began in earnest when Neville Chamberlain appointed a commission headed by Lord Barlow to consider the location of industry. Osborn was not a member, but he "camped on their doorstep" and helped to write the commission's strong recommendations for the planned decentralization of industry.[5] The recommendation was given added urgency by the date of its publication: 1940. Osborn redoubled his efforts because he believed that substantial reconstruction was inevitable after the war. The problem was to decide on a national policy so that the pressure for immediate housing would not overwhelm planners at the war's end. He patiently pushed his proposals through a series of wartime committees. The most important, the Uthwatt Committee, established the principle of government action to regulate land use—zoning on a national level.[6]

Osborn's arguments permeated both parties, and the great Labour victory in 1945 did not slow the progress of his ideas. Lewis Silkin, the new Minister of Town and Country Planning, appointed a committee headed by Lord Reith to pursue the creation of new towns. The Reith Committee established the basic features of the New Towns program.[7] In this plan the government takes the place of Howard's "gentlemen of responsible position and of undoubted probity and honor"; it raises the money to purchase land and design the new city, and then offers leases to homeowners and to industry. As in Howard's scheme of philanthropic land speculation, the income from the leases pays off the government's investment.

The Reith Committee reports were embodied in the New Towns Act of 1946. Construction of the towns themselves soon followed: the latest report of the Commission for the New Towns lists thirty-four cities.[8] One of them, however, is Ebenezer Howard's second Garden City. In 1948 Welwyn was purchased under the provisions of the New Towns Act and incorporated into a system of satellite cities around London. In the 1960s Howard's first Garden City provided convincing —if ironic—proof of the practicality of his scheme. The First Garden City Ltd. still owned all the land on which Letchworth stood. Some real estate speculators attempted to buy the company, raise the rents, and thus collect for themselves the "unearned increment" that Howard had intended the community itself receive. Howard had foreseen this danger. In 1907 he predicted that the citizens could easily surmount it by banding together to exercise their rights to buy the stock themselves.[9] In 1962 the citizens did organize—they organized a pressure group to present their problems to Parliament. In that year Parliament authorized the purchase of the old company, and on January 1, 1963 the First Garden City Ltd. was replaced by a public corporation.[10] Letchworth, Howard's "working model of a new civilization," is now part of the British welfare state.

8

Summation

NOTHING is more discouraging to any idealistic movement than partial success. Howard's experience at Letchworth and Welwyn led his followers to abandon his methods and make their peace with the welfare state. The welfare state has since disappointed those who expected order and justice from it; in comparison, Howard's original goal of a genuinely multi-centered society seems surprisingly fresh and exciting. In an age of centralized bureaucratic planning, we can better appreciate the wisdom of Howard's modesty, his understanding of the limitations of outside control, his concern to leave the final development of a city to the citizens themselves, and his careful balance of cooperation and individualism.

We can also appreciate, if not share, the radical optimism that marked Howard's ideas. He always refused to recognize the existing cities or the existing social order as the necessary context for planning. The enormous *fact* of London and the other great urban centers never impressed him. In the name of progress he called for the dismantling of the very cities that sheltered the most advanced centers of art and science. His faith in evolution had convinced him that man could and must outgrow any environment that thwarted human brotherhood. In Howard's thought the transformation of the environment became the central act in the creation of a new civilization. To the planner—the man of imagination and justice—he assigned the task of designing homes and cities that would make cooperation among men and contact with nature the basis of daily life. The planner thus became the real founder of the new society. The responsibilities of this role were too great for Howard's successors, who sought to redefine themselves as technicians for the welfare state. Only Frank Lloyd Wright and Le Corbusier, two architects of genius, formulated in their own thought a conception of planning as ambitious as that conceived by the modest stenographer who invented the Garden City.

II

Frank Lloyd Wright

9

Truth Against the World

IN APRIL 1935, Frank Lloyd Wright exhibited a meticulously detailed scale model of Broadacres, his ideal city, at an
industrial arts exposition held in Rockefeller Center. There,
deep within the complex of skyscrapers that concentrated
wealth and power had built—inside the "entrails of enormity,"
as he put it—he showed for the first time his three-dimensional "cross section of a whole civilization" that had been
radically decentralized. New York and every other city larger
than a rural county seat no longer existed, nor did the large
organizations that had made the metropolis their home.
Everything "big business built to be big" had withered away;
there were no urban centers or any need of them. In Wright's
words, the city had "gone to the Countryside."

Like the Garden City, Broadacre City is an application of
the principle of decentralization, but an application so bold
that beside it the Garden City seems staidly traditional. For
Howard's advocacy of decentralization had stopped with the

Garden City itself. Although he talked of the "marriage of town and country," his plan preserves the accustomed separation of the two. Within the clearly defined borders of Howard's city, everything is compact, symmetrical, urban—in a word, *centralized*. One can look at Wright's model of Broadacres, however, and not see a city at all. There is no recognizable center, no point at which the natural world gives way to an environment dominated by man. In Broadacre City, decentralization reaches the point at which the urban/rural distinction no longer exists. The man-made environment is distributed over the open countryside until its structures appear to be natural, "organic" parts of the landscape. Rather than Howard's or Unwin's close-knit neighborhoods, there are hundreds of separate homesteads in the midst of fields, each the site of an inward-turning domestic and economic life. In Broadacre City homesteading is the dominant way of life. Each citizen has the right to as much land as he can use—a minimum of one acre per person—and everyone would be at least a part-time farmer.

Yet Broadacre City is not a plan for a return to a subsistence economy. On the contrary, it represents Wright's vision of the true form for the Machine Age. The metropolis with its centralized institutions was not, Wright asserted, the greatest embodiment of progress but the greatest barrier to it. He saw the big city as a monstrous aberration built by greed, destructive both to efficient production and to human values. Man would reap the benefits of the Machine Age, Wright proclaimed, only when he returned to his natural home, the land. Scattered among the farms of Broadacre City, therefore, are all the institutions of an advanced society: factories, schools, stores, professional buildings, and cultural centers. They are all small-scale and placed to ensure that there would be no central point around which people and power could cluster. Office buildings rise beside quiet lakes; factories nestle in the woods; a few shops gather at a country crossroads; churches, hospitals, and schools seem to grow from the fields. With its network of highways, such a city might cover 100 square miles or more.

This extreme dispersion would have been literally inconceivable to Ebenezer Howard. Working at the turn of the century, Howard freely invented complicated networks of interurban railways and even canals, but he never imagined anything like the automobiles and superhighways which make possible Wright's concept of a radically decentralized community. The Garden City citizen is still a man on foot who must be within walking (or perhaps bicycling) distance of every part of the town. Railroads make possible rapid movement from the centers to the countryside, but this movement must follow the railroad lines; at the same time, the discontinuous stops reinforce the need for people to gather close to a central point—the station—where shops, offices, and other meeting places can be found. The result is the Garden City pattern of open countryside dotted with compact planned cities.

If the Garden City had its genesis in the railroad era, Broadacre City belongs to the still-optimistic beginnings of the automobile age. Wright saw that the personal car provides a new mastery of time and space on which a new kind of city can be built. Traveling at 60 miles per hour, the motorized citizen can cross Broadacre City as rapidly as Howard's pedestrian can traverse the Garden City. Not only does the automobile thus make possible a dramatic new urban scale, but it also introduces an unprecedented freedom of design. With a modern road system, the car is not restricted to a few lines or stops. Since virtually any point is as accessible as any other, people need not cluster into compact areas.

But Broadacres is more than an ideal city for automobiles. As with the Garden City, its plan is an expression of its designer's deepest values. Howard's fundamental commitment was to cooperation, so it was appropriate that his ideal city take the form of a physically compact community where sharing and fellowship would be the basis of everyone's life.

Wright's central belief was individualism. Where Howard and his followers looked back to the close-knit English village, Wright took his inspiration from the Jeffersonian tradition in American thought which celebrated the self-reliant rural proprietor. If he broke up Howard's well-organized city, it was to permit each citizen and his family to live their own lives on their own ground. Wright never doubted that the only firm foundation for the democracy to which he was so ardently attached was the physical and economic independence of its citizens. Only radical decentralization could lay this foundation, and yet Wright believed the goal to be not merely possible but almost inevitable. Already the automobile had undermined the justification for centralized cities. Advanced technology, which seemed to have destroyed the kind of independence Wright advocated, was in fact leading directly to its rebirth. Broadacre City, he announced, was not just the destiny of a mature industrial society. It was "the plastic form of a genuine democracy."

Wright's model had no sponsors. He was then an isolated figure in American architecture, an aging prophet of 67 still crying in the wilderness, a man who seemed to have outlived his period of creativity and influence. Most of his finest work had been done in the 1890s and 1900s, before he turned forty. Since 1909, when he fell in love with the wife of a former client and deserted his own wife and children, his career had been plagued by his marital difficulties. In the mid-1920s his professional and personal life reached a crisis, and from 1925 to 1935 he built virtually nothing.

Broadacre City was one product of Wright's crisis years. If it reflected his deep alienation from the America of his time, it also embodied the hopes for the future that enabled him to overcome his isolation. Along with such works as "Fallingwater" (the Kaufmann House) and the Johnson Wax Building, Broadacre City marked a dramatic new phase in Wright's creative life. He cast aside the doubts that had assailed him and exhibited his ideal city to the American people in the belief that it was not his alone. The great tide of centralization, he proclaimed, was about to reverse. The economic forces that had created the great city were now working to destroy it. The technology that had fostered concentration could now be used for planned dispersion. The big city owed its survival only to inertia, the inability to conceive the true alternative. Here was the function of the Broadacre City model. The American people must be reminded of their deepest values and shown the way to the fulfillment of those values. Once the alternative had been *seen*, then the path to Broadacre City would be open.

Wright, as we shall see, had a very different idea of action than Ebenezer Howard. Where Howard looked to the power of cooperation to change the world, Wright relied instead on an "appeal to imagination." Howard had worked patiently to assemble diverse coalitions of supporters, adjusting his goals as conditions changed. Wright's major concern was to perfect his vision of the future and to construct ever more inspiring visions. He had no interest in working out a day-to-day strategy for moving from the ideal to the reality. "I am not guilty," he once remarked, "of offering a plan for immediate use."[1] The effort that Howard had put into organizing, Wright and his students devoted to the intricate details of planning, assembling, and painting their scale model of Broadacres.

This activity reflected Wright's conception of the artist's role in society. He maintained that the creative artist, although he appears to be society's natural rebel, is in fact its "natural interpreter." In a world of false forms spawned by anarchic mechanization—sprawling cities, overgrown institutions, inhuman housing—he must bring true form. The artist has the vision to see farther into the future than his fellow citizens. He has the imagination to embody their inchoate desires in concrete form, giving meaning and direction to social change. The artist is thus the real planner and the natural leader of society.

Wright insisted that his particular mission was to proclaim true form in all its purity. In sharp contrast to Howard, he had no interest in working out a method to move from the reality to the ideal. In his architecture and in his social thought Wright took up as his own a motto he had inherited from his grandfather, a Unitarian preacher: "Truth Against the World." Wright held that true form arose in isolation; its only source was an individual's confrontation with his imagination and his conscience. But he also shared his grandfather's belief that no real truth can remain forever "against the world." The individual's uncompromising assertion of his own faith—even if it goes against the opinions of the moment—must ultimately put him in harmony with the deepest beliefs of his fellow citizens. Wright, therefore, was not daunted by his isolation; nor intimidated by the population trends which seemed to be moving against his predictions; nor awed by the massive power of centralized institutions, so aptly symbolized by Rockefeller Center's mass of steel and concrete surrounding his painted wooden model. He was convinced that expounding true form could become a form of leadership—prophetic leadership—more powerful than the largest institutions.

Ralph Waldo Emerson, an inspiration both to Wright's grandfather and to Wright himself, says in *Self-Reliance*: "To believe your own thought, to believe that what is true for you in your private heart is true for all men,—that is genius. Speak your latent conviction and it shall be the universal sense."[2] This was the faith that sustained Wright, even in the bowels of Rockefeller Center.

10

An American Boyhood

WRIGHT'S *Autobiography* begins with a lyric depiction of the family farm where he was born in 1867 and ends with his vision of Broadacre City.[1] These two agrarian tableaux, both celebrating the values of family unity, economic security, and contact with the land, form the prologue and the epilogue to the story of his life. They also provide the frame of reference for the middle chapters, dealing with Wright's career as an architect. The structure of the autobiography reflects Wright's hope that his architecture would become the link between the rural America of his youth and a new agrarian future.

Wright was born near Spring Green, Wisconsin, on the farm that his grandfather Richard Lloyd Jones, the Unitarian preacher, had founded in the 1840s. Soon after his birth, however, his parents moved to Weymouth, Massachusetts, where his father was a Baptist minister. Wright returned to the "Valley," as his grandfather's farm was called, during summer vacations. His idealization of a rural childhood was wholehearted, even if he had been, in fact, only a part-time farmboy.[2]

Wright organized the account of his boyhood in the *Autobiography* around the contrast between his winter and summer experiences. His grandfather and uncles owned and farmed almost all the land in their Valley; theirs was a life of constant physical toil—"adding tired to tired," as Wright's grandfather put it—rewarded by a measure of economic abundance. In Weymouth his parents had settled into a life of suburban intellectuality and genteel religion; it was a quiet existence composed of poverty, prayer, Beethoven, Goethe, and Graham bread. Wright's father, William Russell Cary Wright, was related to two distinguished Boston families from whom he inherited his middle names and little else. A man of intelligence and sensitivity whose talents never found an outlet, he took up and then abandoned several careers—doctor, lawyer, music teacher, preacher—without achieving success in any of them. Wright credited his father only with instilling in him a love of music. He sympathized with his father's "vain struggle of superior talents with untoward circumstances," but he despised the weakness that made his father's career a "sacrifice to sentimentality."[3] His father came to represent to him exactly what he wished to avoid in his own life: sensitivity without strength, independence, or originality.

William Wright had moved to Wisconsin in 1859 where he met Anna Lloyd Jones. The architect's mother was a teacher, "imbued," he recalled, "with the idea of education as salvation." William Wright "satisfied her ideal of 'Education.'"[4] This, at least, was Wright's opinion of his parents' love affair; they were married in 1866. It was not a happy marriage. Wright asserted that from the time of his birth his mother withdrew her affections from his father and gave them to him. He could not believe, it seems, that he was ever his mother's second choice. In the *Autobiography* he claimed that even before he was born his mother had resolved that he would become a great architect; the rooms of his nursery were decorated with engravings of English cathedrals to inspire him in this calling. One may doubt the literal truth of this assertion, but there can be no doubt that Wright's mother had focused her hopes on her son and made his education her special mission. After a visit to the Centennial Exposition in Philadelphia, she brought back for him a set of Froebel "gifts," the original educational toys invented by the founder of the kindergarten to train children in the perception of form.[5] She sacrificed to send him to private schools in Weymouth and, in 1878, insisted that the family move back to Wisconsin so that Frank and she could be closer to the salutary influence of the Lloyd Jones family. Throughout his life Wright had that absolute self-confidence which, as Freud says, comes of being the best beloved of one's mother.

The alliance between mother and son turned increasingly against the father. The move to Wisconsin had not been a happy one for William Wright. He started an "Academy of Music" in Madison and preached occasionally as a Unitarian. Neither occupation was financially rewarding; the family grew increasingly dependent on aid from the Lloyd Joneses, and the father's position within the family was further eroded. As a child Wright had aroused his father's jealousy; as a teenager he began actively defying his authority. "For some disobedience about this time," he recalled, "the father undertook to thrash the young man. It had happened in the stable and the young rebel got his father down on the floor, held him there until his father promised to let him alone."[6] In 1885 came the final break between the parents:

> One day when difficulties between mother and father had grown unbearable the mother, having borne all she could—probably the father had borne all he could bear too—said quietly, "Well, Mr. Wright,"—she always spoke of him and to him so—"leave us. I will manage with the children. Go your way." . . . So the boy himself, supersensitive, soon became aware of the "disgrace." His mother was a "divorced woman."[7]

The alternative to this domestic failure was the Valley where Wright spent his summers. He could not help observing that the Lloyd Jones family had escaped the divisions that beset his own. "These sons and daughters of Richard Lloyd Jones, Welsh Pioneer, in his Valley," Wright recalled, "had already gone far toward making the kind of life for themselves that he [Wright] would have approved. The united family had its own chapel, its gristmill (Uncle John's), and owned, cultivated or pastured pretty much all the land in sight in the Valley and in its branches."[8] The farm was a "hive of work, prayer and song" all centered on the family. Wright's grandfather and uncles had, through their own labor, provided the family with economic independence. His aunts ran a school for their own and their neighbors' children. And the family had its own chapel where it could worship according to Wright's grandfather's precepts.

Richard Lloyd Jones, whose radical Unitarianism had made him an outcast in his native land, founded the Valley in order to create an absolute refuge to protect his truth against the world. The vitality of family life at the Valley was a result of his decision to isolate himself and his kin. It was this aspect of the Valley that exerted the strongest influence on Wright. His parents' troubles seemed an apt illustration of what could happen to a family that lacked the economic and cultural independence of the Lloyd Joneses. The failure of the Wright family and the success of the Lloyd Joneses—the contrasting winter and summer experiences of Wright's boyhood—both contributed to this first principle of Broadacre City: the family, if it is to survive, needs a place of its own, an opportunity for work, an inviolable sanctuary, its own land.

Wright never saw his father after his parents' divorce. He continued to live in Madison with his mother and two younger sisters. He was not tempted by full-time farm work at the Valley. His mother had succeeded in imbuing in him her own ambition: that he become an architect. She chose this profession, which no other member of her family had ever practiced, because it answered her hope that her son would be both "spiritual" and successful. She encouraged him to develop his gift for drawing and communicated to him her love of reading. Rousseau, Goethe, Carlyle, and Hugo were among the authors that Wright remembered reading as a teenager. Throughout his life he remained an ardent lover of books. In a curious afterword to *An Autobiography*, he compiled a list of the authors he had "long ago consulted and occasionally remembered" in writing the story of his own life.

> Pythagoras, Aristophanes, Socrates, Heraclitus, Laotze, Buddha, Jesus, Tolstoy, Kropotkin, Bacon, William Blake, Samuel Butler, Mazzini, Walt Whitman, Henry George, Grundvig, George Meredith, Henry Thoreau, Herman Melville, George Borrow, Goethe, Carlyle, Nietzsche, Voltaire, Cervantes, Giacosa, Shelley, Shakespeare, Milton, Thorstein Veblen, Nehru, Major Douglas and Silvio Gesell.[9]

Although the list is unreliable as a guide to the real influences on Wright's social thought, it demonstrates both the range of his readings and his even greater pride at having read so widely.

After Wright left high school in 1885, his mother arranged a part-time job for him assisting a member of the civil engineering department at the University of Wisconsin. At that time the university had no school of architecture, so Wright enrolled as a freshman in the school of engineering. He never received any formal training in architecture and studied engineering for less than a year; he was avid for "experience." Although his mother insisted that he stay for a degree, he disregarded her plea in his haste to fulfill her hopes. In the spring of 1887 he pawned his father's leatherbound copies of Plutarch's *Lives* and Gibbon's *Decline and Fall* and bought a train ticket to Chicago.[10]

11

Chicago and Oak Park

> You shall no longer take things at
> second or third hand, nor look
> through the eyes of the dead, nor
> feed on the spectres in books;
> You shall not look through my eyes
> either, nor take things from me:
> You shall look to all sides, and
> filter them from yourself.
>
> WHITMAN, *Song of Myself*

WRIGHT'S "higher" education in architecture and in social problems was gained in Chicago, and Chicago was a challenging school in both fields. The city was in what Theodore Dreiser called its "furnace stage," and its sudden emergence as one of the world's greatest industrial centers was a source of pride and fear to its residents, most of whom, like Wright, had been born in more tranquil settings. The skyscrapers of the Chicago School expressed the explosive sense of growth, power, mastery of industry, and freedom from tradition which constituted the city's grandeur. Its miseries were summed up in the ever-expanding slums, the increasingly bitter unemployment crises and labor unrest. These problems could no longer be dismissed as eastern or European aberrations, irrelevant to the real life of the country. Chicago was in the heart of the region that considered itself archetypally American, and its proud towers seemed a frightening negation of the prairies that surrounded them. The city's concentrations of wealth and poverty raised the question of whether democracy could survive in that environment, a question which provided the major theme for a school of social theorists who made Chicago their archetypal industrial city. Jane Addams founded Hull House two years after Wright came to Chicago; Thorstein Veblen began teaching at the University of Chicago three years later, to be followed shortly by John Dewey. Theodore Dreiser, Lincoln Steffens, and Upton Sinclair all lived and worked there.

Wright, a college dropout of nineteen, won surprisingly quick access to the inner circles of architectural practice and of intellectual society. His lack of a degree did not especially hinder him in his profession; it was not required at that time, and Wright had the appearance of a "college man," which counted more than the baccalaureate. More importantly, he was a natural draftsman, and this talent won him a place first in the office of J. L. Silsbee and then with Adler and Sullivan. An uncle, Jenkin Lloyd Jones, had preceded him to Chicago and had established himself as a prominent Unitarian minister. Wright was a frequent guest at his house. It was there that he first met Jane Addams and made the acquaintance of the Chicago intellectual community.[1]

The man who brought the intellectual and the architectural worlds together for Wright was Louis Sullivan, his "Lieber Meister." Sullivan was the "designing" partner in the firm of Adler and Sullivan that had been commissioned to plan the Chicago Auditorium, which was to be the largest opera house in the world and the symbol of Chicago's emergence as a great city. Sullivan hired Wright to be the "pencil in his hand" —the draftsman who would transform his rough sketches into finished drawings. Then at the height of his creative power, Sullivan was the genius of the Chicago School, the man who gave definitive form to its greatest innovation, the skyscraper. Wright began as Sullivan's "pencil," but soon became his disciple. He made himself the Lieber Meister's apprentice, assistant, and constant companion, the chosen heir to his "Architecture of Democracy."

Sullivan was as much concerned with the role of architecture in society as he was with architecture itself, and many of the ideas which he expounded to Wright in long conversations after office hours survived in Wright's own thought. As a social theorist Sullivan was at once vague and all-inclusive. His interest was in "generalizations so broad as to admit no exception whatsoever."[2] His basic generalization was that just as feudalism was being replaced by democracy, so must the architecture of feudalism (i.e., all traditional architecture) be replaced by new forms which could express the democratic way of life. By "feudalism" Sullivan meant any domination of man over man, a concept that stretched from the Spanish Inquisition to the Armour Meat Trust. Its corollary in architecture was the domination of the "styles" inherited from the past over the creative artist's attempts to find his own way. Democracy, however, meant freedom for individual development and expression. "It is the ideal of Democracy," he wrote, "that the individual man should stand self-centered, self-governing—an individual sovereign, an individual god."[3]

Sullivan was not surprised that the modern captains of "industrial feudalism" preferred architects who gave them their facades in one of the traditional styles. The fashionable architect in his "plan factory" was the exact counterpart of the tycoon who forced economic life to assume the outmoded forms inherited from centralized monarchies. The result was the "incongruous spectacle of the infant Democracy taking its mental nourishment at the withered breast of Despotism."[4] The true architect must free himself from all outmoded forms, looking first to himself and then to the emerging spirit of American democracy, if he was to produce the original works of imagination that his country needed in order to be genuinely independent. "The American architect must himself become indigenous . . . he must absorb into his heart and brain his own country and his own people."[5]

Wright sought throughout his life to become the "indigenous" architect that Sullivan was seeking. His concept of democracy and its relation to architectural innovation were essentially the same as Sullivan's. Perhaps the most exciting implication of the Architecture of Democracy for him was Sullivan's suggestion that the well-being of the republic depended upon the architect; his creative mind must embody the democratic idea in visible, functional form if it was ever to become real to the American people.

Wright was attracted by the grandeur of the concept. In his autobiography he recalled that as a boy he had regarded as the "grandest, saddest story" the prophecy of Frollo in Victor Hugo's *Notre-Dame de Paris*. There Hugo argued that in the Middle Ages architecture was truly "the sovereign art," "the social, collective and dominant art." The master builder of the cathedrals defined and expressed the deepest values of his society in stone and glass: he was its true leader. Hugo went on to state that the dominant role of the architect ended when the printed word replaced architecture as the principal "register of humanity."[6] This last idea Wright could never accept. He believed that architecture would occupy in the modern age the position which Hugo believed it had held in the medieval. He was determined to become the master builder of American democracy.

Wright's attempt to define for himself the role of the artist in society came in a lecture he delivered at Hull House in 1901, "The Art and Craft of the Machine."[7] This beginning of his "indigenous" social thought was a reaction against that fashionable foreign import, the theories of Ruskin and Morris. It was the ironic fate of a movement dedicated to reviving the medieval crafts that it proved to be an important source of the modernist theories of the Machine Age. Not only Wright but Le Corbusier and the Bauhaus theorists formulated their ideas as reactions against the doctrines of Ruskin and Morris; and like all reactions, they were deeply marked by the ideas that provoked them. Wright figures as both the severest critic of the arts-and-crafts movement in America and as one of its aptest pupils.

The significance of the machine was perhaps the first question that faced any Chicago artist who wished to take a "broader" view. The battle lines were sharply drawn between the partisans of mechanization à outrance, like the architect Daniel Burnham, and the proponents of William Morris's attempts to base the modern economy upon handicrafts. Occupying the middle ground were the social workers at Hull House, many of whom were seeking to revive the Old Country crafts of the Chicago immigrants as an antidote to factory life. Jane Addams supported these attempts insofar as they re-established ties between the young workers and their immigrant parents. She feared, however, that the handicrafts movement "begged the question" of industrial reform and that its patrons, most of whom had grown rich from the very industrialization they professed to despise, were more interested in collecting objets d'art than in changing society.[8]

With Jane Addams's encouragement, Wright began to question whether industrialization was the necessary enemy of art and democracy. He presented his conclusions before an audience at Hull House of devoted followers of the arts-and-crafts movement. The lecture, a fervent defense of the machine, was received like a talk on the joys of whiskey delivered at a temperance meeting. What was most disturbing was that Wright defended the machine on the basis of the ideals of the handicrafts movement. Wright was drawn to Morris's theories; he understood them more thoroughly than Morris's self-proclaimed advocates, and he used Morris's ideas against his own movement. As Wright once admitted, he was a "natural heretic."[9]

He began by agreeing with Morris that the machine had destroyed or degraded "every type or form sacred to the art of old," leaving only a "pandemonium of tin masks, huddled deformities and decayed methods."[10] His critique of the uses to which machines had been put was essentially the same as Ruskin's: that the machine, in its automatic imitation of handicrafts, had debased the decorative arts and dehumanized the workers who were forced to tend it. Morris's solution was that the machine be restricted to the most arduous and degrading tasks and that man's joy in his labor and his capacity to produce beautiful things be recreated through the restoration of the old handicrafts techniques, with workers organized into cooperative guilds.

Wright was impressed with Morris's democratic idealism, but his own concept of democracy was closer to Sullivan's triumphant individualism than to the spartan cooperation of Morris. Democracy for him meant independence and abundance for everyone, "the highest form of Aristocracy conceivable." He realized that only the machine—"Intellect mastering the drudgery on earth"—could provide the material conditions on which such a democracy could be based. Wright thus rejected any return to older methods. "Every age has done its work, produced its art with the best tools or contrivances it knew, the tools most successful in saving the most precious thing in the world—human effort."[11]

He also rejected the contention that a society based on machines would be a world deprived of beauty. He believed that the artist-designer could find the "poetry of this Machine Age" by understanding and mastering the newest techniques. "Multitudes of processes are expectantly awaiting the sympathetic interpretation of the master mind," he exclaimed.[12] He called for experimental workshops where designers, working with scientists and industrialists in such fields as welding, electro-plating, or lithography, would create a Machine Age aesthetic based on Morris's ideals of simplicity and respect for the nature of materials.

It is difficult to recapture the excitement Wright felt at what was then an original and even shocking formulation of the relationship of the artist to the machine. "My God is machinery," he told the English handicraftsman Charles Ashbee in 1901. "The art of the future will be the expression of the individual artist through the thousand powers of the machine, the machine doing all the things that the individual worker cannot do, and the creative artist is the man that controls all this and understands it."[13]

Wright and Morris agreed that the Industrial Revolution had given the artist a special social function to perform. For Morris the artist's mission was to be the implacable enemy of the machine; his ability to humanize labor by restoring handicrafts was the origin of his authority. For Wright, however, it was the artist's capacity to shape and to promote industrialization that was the source of his power. In the Hull House lecture he distinguished two stages in the Industrial Revolution: the first, in which the machine was "in the service of greed"; and the second, about to begin, in which it was "under the control of the creative artist."

Of all creative artists, the architect was most affected by this new responsibility because his craft was most closely tied to the new technology. Wright found poetic justice in this fact. He recalled Victor Hugo's prophecy of Frollo from *Notre-Dame de Paris* in which the architect had been displaced from his preeminent place in society by the printing press, the first and most influential of the modern machines. Now the time had come for the architect to reassert his control over the machine and thus recapture the vitality of his art and the social significance of his efforts.

Wright ended the lecture with a dramatic image: the Architect atop his new cathedral, the skyscraper, looking down upon "man's glory and menace . . . this monstrous thing . . . a great city." Wright depicted the Architect as both repelled and excited by the "muffled persistent roar . . . the ceaseless activity" of the "monster leviathan . . . whose heavy breathing, murmuring, clangor . . . rose to proclaim the marvels of the units of its structure." The city was a monster but a magnificent one—magnificent because of its concentrated power—and thus a fitting antagonist. The creative artist, he concluded, must dominate and transform this "greatest of machines, the city" and give it "A SOUL."[14]

In the Hull House lecture, delivered more than thirty years before he began planning Broadacre City, Wright announced his conviction that the architect's highest mission was to master the city. He offered no specific ideas for a new city or a new social order. It was the grandeur of the architect's *role* that Wright emphasized. The architect combined the engineer's understanding of technology with the artist's intuitive grasp of the deepest values of his culture. He thus had the capacity to use the machine wisely. In a society torn apart by the stress of industrialization, this capacity made the architect a natural leader. He alone could give humane form to the city. Wright's conception of the architect as leader lacked only this most important element: a goal. He had no alternative society of his own to put forward, just the hope that the creative artist could formulate one. The idea of the Planner preceded the Plan.

When Wright delivered the Hull House lecture, he had in fact moved his architectural practice from the city he dreamed of dominating to Oak Park, a suburb where he concentrated on building luxurious private houses. He had moved there soon after his marriage in 1889 to Catherine Lee Tobin, the daughter of a prominent businessman. In 1892 he quarreled with Sullivan after the Lieber Meister objected to his designing houses on his own, and the following year he left the firm of Adler and Sullivan. Although Wright continued to maintain an office in Chicago, Oak Park became the center of his professional and his family life.

The houses he designed for his suburban neighbors made Oak Park, as Henry-Russell Hitchcock put it, "a pilgrimage spot, the Ile-de-France of modern architecture."[15] They also represent a significant stage in his social thought, for they mark the beginning of his commitment to the single-family house as the only permissible shelter for a free society. The single-family house was as central to Wright's conception of the ideal city as cooperative housekeeping had been for Howard and *Unité d'habitation* was to be for Le Corbusier. The values that dictated Wright's choice—the supreme importance of individuality based on private proprietorship—became the values of the whole planned city. Each American, he wrote in 1910, had "the peculiar, inalienable right to live his own life in his own house in his own way."[16]

Wright's move to the suburbs was not, therefore, a simple retreat from the responsibilities he had outlined in the Hull House lecture. His thought at this time was divided into two separate tracks. The first was his very general concept of the Artist-Planner, the master builder of the new society; the second consisted of his specific attempts to design houses which would be ideal environments for the preservation of the family and individuality. The two tracks eventually met in his vision of a planned community organized around the single-family home, Broadacre City.

Wright's preoccupation with the house stemmed partly from the extreme individualism of Sullivan's Architecture of Democracy and partly from his personal fears for the fragility of the family. It also reflected the concerns of his neighbors. Oak Park was a "family" suburb. "The people," Wright recalled in *An Autobiography*, "were good people, most of whom had taken asylum there to bring up their children in comparative peace, safe from the poisons of the great city."[17] Wright's mother, who lived with the young couple, once told him that she liked Oak Park because it was a small town, another Madison. Its citizens were indeed typical small-town notables—professional men, merchants, small manufacturers. But they worked in the city, and their careers were a constant struggle to maintain their independence against the great forces of Chicago. The tree-lined streets of Oak Park preserved the illusion that the United States was still a nation of small towns and local elites. Oak Park was their asylum against the world of Trusts and immigrants where they earned their living, and their homes were their special refuge. As Richard Sennett has pointed out, the characteristic response of the middle class to the disorder of Chicago was to retreat to the nuclear family as the "bulwark against confusion," the "only sphere of interpersonal engagement that men wanted and certainly the only sphere they had."[18]

Wright's revolutionary innovations in design found support among his solid neighbors because his clients recognized them as responses to their own hopes and fears. The houses enshrined their threatened independence. Wright rejected the "Queen Anne" style whose elaborate ornamentation was associated with imitation of the very rich. Instead, he emphasized honesty and simplicity in the use of materials, qualities more appropriate to the self-image of the Oak Park citizens. His houses bespoke a democratic individuality, horizontal and unpretentious, yet prosperous and secure. He eliminated the small, separate rooms of older houses, the parlors and dens redolent of faded proprieties and divided families. His relatively "open plan"—the flow of living room, dining room, and den into a "great space" centered around the hearth—seemed to express the rich and open family life his clients were seeking. Wright gave beautiful form to the middle class ideals of affection and abundance. This, he believed, was the Architecture of Democracy.

For Wright at the turn of the century maintained that the "American man of business with unspoiled instincts and untainted ideals" was the natural ally of the creative artist seeking to found a modern American culture. The rich were too greedy and too snobbish to accept anything but expensive European imitations. The poor had neither the means nor the education to assert their own taste. Both the rich and the poor thus lived in a world of copies. Only the independent professional or businessman had "the faculty of judging for himself" and the means to make his judgment count.

Wright's faith in the businessman's taste was analogous

to the Progressive Era's faith in his politics. His reasoning paralleled the Progressive idea that the United States should be led by those whom Woodrow Wilson called "independent men of affairs," honest, well educated, financially sound but free from the plutocracy. Wright looked to the same class of "independent men of affairs" for support in his architectural innovations that the Progressives called upon for support in their legislative reforms. His optimism in the Oak Park years was based on the hope that men of "unspoiled instincts and untainted ideals" were about to take the initiative in all areas of American life.

The clearest example of Wright's trust in the businessman was his proposal (put forward in the Hull House lecture) for the establishment of "experimental stations." These "stations," or workshops where the artist could learn the new industrial techniques, were to be established by business. "Once the manufacturers are convinced of due respect and appreciation on the part of the artist, they will welcome him and his counsel gladly," Wright predicted.[19] The artist would create the new forms that the enlightened manufacturer would mass-produce. This victory for the artist allied to the "independent man of affairs" would also be a defeat for the forces of "greed" that had previously controlled the machine.

Wright found many willing clients at Oak Park and throughout the Midwest, but he was disappointed in his search for enlightened businessmen to carry out his program. The experimental stations were never established; nor was the Creative Mind offered control over the Machine. Wright was forced to acknowledge that Oak Park was indeed an "asylum" and that its citizens were independent only within a very limited sphere. He began to think of the house as a complete work of art in which every detail—design, fixtures, furniture, sometimes even the clients' wardrobes—would be determined by the architect. The concept betrayed a desire to assume total control over one piece of the environment, perhaps as a compensation for his failure to achieve any influence over the rest.

There was certainly a strong element of defensiveness in his will to determine "the character of every detail in the sum total, even to the size and shape of the pieces of glass in the window."[20] It reflected a growing fear of a world whose ugliness and vulgarity he could not redeem.

The contrast between his mastery of domestic architecture and his powerlessness to shape the larger environment in which his houses existed was probably an important cause of the intense feelings of frustration and weariness from which he began to suffer in 1908, after fifteen years in Oak Park. "I was losing my grip on my work and even my interest in it," he recalled. "Every day of every week and far into the night of nearly every day I had 'added tired on tired' . . . continuously thrilled by the effort but now it seemed to leave me up against a dead wall. I could see no way out."[21]

He was then forty years old, the most honored American architect of his generation. Yet the revolution in architecture he had achieved had brought him no closer to the larger role in society he had outlined in the Hull House lecture. If anything, the houses had identified him, as he was beginning to acknowledge, with the suburban "asylum" whose residents were either unwilling or unable to change the conditions from which they had fled.

His alienation was sharpened by a more personal cause. In 1907 he had fallen in love with Mamah Borthwick Cheney, the wife of a former client. Wright was perhaps too great a believer in marriage to wish to maintain the illusion of union with a wife he no longer loved. Like his mother, he preferred an open break to continued strife and hypocrisy. Catherine, the mother of his six children, was more sensitive to the community's proprieties. She refused to give him a divorce.[22]

Wright's immersion in the legalities of marriage and divorce completed his disillusionment with Oak Park. His houses had been designed to express his community's ultimate concern for love and the family, but now he came to believe that this concern had always been subordinated to legality and property.

In his struggle to free himself from the ties that bound him, he turned against the "hypocrisy" of Oak Park, its vicarious culture and separation of work from life. In 1909, Wright decided to defy legality and his neighbors' taboos. He assigned his architectural practice to a young colleague he hardly knew and departed with Mrs. Cheney for Europe.

Wright had gone to Oak Park to become an indigenous member of a democratic community. He left a rebel.

Ebenezer Howard at 50.
From *Garden Cities
of To-morrow*, (1902).

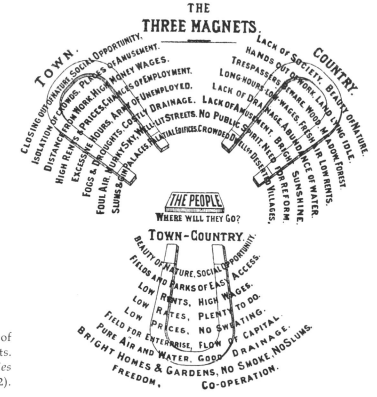

Howard's Diagram of
the Three Magnets.
From *Garden Cities
of To-morrow*, (1902).

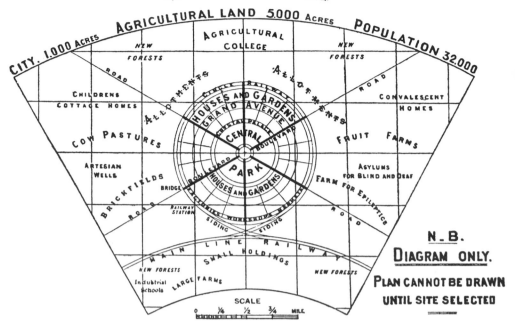

The Garden City surrounded by its agricultural belt. The notation "Diagram only. Plan cannot be drawn until site selected" was added in the second edition (1902). From *Garden Cities of To-morrow*, (1902).

One slice of the circular pie. A typical ward and the center of the Garden City. From *Garden Cities of To-morrow*, (1902).

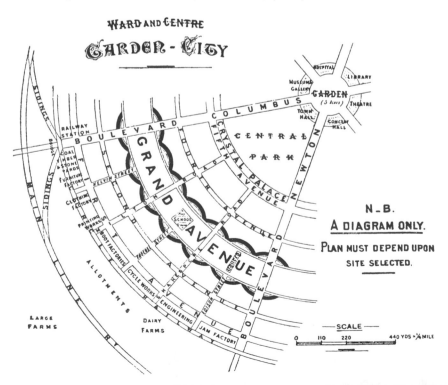

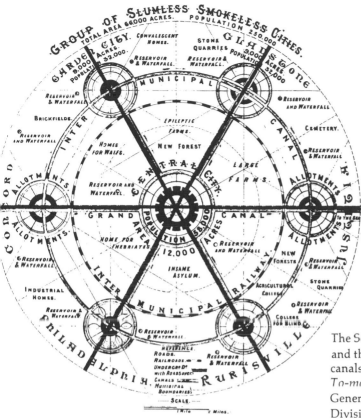

The Social City, six garden cities and the central city, connected by canals and railways. From *To-morrow*, (1898). Courtesy of General Research and Humanities Division, The New York Public Library, Astor, Lenox and Tilden Foundations.

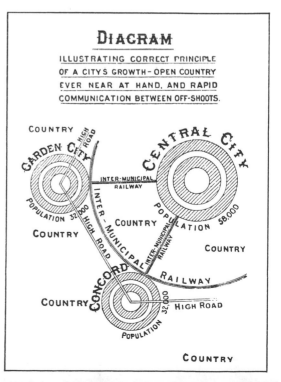

The Social City in its more limited realization in *Garden Cities of To-morrow*, (1902).

Sir Ralph Neville, lawyer, judge, and Ebenezer Howard's most efficacious supporter. From *The Speeches and Papers of Ralph Neville*, (1919).

Parker and Unwin's plan for Letchworth. An echo of Howard's geometrical formality is retained in the area around the town square (M). From *A Guide to Letchworth*, (1907).

PLAN OF ESTATE

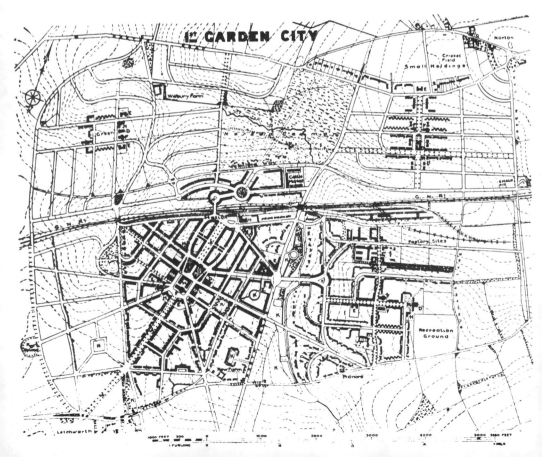

Organic unity. Raymond Unwin's evocation of an idealized English village (as drawn by his associate G. P. Wade). R. Unwin, *Town Planning in Practice*, (1909).

Unwin's original drawing of his "cooperative quadrangle." From *Cottage Plans and Common Sense*, (1902).

A pair of semi-detached villas for the middle class, built by Parker and Unwin. From *Letchworth Garden City in Fifty-Five Pictures*, (1911).

Cleanliness, simplicity, and the honest use of materials. This interior of a Letchworth house designed by Parker and Unwin was intended as an aesthetic and moral lesson after the excesses of Victorian decoration. From *Letchworth Garden City in Fifty-Five Pictures*, (1911).

Organic unity. Parker and Unwin's designs for working class housing in Letchworth. R. Unwin, *Town Planning in Practice*, (1909).

Letchworth cottages for the working class, designed by Parker and Unwin to express the Garden City philosophy. From *Letchworth Garden City in Fifty-Five Pictures*, (1911).

Family life around the hearth. Raymond Unwin's drawing of his combination living-dining room for working class cottages. From *Cottage
Plans and Common Sense,* (1902).

The marriage of town and country. A street in Letchworth. From
Letchworth Garden City in Fifty-Five Pictures, (1911).

Frank Lloyd Wright at 70. Photo by Peter Stackpole.

A suburban house for the "independent man of affairs." South side, the Arthur Heurtley House, Oak Park, Illinois, 1902. From *Ausgeführte Bauten*, (1911).

Open spaces centered
around the hearth.
Living room, the
Isabel Roberts House,
River Forest, Illinois, 1908.
From *Ausgeführte Bauten*,
(1911).

The hand written
wedding announcement that
Wright and Olgivanna sent
to friends. Iovanna,
their daughter, had been
born in 1925.
From the W. R. Heath papers,
Library of Congress.

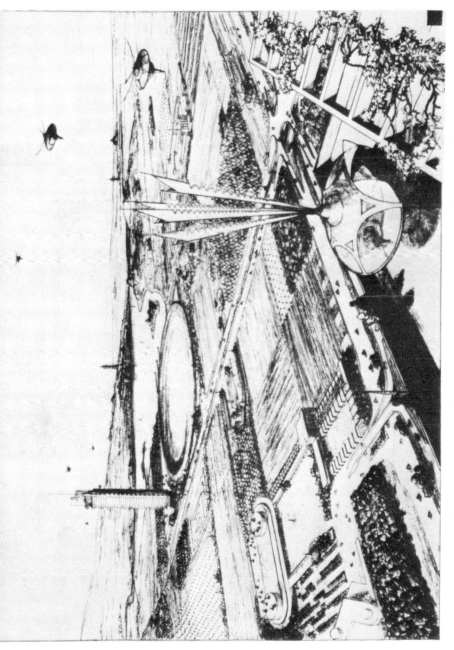

Broadacre City seen from above. The county seat is in the background, the "roadside market" and cultural center in the foreground. The personal automobiles have been supplanted by personal helicopters. From *The Living City*, (1958).

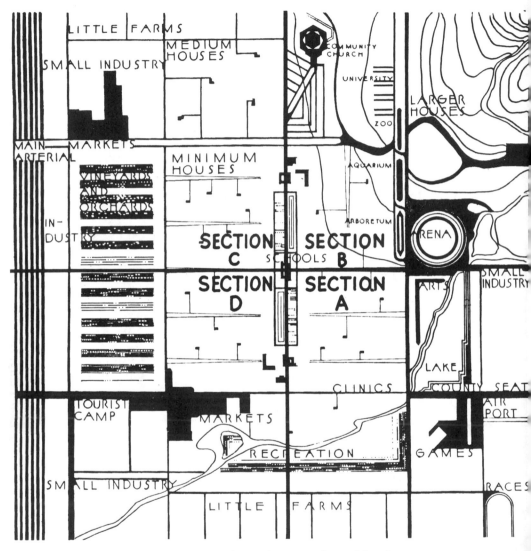

Plan of the center of Broadacre City. The grid pattern formed by the roads is typical of the American midwest. From *When Democracy Builds*, (1945).

Wright's pencil drawing, c. 1950, of a Broadacre City landscape. The cars and helicopters are, of course, his own designs. From *The Living City*, (1958).

Wright, wearing beret at left, supervises the construction of the Broadacre City model. From *Architectural Record*, (1935).

The Broadacre City model. The circus for county fairs and pageantry, behind which stands a "monumental pole" for announcing festivities. From *Architectural Record*, (1935).

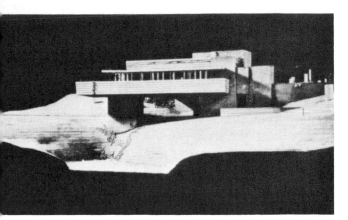

Broadacre City model.
Typical home for
sloping ground.
From *Architectural Record*,
(1935).

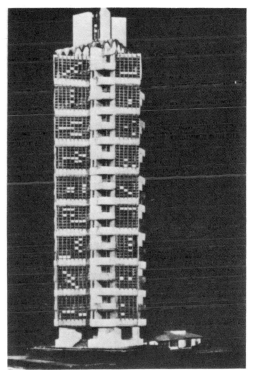

Broadacre City model.
High-rise apartments
for "the city-dweller
as yet unlearned
where ground is concerned."
From *Architectural Record*,
(1935).

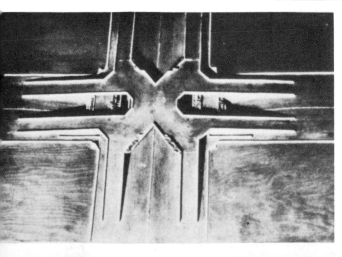

Broadacre City model.
Freeway interchange.
From *Architectural Record*,
(1935).

Berm houses for cooperative workers.
Project "abandoned for lack
of cooperation, 1942."
From *Architectural Forum*, (1948).

Berm house. From *Architectural Forum*, (1948).

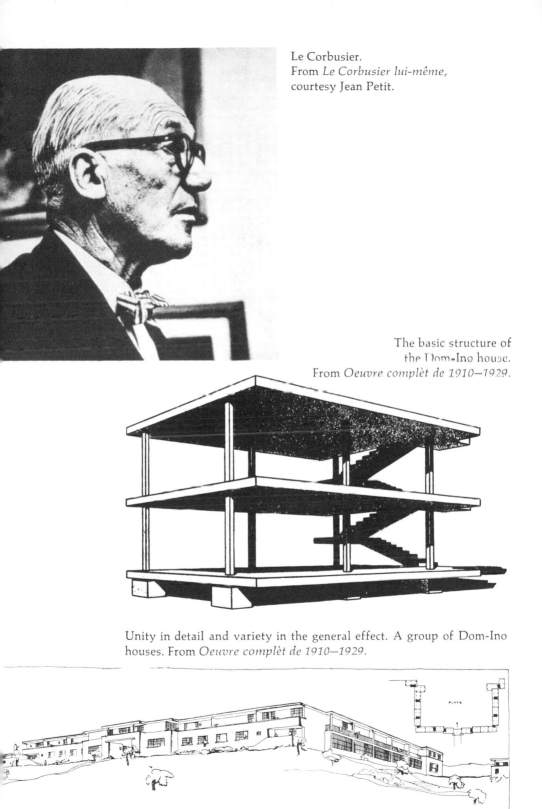

Le Corbusier.
From *Le Corbusier lui-même*,
courtesy Jean Petit.

The basic structure of
the Dom-Ino house.
From *Oeuvre complèt de 1910—1929*.

Unity in detail and variety in the general effect. A group of Dom-Ino
houses. From *Oeuvre complèt de 1910—1929*.

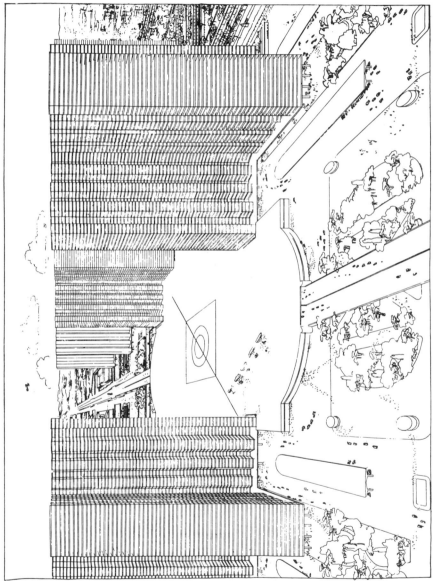

The center of the Contemporary City (1922). Transportation center (with a runway on the roof) flanked by high-rise towers. From *Oeuvre complèt de 1910–1929.*

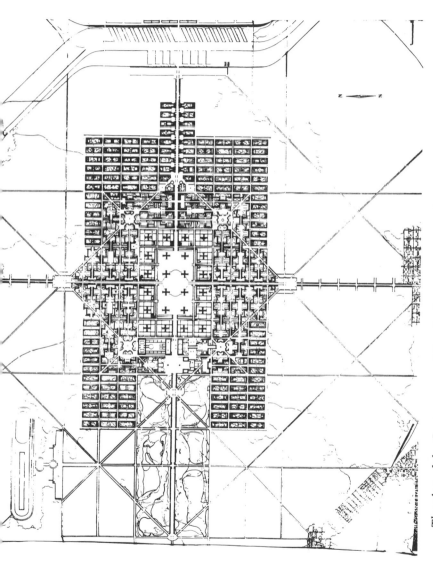

The plan of the Contemporary City. At the exact center is the transportation interchange for automobiles, subways, trains, and airplanes. Around the center are first: the twenty-four towers of administration, and then the luxury apartments for the elite. Beyond the central district lie satellite cities for industry and workers. The north-south, east-west axes are aligned with the points of the compass. From *Oeuvre complèt de 1910–1929.*

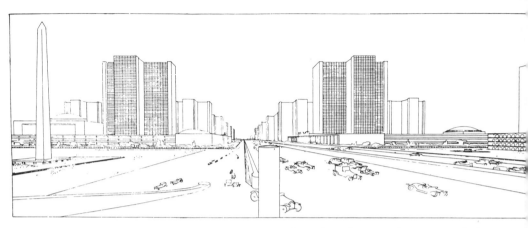

A superhighway forms a triumphal entryway leading directly into the center of the Contemporary City (1922). From *Oeuvre complèt de 1910—1929*.

The vast apartment blocks where the elite of the Contemporary City live, surrounded by parks. From *Oeuvre complèt de 1910—1929*.

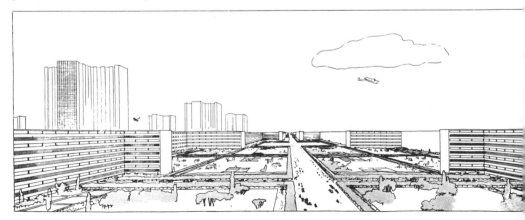

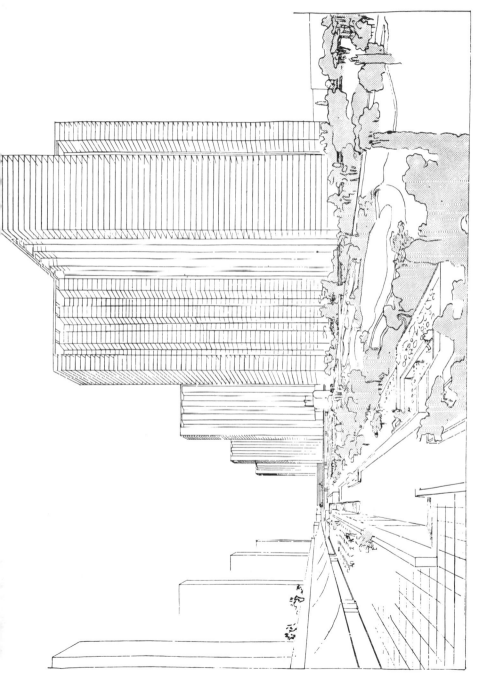

Contemporary City (1922). To the right of the skyscrapers is the multi-tiered pedestrian promenade with its shops, cafes, and restaurants. From *Œuvre complèt de 1910–1929.*

A "Villa-Apartment," (1922), luxury living for the elite of the Contemporary City. From *Oeuvre complèt de 1910–1929*.

Each apartment in the "Villa-Apartment" has a private "hanging garden." From *Oeuvre complèt de 1910–1929*.

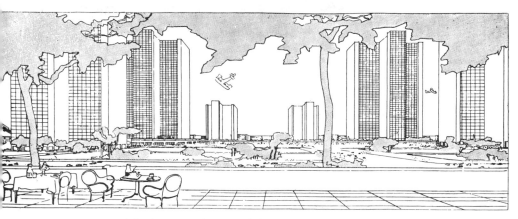

The business district of the Contemporary City as seen from the terrace of a fashionable cafe. From *Oeuvre complèt de 1910–1929*.

The Green City. Juxtaposed with the geometrical city of towers is a world of trees, greenery, and curving lanes. "The rapport between men and nature is re-established." From *Précisions*, (1930).

A scale model of the Plan Voisin (1925). The Seine and Ile-de-la-Cité are at the lower right. From *Oeuvre complèt de 1910—1929*.

The Plan Voisin. Eighteen skyscrapers in the center of Paris opposite the Seine and Notre-Dame. From *Oeuvre complèt de 1910—1929*.

Le Corbusier's architectural history of Paris. Consciousness unfolds. . . .
From *Précisions*, (1930).

But "academicism says No!" From *Précisions*, (1930).

Le Corbusier's vision of the "corridor-street," the ubiquitous urban form which he regarded as ugly and outmoded.
From *La maison des hommes*, (1941).

The pyramid of society. Only the elite at the top can comprehend the new spirit. The rest are immured in "academic or romantic" ideas.
From *Précisions*, (1930).

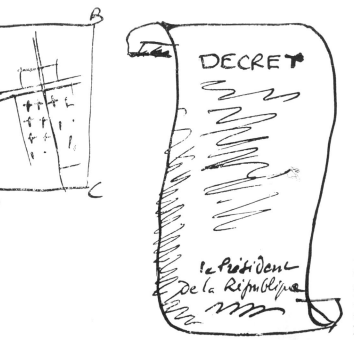

Le Corbusier's fanciful drawing of the decree from the President of France authorizing him to begin the *Plan Voisin*.
From *Précisions*, (1930).

The visible hand. The finger of authority points—but it is only Le Corbusier's own hand reigning over a scale model. From *La ville radieuse*, (1935).

The correspondence of destruction (war) and construction (planning and urbanism). Both achieve their victories through hierarchy, authority, enthusiasm, and unity. The result of war is death and shame, but urbanism yields "activity, progress, and the creative joy of a new era." From *La ville radieuse*, (1935).

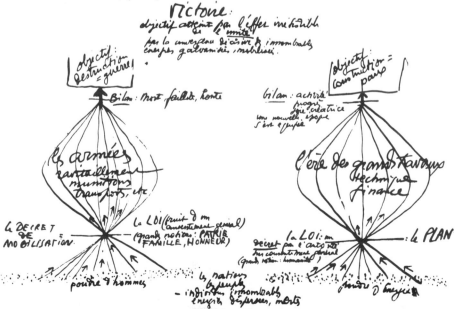

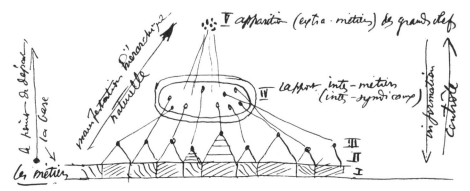

Architecture reconciles individual liberty with collective power. The alternative is "? ? ?" From *Quand les cathédrales étaient blanches*, (1937).

Le Corbusier's diagram of a Syndicalist state. This "manifestation of a natural order" begins with citizens organized into unions (I) who elect their natural leaders (II). The heads of each trade (III) meet in a council (IV) which governs the country. This council promulgates a National Plan devised by their expert advisors (V), who, significantly enough, occupy the uppermost position in this diagram. From *La ville radieuse*, (1935).

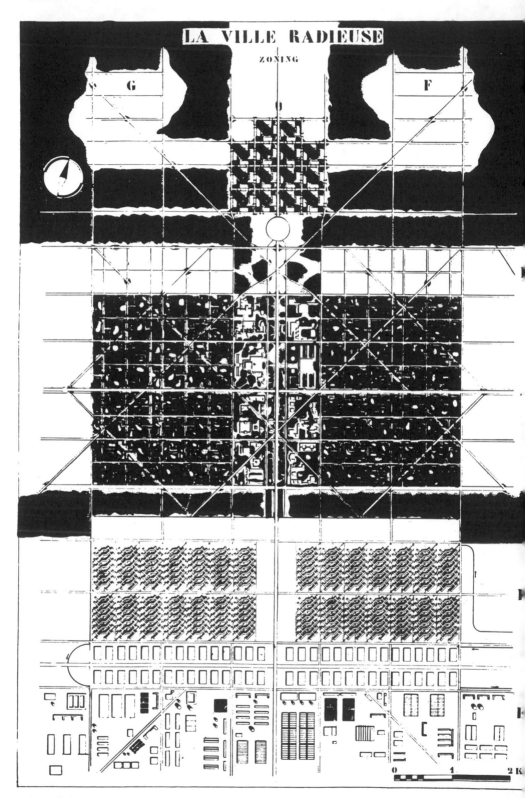

Plan of the Radiant City. The central district is now residential; above
it is the business district and below are the industrial sites. From *La
ville radieuse,* (1935).

A Radiant City. Le Corbusier's Plan for Antwerp (1933), never built. From *La ville radieuse*, (1935).

The National Center of Collective Festivals for 100,000 People, 1936. From *Des canons, des munitions?* (1938).

The Directive Plan for Algiers, 1942. From *Oeuvre complèt, 1938—46.*

Le Corbusier's conception of a business center of Algiers, 1938—39, later incorporated into his Directive Plan. From *Oeuvre complèt, 1938—46.*

12

In the Wilderness

> But you see I am cast by nature for
> the part of the iconoclast. I must
> strike tear down, before I can
> build my very act of building de-
> stroys an order.
>
> FRANK LLOYD WRIGHT,
> letter to Charles Ashbee (1911)[1]

IN 1908, Wright had written of his architecture: "Radical
though it be, the work here illustrated is dedicated to the
cause conservative in the best sense of the word."[2] His
rhetorical juxtaposition of "radical" and "conservative" well
described the combination of rebelliousness and respect that
marked both his life and his work. His great rebellions against
conventional practices were all intended as restorations of the
ideals that the conventions had betrayed. In architecture he
attacked the classical "styles" to affirm his respect for the
classical tradition. In politics he was to propose a radical redistribution of property and power to create what he called
"true democracy" and "true capitalism."

His rebellion against marriage was part of this pattern. He
deserted his wife and six children in order to affirm his belief
in the ideal of marriage based on love. "Love should be its own
protection or its own defeat," he wrote.[3] Wright was well
aware of the difficulties of his position. "I loved my children. I

loved my home. A true home is the finest ideal of man, and yet—well, to gain freedom I asked for a divorce."[4] He always insisted on his untrammeled individuality, his freedom to destroy. Only then could he create the new forms he was seeking. After Catherine refused to give him a divorce, Wright believed he could begin a new life with Mrs. Cheney outside the bounds of legal marriage. The tragic frustration of this hope forced Wright to confront the possibility that his rebellion was an act of selfishness necessarily opposed to the values he wished to preserve. In the twenty years of exile and rootlessness that followed his decision to leave Oak Park, he often feared that he had destroyed more than he could create.

When Wright returned from Europe with Mrs. Cheney in 1911 he began to build a new house to protect his truth against the world. He picked an appropriate site for this purpose: the Valley of the Lloyd Joneses. "I turned to the hill in the Valley as my grandfather before me had turned to America—as a hope and a haven."[5] Taliesin, named for an old Welsh poet, was to be a residence, an architectural studio, and a farm with its own water and power supply. It was thus a true successor to the self-sufficiency of the Lloyd Jones settlement. It was also the logical conclusion to Wright's attempts at Oak Park to create an environment which he controlled completely; it was a more impregnable asylum than any he could have built there. But Taliesin was a hope as well as a haven. If the house reflected Wright's desire to return to a womblike security in the Valley where he was born, it also embodied his emerging conviction that the democratic way of life required some firmer foundation than a suburban lot.

"It was still a very young faith that undertook to build that house," Wright recalled in *An Autobiography*.[6] He intended Taliesin to be the perfect shelter for a family based on the ties of love, not legality. By including a studio and a farm in the plans he eliminated the suburban separation of professional from family life. Taliesin was to be a place where "life and work were one." Finally, the house was designed to express the close and intimate contact of its residents with nature. It was tucked into the brow of a hill overlooking the Valley, so closely integrated with its site that Wright claimed it was "not so easy to tell where pavements and wall left off and ground began."[7]

Wright's hope was virtually destroyed in August 1914. A servant who went mad set fire to Taliesin, killing Mrs. Cheney and three of her daughters. (Wright was in Chicago at the time.) After a period of total despair he found the strength to begin rebuilding Taliesin, but not the strength to try to continue the life he had hoped to lead there. He already had a commission from Japan to build the Imperial Hotel for foreigners. Wright had a connoisseur's knowledge of Japanese prints; he had visited Japan in 1905; and in 1916 he eagerly embarked upon the commission. He spent most of the next six years in voluntary exile in Tokyo, a period in his life about which very little is known.[8]

Wright was over fifty when he shifted the focus of his activities back to the United States. He returned in the hope that he could resume both his architectural practice and his efforts to create his own life at Taliesin. Catherine was finally ready to grant him a divorce, and Wright was preparing to wed Miriam Noel, a sculptress with whom he had been living in Tokyo. He had, moreover, a client of impressive taste and even more impressive wealth, Aline Barnsdall, who had commissioned him to build a magnificent house and related buildings on a hill she owned in Hollywood.

The decade of the 1920s, however, proved to be the most difficult in Wright's life. His achievements in architecture, now so much admired and copied in Europe, seemed to lose all their appeal in the United States. Like so many other bright hopes of the Progressive Era, the Architecture of Democracy appeared dead in the America of Harding and Coolidge. Only the traditional styles were stylish. After he had completed his designs for Miss Barnsdall—most of which never materialized —he experienced a neglect which even the miraculous and much-publicized survival of the Imperial Hotel in the 1923 earthquake did not remedy. In that year he built only two houses, one of which was essentially a renovation of one of his Oak Park houses which had been damaged by fire. In 1924, 1925, and 1926 he built nothing at all.[9]

At this time he was also experiencing a severe crisis in his personal life. His relations with Miriam Noel had never been placid. After his divorce from Catherine in 1922 he married Miriam in 1923 on the middle of a bridge in Taliesin. This symbolized their hope that the marriage would bridge their growing differences. In fact, it sealed them. They were formally separated in 1924.[10]

Alone again, Wright met Olgivanna Milanoff, granddaughter of a duke, daughter of the Chief Justice of Montenegro, a teacher and disciple of the philosopher Gurdjieff.[11] They fell in love, and he brought her to Taliesin. In 1924 the house was again seriously damaged by fire. There were no injuries, and Wright resolved to rebuild on an even grander scale. Since he had no income from commissions, he began by mortgaging everything at Taliesin that had survived the blaze. Wright had little sense of money and none of thrift. "Give me the luxuries," he once said, "and the necessities will take care of themselves."[12] In this case they did not. His financial straits made it difficult for him to find money for Miriam's alimony. This and his unwillingness to assume the legal role of the "guilty party" led him to break off divorce proceedings in November 1925.[13] The decision left him vulnerable to Miriam's increasingly vindictive and irrational jealousy of Olgivanna.

Married to one woman and living with another, Wright was subject to the laws against adultery. Miriam obtained a warrant for his arrest in September 1926 and Wright fled—to Mexico it was rumored, but to Minneapolis in fact. There he lived secretly with Olgivanna, Svetlana (Olgivanna's daughter by a previous marriage), and Iovanna, the eight-month-old daughter of Wright and Olgivanna. The police found them a month later, and Wright was jailed briefy as a "fugitive from justice," charged with criminal adultery and violation of the Mann Act—transporting Olgivanna from Wisconsin to Minnesota for immoral purposes. He was then almost sixty.[14]

The crisis, having reached its peak, gave way to solutions. Miriam decided to relent and agreed to a divorce. Her lawyers, who had initiated the criminal charges against Wright, now pressed for their dismissal, and all the indictments were dropped. The divorce was granted in August 1927, and Wright and Olgivanna were married after the required waiting period of one year.[15] Meanwhile, Wright's remaining friends had banded together to bring some financial order into his life. They "incorporated" Wright by discharging most of his debts in return for shares in a corporation which would receive its income from Wright's future earnings. Although the Bank of Wisconsin had taken possession of Taliesin, its agents were unable to sell it; in the fall of 1928, Wright's friends arranged for him to return to his "hope and haven." There he attempted to rebuild his architectural career until the Great Depression indefinitely postponed that possibility.

Wright had been severely shaken by the crisis. He resented especially the publicity that presented him as a jaded bohemian and irresponsible destroyer of families. His architectural achievements may have been forgotten, but he still made good copy. Olgivanna, Wright's "housekeeper" in the newspaper accounts, was identified in the *New York Times* as a "Montenegrin danseuse";[16] Taliesin figured as the "Love Bungalow" where the statutory crimes took place. Everything was presented with that combination of prudery and salaciousness in which even the respectable press reveled. Wright was deeply hurt by this coverage, perhaps in part because the image of himself the press presented corresponded too closely to his own private fears. Instead of the security and honors to which his achievements had entitled him, he found himself destitute, forced into hiding, remembered only for his scandals. This was far from the noble vision of the Artist with which he had closed the Hull House speech. Not surprisingly, Wright began to doubt himself, to mistrust his highest gifts. "I have been so badly whipped for my ignorance and willful disregard of the fact," he wrote to W. R. Heath in 1927. "I have lived and had my being in 'motifs' and speculations and surmises—Too many fairy tales when a boy maybe —Too gushing a fountain of creative energy to be safe as a man."[17]

Nevertheless, he emerged from his difficulties not destroyed but strengthened. Since leaving Oak Park he had tried to "go it alone," but the shocks of the 1920s awakened him to the dangers of the self-destructive isolation into which he had drifted. Olgivanna and his remaining friends taught him the value of the human ties he had so badly frayed. As he wrote to Alexander Woollcott, one of those who stuck by him:

> I think about the only thing I really learned from the gratuitous punishment and grueling experience of the past four years is the value of an honest friendship based on mutual liking. I got, naturally, into a hell of a fix,— where I needed my friends and hadn't really myself earned the right to make any demands on friendship let alone laying a tax upon "friends." Not only had I never made any financial investment of any kind that would bring me a cent, but I had never really invested anything deepheartedly or seriously in "friendship" either.[18]

Unlike Louis Sullivan, who succumbed to the bitterness born of undeserved neglect, Wright found the strength to reestablish his life without cutting off his "fountain of creative energy." He survived to disprove F. Scott Fitzgerald's dictum that there are no second acts in American life.

Wright's regeneration began when he was still a "fugitive from justice." Unable to pursue his architectural work, he began both his autobiography and the preliminary studies for Broadacre City.[19] The two were intimately connected. At this point of greatest isolation—without a home, without income, his reputation destroyed, pursued by the law—he began to recapture himself. The autobiography was his attempt to banish the destructive image that had been imposed on him, to regain his own identity and establish the ideas he lived by. In the Broadacre City studies—originally called "The Usonian City," after Usonia, Samuel Butler's name for the United States[20]—he tried to redefine his relationship to his fellow citizens. He was unilaterally declaring an end to his isolation, not by joining the America that had rejected him but by declaring his membership in the democracy of the future he would help to build. He began planning an American city in which he could be a citizen, a city which expressed his faith that he still represented the true spirit of his country. Wright resolved to prove that his life and art were not eccentric but prophetic. He would speak his latent conviction and work to make it universal sense.

13

Broadacre City

> A good plan is the beginning and
> the end, because every good plan is
> organic. That means that its de-
> velopment in all directions is in-
> herent and inevitable.
>
> FRANK LLOYD WRIGHT, "In
> the Cause of Architecture"
> (1928)[1]

IN the late 1920s, Wright expanded his plan for a new
Usonian city until it became a complete alternative society—
Broadacre City. He read widely in social theory and economics,
seeking the proper form for all the institutions of the new
civilization. The ideal city was a useful intellectual tool; it
enabled him to show the workings of government, education,
religion, the economy, and the home as integral parts of the
total environment he wished to create. The Great Depression
gave an added urgency to his work and provided him with the
enforced leisure to pursue it. The stock-market crash of 1929
strengthened his conviction that the nation needed a radical
change both in its physical and in its economic organization.
Wright first advanced a summary of his plan in the Kahn
Lectures he delivered at Princeton University in 1930. The
complete plan was expounded in a book, *The Disappearing
City*, published in 1932.

Wright's book depicted a time when the great urban centers

were not merely "disappearing"; they had already ceased to exist. This, Wright believed, was inevitable. In the age of the automobile and the telephone the great cities were doomed: they were "no longer modern." The expensive concentration of people was merely wasteful when modern means of communication could overcome distance. Nor was there any further need for the large, centralized organizations which were based in the cities. Their functions could be accomplished far more economically in decentralized units spread over the countryside.

Wright gave little attention to the mechanics of this process. He was convinced that the big city was as obsolete as the horse-and-carriage, and therefore destined to be replaced by something better. Like so many other Americans of his time, Wright was fascinated by the automobile, convinced of its potential to revolutionize modern life and blind to its limitations. He assumed that modern man had an inherent right to own a car and to burn as much gasoline in driving it as he desired. He knew only that the automobile had created the possibility of new communities based on a new mastery of time and space. Thus, the only questions were: what form would these communities take, and what opportunities for a new American civilization did they offer?

Wright's essential insight was that decentralization, if taken to its logical extreme, could create the material conditions for a nation of independent farmers and proprietors. If properly planned, cities could spread over the countryside and still not lose their cohesion or efficiency. The diffusion of population would create conditions for the universal ownership of land. The world of concentrated wealth and power would be replaced by one in which the means of production would be widely held. The most advanced technology thus pointed the way for a revival of the democratic hopes of the eighteenth century: Edison and Ford would resurrect Jefferson. The individuality which Wright had been preaching would have its base in the very structure of the country. A society of proprietors, Wright believed, was a society of independent men—a democracy. "When every man, woman, and child," he proclaimed, "may be born to put his feet on his own acres, then democracy will have been realized."[2]

Broadacre City was thus a juxtaposition of the past and the future: the ideal of Jeffersonian democracy given new meaning in terms of the technology of the future. This hybrid provided the standards of efficiency and humanity against which Wright judged the cities of the present and, not surprisingly, found them wanting. "To look at the plan of any great city is to look at the cross-section of some fibrous tumor," he remarked.[3] Wright's critique of the modern city was often intemperate in tone, and occasionally incoherent in substance. A representative sample will suffice.

> Tier upon tier, the soulless Shelf, the interminable empty crevice along the winding ways of the windy unhealthy canyon. The heartless grip of selfish, grasping universal stricture. Box on box beside boxes. Black shadows below with artificial lights burning all day long in little caverns and squared cells. Prison cubicles?[4]

There is surprisingly little accurate observation of city life in Wright's anti-urban books. He relied upon massed clichés and stereotypes to convey his indignation.

Out of the clichés he managed to fashion a theory of the city. Its relevance to actual conditions is debatable, but it is certainly an excellent introduction to Wright's own preoccupations. Wright believed that the psychology of urban life was as dangerous to the nation's mental health as urban economics was to its physical well-being. He summed up his analysis of the evil of the city in the term "Rent," Wright's word for exploitation. He distinguished three forms: rent for land, rent for money (interest), and rent for ideas (control of inventions).[5] All three are the support of the "vicarious" life of the rentier, whose existence is vicarious in the economic sense because it is based on the labor of others, and vicarious psychologically because the rentier can have no sense of himself as a productive individual. The city is the great locus of Rent, and hence the natural center for the vicarious life and the "herd instinct." Not only does the moneylord have his headquarters there; it is also the natural home of the "satellites of rent"—the experts who direct the artificial economy of cities and the "white collar armies" who carry out their commands. Both the leaders and the troops in this army are victims of city life. Their narrow and fragmented tasks reflect the lack of independence that characterizes the urban economy.

In an urbanized world, Wright held, there is no truly productive labor, only the struggles over spoils. "The properly citified Citizen has become a broker, a vendor of gadgetry, a salesman dealing for profit in human frailties, or a speculator in the ideas and inventions of others."[6] The victims (and even the so-called successful) cannot call their lives their own:

> The city itself is become a form of anxious rent, the citizen's own life rented, he and his family evicted if he is in arrears or the system goes to smash. Should this anxious lockstep of his fall out with the landlord, the moneylord, or the machinelord, he is a total loss.[7]

The city, he concluded, has "made of the Man a piece of cheap speculative property."[8]

Broadacre City is the place where there is no Rent. Wright meant to abolish all forms of vicarious life—economic, psychological, or intellectual. The means to this end was the reforming of the environment through the abolition of rent for land. Wright's emphasis on the land question derived in general from the Jeffersonian tradition and in particular from the foremost representative of that tradition in the late nineteenth century, Henry George. "Henry George's analysis of poverty has never been refuted," Wright maintained in 1932.[9] He was still defending George against academic economists as late as 1958.[10] Wright was one of those Progressives for whom

Progress and Poverty was an underground classic, deeply influential in its principles yet too radical in its immediate implications to be openly embraced.

Wright's interpretation of George forms an interesting contrast with that of another reticent disciple, Ebenezer Howard. Wright and Howard both adopted the basic principles of their economic thought from George: the idea that the conflict between capital and labor was not fundamental to industrial society, and that this conflict, along with depressions and even poverty itself, could be eliminated if the root cause—inequities in land ownership—were eliminated. George's theory gave to both Howard and Wright the confidence to believe that their planned communities would provide the necessary environment for social harmony.

Wright and Howard both mistrusted George's proposal for a Single Tax on land as the single solution to the land question. George believed that all subsequent improvements, including a more rational pattern of land use and community development, would follow automatically from the beneficent operation of the laws of economics. Wright and Howard believed that this pattern must be *planned*, and its form established in advance. They held, moreover, that the form of the community must reflect and protect the equitable distribution of land on which it is based.

Howard and Wright disagreed, however, on how to achieve the universal land ownership that George had advocated. Howard, as we have seen, wanted the land to pass gradually and legally into the hands of the community, i.e., the individual Garden Cities, which would devote the rents to the common good. Cooperation was Howard's greatest good, and his scheme reflected his hope that the cooperative nature of society would be assured once the land—the most important determinant—was held in common.

On this issue Wright showed himself to be at once more radical and more conservative than Howard. Wright called the Single Tax "only an expedient"; nevertheless, it was an expedient he was anxious to use.[11] His plans for Broadacre City clearly presupposed legislation that would expropriate all landholdings larger than any one family would need. This radical attack on property was in Wright's mind only a means to a conservative strengthening of the property rights that remained. Everyone would have an absolute right to the area he used and improved. (We should remember that, given Wright's prescript of an acre of land per person, the entire population of the United States in 1930 could have fitted comfortably inside the state of Texas.) Neither banks nor the government could challenge the individual's claim to his homestead. For Wright as for Howard, property served to define and to protect the society's greatest good. This, in Wright's view, was individuality. He believed that the independence he wished to safeguard rested in the last analysis on the individual's absolute right to property.

This right, translated into the innumerable homesteads that dot the plan of Broadacres, determined the shape and scale of Wright's ideal city. Neither shape nor scale appear recognizably urban: one "city" might sprawl over 100 square miles without any recognizable center. Yet Wright insisted that he was presenting a coherent planned community. He based his claim on the new sense of time and space he was introducing. As we have seen, when Howard fixed the size of the Garden City, he was thinking in terms of pedestrians (or perhaps bicyclists). The 30,000 inhabitants of the Garden City could walk across the city in fifteen minutes or less. The motorized citizen of Broadacres could make a similar claim: traveling at 60 miles per hour he too could reach any of his 30,000 neighbors in fifteen minutes.

However, the "open plan" of Broadacre City was a genuine departure from the neat concentric circles of the Garden City. Although Howard spoke of the "marriage of town and country," he sharply distinguished the two realms in his plan. He wished to preserve within the confines of the city a genuine urban life. Wright's hopes for Broadacre City were the exact opposite. His fundamental tenet was that there must be no more distinction between urban and rural life-styles. Therefore, there must no longer be a physical separation between urban and rural areas. Broadacre City was planned to ensure this; the houses, the factories, the stores, the office buildings, and the cultural centers are all in the midst of farmland and forests. At the same time, the transportation system unites the citizens with the many points of community exchange that provide the urban experience.

The real union of the urban and rural would take place at work. William Morris had taught Wright that the truest measure of any society was the opportunity it provided for creative labor. Wright sought to eliminate any rigid specialization of the Broadacre City citizens into farm workers, factory workers, or office workers. In Broadacre City both physical and mental labor would be part of everyone's daily experience. Everyone would have the skills to be a part-time farmer, a part-time mechanic, and a part-time intellectual. Only drudgery would be absent from work. The small farms that surrounded each homestead were the natural extensions of the gardens. If the machine were in the service of man, factory labor could become an exercise in mechanized craftsmanship. The daily variety of tasks would blur the line between work and leisure.

The merging of town and country, physical and mental labor, work and leisure—these were all part of Wright's attempt to eliminate the fragmentation of modern life from Broadacre City. Schiller, one of Wright's favorite thinkers, had posed the problem in his great "Sixth Letter on Aesthetic Education":

> Eternally fettered only to a single little fragment of the whole, man fashions himself as a fragment; ever hearing only the monstrous whirl of the wheel he turns, he never displays the full harmony of his being.[12]

In Wright's ideal city everyone could display each day the "full harmony of his being." The purpose of Broadacre City, he wrote, was not merely to create

> a better livelihood but to recreate the framework of our modern life that our leisure, our culture and our work will be our own and as nearly as possible One. Men must desire to qualify to go forward to their original inheritance—The Good Ground—so that each man may again be a whole man in himself living a full life. That does not mean that every man must be a genius or a farmer, but there is no longer excuse for him to be the kind of parasite that machine centralization has been busy making of him. . . .[13]

Wright believed that this new way of life would necessarily strengthen the family. In urban society the home was merely the locus of one of the disconnected fragments of modern life. In Broadacre City the family would take the offensive. As a base for production, education, and culture, the family would recapture the centrality which it had surrendered to urban institutions. "The true center (the only centralization allowable) in Usonian democracy," Wright held, "is the individual in his true Usonian home."[14] The family-centered economy which Wright had respected among the Lloyd Joneses and the domestic architecture which he had created at Taliesin would become the universal norms.

In Broadacre City Wright was finally able to conceive of his houses not as isolated or artificial retreats but as integral parts of the new environment. The revolutionary features of Wright's architecture take on a "conservative" meaning in Broadacres. The open plan of the interiors is the natural and functional setting for the family's shared economic and social responsibilities. The intimate contact between the house and its surroundings expresses the residents' intimate contact with their own land in work and leisure. The "Usonian House," horizontal and unpretentious, honest and sparing in its use of materials, reflects the new society's respect for nature and its egalitarian ethos. In Broadacre City the house is a natural feature of the landscape.

Wright hoped that Broadacre City would begin with the house. After the great land reforms had made property available for everyone, the urban factory worker could move to the countryside and, with his former rent money, purchase and assemble the essential mass-produced components of a house. These components would be sufficiently flexible to enable everyone to put them together in his own way. With income from part-time farming and part-time work in local factories, the worker could afford to enlarge his house. Wright remarks that it "should grow as the trees around the man himself grow"; its shape would be determined by the individual's resources, the needs of his family, and his understanding of his own land. Every citizen, Wright predicted, could "make his house a harmonious whole, as appropriate to him as to his purse, to his ground as to his God."[15]

Once the homestead was complete, the worker would cease to be a propertyless proletarian. On this own land he could never be "unemployed or a slave to anyone." This independence increased his economic power even when he was working part-time for others. Since he could live by his own labor if necessary, he did not have to submit to exploitative wages or poor working conditions.

Thus, the return of the family as the basic economic unit would solve the labor problem. Wright's reasoning here shows the tremendous weight of social responsibility his theory places on the family. The solutions to all social problems rest on its capacity to create its own world of stability, prosperity, and love. It is the one wholly independent unit in society; its members are expected to spend the bulk of their time living and working together. Yet Wright knew from bitter experience the inner forces that tear families apart. The homesteads of Broadacre City recall his previous attempts to find a refuge for the family from outside pressures, though in Wright's ideal city these pressures should no longer exist. There is, however, a psychological truth in Wright's placing so much emphasis on an institution he knew to be tragically weak. The members of a Broadacre City homestead could not disguise the importance of their role. This responsibility, Wright hoped, would be a crucial source of the family's strength.

Factories and other economic institutions were thus cast explicitly as "support units" for the family. Wright believed that factories in Broadacre City could be either privately or cooperatively owned. The important factor was that they be small and located within convenient driving distance of the homesteaders who were employed in them. In fact, Wright usually favored private enterprise as more consistent with his ideal of individualism, but he always opposed any centralization of industry which would overwhelm the homestead. He supported a limited measure of inequality: the houses he designed for Broadacre City ranged in size from "one-car houses" to "five-car houses." Strict equality, he held, would threaten individuality, but no family could be true homesteaders if they were too poor to afford one car or rich enough to maintain more than five. Within these limits there was no rigid hierarchy because "quality is in all, for all, alike. The thought entering the first estate or the least estate is of the best. . . . There is nothing poor or mean anywhere in Broadacres."[16]

As long as the homestead supplemented by the small factory remained the foundation of the Broadacre City economy, Wright saw no need for government regulation. All that was required for the economy to function properly was an adequate system of banking and currency. Wright's own unhappy experience with the banking system made its reform a special concern of his. Both as an architect and as a radical he despised what he called "the grandomania of the pillared 'Temples-of-the-Unearned-Increment.' "[17]

In Broadacre City, credit would be decentralized: everyone could command the resources to set himself up as an independent farmer or businessman. To accomplish this goal, Wright advocated a curious monetary reform which had first been proposed by the Swiss economist Silvio Gesell at the turn of the century. Gesell, whose writings were enjoying a revival in the 1930s, had been impressed by the fact that a commodity like new potatoes declines steadily in value after a harvest because potatoes are perishable; in contrast, the money or gold used to purchase the potatoes never decays. This, he claimed, gives the holders of money an undue advantage over the producers of commodities. He therefore proposed to make money perishable: a banknote issued at the beginning of the year would lose a fixed percentage of its face value by the end of the year. This would prevent hoarding, encourage spending, and reduce interest to a minimum.[18]

Wright's enthusiasm for this monetary "reform" does little for his reputation as an economist, but it does reveal an important aspect of Broadacre City. Gesell was an admirer of Henry George; like George, he emphasized that the economic order could be based on self-interest and the laws of supply and demand once the crucial changes had been made. This radical vindication of laissez-faire—that is, laissez-faire *after* the revolution—was very attractive to Wright. It assumed, as he did in his plans for Broadacre City, that extreme individualism could lead to a genuine order. It expressed in the economic sphere his conviction that the individual's truth was finally the world's truth.

Wright differed from George and Gesell in his belief that a planned physical structure of decentralization must be the basis of all the other reforms. The unnatural environment of the cities set man against man; only in Broadacres would the natural harmony of interests be revealed. Broadacre City, Wright asserted, would be an "organic" society. Wright's use of the word "organic" in this context had nothing in common with its use in classical political theory to refer to a society whose members are as subordinated to the whole as the individual organs to the body. Wright had in mind, perhaps, an image borrowed from the Romantic landscape artists: an organic order in which every living thing has a place and shape all its own, and yet contributes to the harmony of the whole. This "organic" reconciliation of individualism and order was Wright's aim in Broadacre City. He believed it was more than a theoretical possibility: it was the necessary end of mankind's and the machine's evolution. Broadacre City could replace all existing cities in three or four generations— if only the ground were cleared.

Wright's concept of the natural economic order found architectural expression in his plan for "the great Roadside Market." In Broadacre City there were no department stores or "congested crowds senselessly swarming in from the country on to hard pavement and back again." Instead, at a junction of two highways, there was a permanent "County Fair" under a huge shed. The Roadside Market brought together under one roof the multitude of small transactions in a decentralized economy. Each producer had his own stall. There the small farmer sold his fresh produce, the craftsman his handiwork, the manufacturer his articles of machine production. Close by were cabarets, cafes, and good restaurants. As Wright commented, the Roadside Market would be "the most attractive, educational and entertaining single modern unit to be found among all the features of the Broadacre City."[19]

At the Roadside Market the impersonal laws of supply and demand which regulate the economy of Broadacre City are dramatized in countless face-to-face transactions. These laws, however, are no longer the regulators of scarcity; in the natural economy of Broadacre City they apportion abundance. Where poverty and class conflict have been overcome, competition loses its grim, destructive aspect. Buying and selling at the

Roadside Market become a form of entertainment, a game of mutual enjoyment, and a ritual of social solidarity. The Roadside Market makes the functioning of the community's economy a public event. The exchange of goods and services is transformed into a daily festival, the celebration of the fruits of the community's labor.

14

Community and Culture

THE Roadside Market was only one of Broadacre City's meeting places. Wright realized that the theme of Broadacres —daily life centered around the home—required its counterpoint: festive public centers and impressive public institutions. Ebenezer Howard had grouped these assembly points into one Center whose position expressed his hope that the Garden City would unite in cooperation. Wright, however, believed that such axial symmetry was a relic of what he called "monarchical planning" and a remnant of the time when men were forced to organize their lives around some exalted power outside themselves.[1] He was careful not to create any single focus for community life which might undermine the "true center," the individual home. What he called the "Community Center" was in fact an entertainment center. It was an "attractive automobile objective" with a golf course, a racetrack, a zoo, an aquarium, a planetarium, an art gallery, theaters, and restaurants.[2]

Wright was most comfortable with this kind of Community Center. It was voluntary, cooperative, and claimed no power over those who enjoyed it. He recognized, however, that Broadacre City needed more authoritative institutions to maintain order, learning, and religion. The question he faced in planning them was: to what extent could the "organic unity" of Broadacre City be embodied in institutions? He was always afraid that these institutions could become coercive bodies and enforcers of mediocrity. Even in his ideal city, Wright was forced to compromise between his conservative wish for stability and his radical fear of any power that might threaten individuality.

Wright was most afraid of government. The Hegelian concept of the state as the institution that embodies the common good and the highest ideals of the society was absolutely foreign to him. Although Wright considered himself a great democrat, he had no desire to encourage participatory democracy. He preferred to be left alone.

In Broadacre City the county offices occupy a functional high-rise building by the side of a lake. They are accessible but hardly the focus of the community, as they are in the Garden City. County government would be virtually the only government in Broadacres. The national government had withered away until it concerned itself only with regulating natural resources and other administrative matters.[3] The county government, too, was largely concerned with administering basic services. The important questions, as we shall see, were resolved outside the political process. The independent citizens of Broadacre City thus had little cause to concern themselves with politics. "No politician as such could make a living in Broadacre City," Wright proudly boasted.[4]

He could not, however, minimize educational institutions as easily as he minimized political ones. The whole life of Broadacre City was dependent on education. Like his mother and father, Wright regarded education as salvation. Broadacres could not survive unless the citizens appreciated the moral and economic principles on which it was founded. The individuality that Wright prized so highly was dependent on the citizens' mastery of technology and their understanding of the wisdom of the past.

At the same time, Wright feared that educational institutions were a grave threat to individuality and the greatest promoters of the vicarious life. The schools, he complained, were mere "knowledge factories"; standardizing their students, they turned "perfectly good plums into perfectly good prunes."[5] Their emphasis on specialization meant they were structured to graduate recruits for the white-collar army that swelled the cities. "There are enough partialities," he complained, "to fill all the pigeonholes in the capitalist bureau of this mechanized nation. . . . In any genuine democracy, were Education adequate, the 'Expert' would be kept in a cage as some abnormality to be publicly exhibited as a warning."[6]

Wright maintained his hope that the principles of Broadacre City could save education. The first, of course, was decentralization. "The *big* American knowledge factory, the *big* school, the *big* anything was always a self-defeating institution."[7] Each elementary school would have perhaps twenty-five, at most forty, students. There would be no fixed curriculum; the emphasis would fall on individual activity. The fatal separation between handwork and brainwork which Wright saw as the curse of industrial society would never develop in these schools. Instead, active pursuits like cooking, gardening, and especially drawing would replace rote learning.

> Perfect correlation of the faculties, active and potential, of the human being—this it would be that constituted the most important aim of all Broadacre City education. Eye and hand, body and what we call Mind thus becoming more and more sensitive to Nature. . . . Spiritually and physically the Broadacre boys and girls would become the coefficients of a *naturally* Creative humanity.[8]

Wright did not anticipate many Broadacre City citizens continuing their education beyond high school. He wished, in fact, to close most of the existing universities and to turn them into community centers. Higher learning would then be pursued in small institutes whose fellows did pure research and functioned as the "Vision of Society."[9]

Another form of higher education which Wright foresaw for Broadacre City was the Design Center. This was an adaptation of the Experimental Stations which Wright had called for in the Hull House lecture. At the Design Center the creative artists of Broadacre City would experiment with the most advanced industrial techniques in use at local factories and create an indigenous style for their community. The Design Centers would preserve the creative artist's mastery over the machine—the original purpose of Broadacre City. They would maintain the community's sense of organic form and thus protect the balance between man and nature on which the whole society rests.

Wright himself actually founded a Design Center. In 1932 he recruited twenty-three apprentices to study with him at Taliesin. The Taliesin Fellowship, as the school was called, never possessed the equipment to experiment with the full range of machine crafts. Nevertheless, the Fellowship offers a working model of Wright's ideal of education.

"So we begin this Working Fellowship as a kind of daily work-life."[10] Wright thus defined the basic principle of the Fellowship: the union of physical and mental labor which he had prescribed for Broadacre City would become an immediate reality at Taliesin. The apprentices built their own quarters, constructed drafting rooms, farmed, cooked, and cleaned. Manual labor occupied about half their day. The rest was spent in the drafting rooms under Wright's supervision. Each apprentice began with the simplest forms of drawing and lettering and worked gradually until he could prepare plans for Wright's buildings and projects of his own.

The apprentices became Wright's extended family, sharing

his work and his leisure. The Fellowship permitted him to realize his dream of making Taliesin truly self-sufficient. The apprentices provided the labor for the farm and the buildings; they also formed an orchestra, a chorus, and a theater group. The Fellowship thus provided the full range of mental and physical experience which Wright believed was essential to all education. It was not, he emphasized, a professional school. "If you are a professional you are dead," he told the apprentices. "Taliesin aims to develop a well-correlated human being."[11]

Wright presided over the Fellowship as master and patriarch. He was an able, if demanding, teacher. Olgivanna recalled that

> often he would lean over the drawing board of a young man and then, becoming interested, he would sit down. "This is very good, you know, this is very good, but . . ." meanwhile erasing practically all the drawing while the poor student stood there, not quite knowing what was happening. Then he would say again: "It is all right; it is still good. The idea was good. . . ."[12]

Wright's administration of the Fellowship was far from democratic. He had the right to dismiss any apprentice at any time. He appointed one apprentice to be "foreman" while he himself supervised the daily activities, which stretched from breakfast at 6:30 A.M. to "lights-out" at 10:30 P.M. He refused to listen to what he called "premature (which is always immature) criticism," the category to which he relegated almost all complaints. There was no "apprentice power" at the Fellowship; the students were expected to obey his orders on almost all subjects. When he was over seventy he decided that three meals a day were a senseless luxury. The apprentices, who were in their twenties, were then served only two. He banned first cigarettes and then pepper from Taliesin.[13]

These idiosyncrasies were one expression of Wright's philosophy of higher education: the personal authority of a master must replace the bureaucratic regulation of the "knowledge factory." The Taliesin Fellowship awarded no degrees, only "personal testimonials" from Wright himself. He had conceived the Fellowship as a model of education for a new society in which the traditional centers of high culture—the great cities and large universities—no longer existed. There would be no academic ladder to climb, and yet Wright's decentralized society required an ever higher level of intellectual and aesthetic achievement than the old one. His solution was to make higher education an intense encounter between a small group of apprentices and one master. The apprentices would become extensions of the master's family; they would submit to his authority in the hope that they would learn his craft and absorb some of his wider concerns. The "knowledge factory," by presenting the teacher only in his limited role as "expert," trained only "partialities." The master, the whole man acting as teacher, developed "well-correlated human beings."

Although Wright was able to work out his conception of education both in theory and in practice, his ideas on religion in Broadacre City were problematic even in theory. The conflict between individuality and institutions was even more damaging, he believed, to the church than to the school. The son and grandson of Unitarian ministers, Wright was a religious man, but his was an undogmatic religion of the heart. "The Kingdom of God is within you" was his favorite text from scriptures. Theology was "troublesome pettifoggery," an obstruction to the search for truth, to which all the world religions could contribute. Religion united the individual with the great harmony of nature; that was salvation.

Wright believed that all churches distorted real religion by imposing some dogma between the individual and the religion of his heart. They were, moreover, "essentially undemocratic, being by nature some form of hierarchy." The American churches, he asserted, sought merely to "administer to partisanship, conscription, and what is called 'public opinion.' "[14]

If Wright distrusted all institutionalized religion, he still felt the need for some form of shared worship. He wanted a church where "worship would again be more nearly universal" because it was founded "by and for the Free Spirit of Individual Man." Wright called this church the Broadacre City Cathedral. It consisted of the tabernacles of the major faiths grouped around a central courtyard. Wright hoped that the focus of religious activity would shift from the tabernacles to the courtyard. There the universal religion of Broadacre City would be celebrated with magnificent pageantry drawn from the four elements: earth, air, fire, and water. The service would be a union of all the arts, a great communal dance in harmony with the "Organic Whole." The Cathedral "would be a rendezvous with the very heart of nature. It alone could serve the depths and breadths of the universal soul So the Church could again be a Citizen's refuge and no less individual for being more profound and comprehensive than it ever was yesterday."[15]

The Cathedral would thus express the final reconciliation of individuality and order which was the goal of the whole city. Like the cathedrals that Victor Hugo had celebrated, it would embody the deepest values of the society: the union of the individual man with his fellow man and the harmony of the whole society with nature. It was the fulfillment of Wright's hopes to be the master builder of a new society. Yet in his plan for Broadacre City, he did not assign the Cathedral a central position. It stands in a field adjacent to the Community Center. In the three-dimensional model of Broadacre City, Wright specified that all buildings except the Cathedral were presented complete. The Cathedral was "under construction—as always."[16] Perhaps he believed that the harmony he was seeking would always remain an aspiration, even in his ideal city.

15

Prophetic Leadership

The creative artist is by nature and by office the qualified leader in any society, natural, native interpreter of the visible form of any social order in or under which we choose to live.

FRANK LLOYD WRIGHT,
"Broadacre City" (1935)[1]

AMONG the handful of officials that Wright permitted in Broadacre City was one called the county architect. His office was unpretentious, his staff almost nonexistent. Nevertheless, he was the most powerful man in Broadacre City. All the other officials were administrators. He was a genuine planner with authority to enforce his decisions. The physical structure of the city—the basis of the society's way of life—was his responsibility.

The county architect's first duty was to design a beautiful and efficient system of roads. These roads would create the community, uniting the citizens with each other without directing them to any "monarchical" center. The county architect also had full responsibility for land allotment. He decided who should get land and how much; he intervened when he judged that an individual's aggrandizement of land ceased to be self-improvement and became "feudal" exploitation. Furthermore, "all building" was "subject to his sense of

the whole as organic architecture." He had "a certain disciplinary as well as cultural" function. He could forbid anything that marred "the harmony of the whole," structures
whose size threatened to restore centralization or whose
ugliness did not accord with that "deeper feeling of the beauty
of the terrain which would be a fundamental feature of the new
city-builders." The county architect was the guardian of the
principles of Organic Architecture, the man who adapted them
to local conditions and ensured that they were followed. "His
must be one of the best minds the city has," Wright asserted,
and he added that the county architect would be the best-
trained member of his community.[2]

Wright never specified how this architectural Philosopher-
King of the County Seat would be chosen or what his relationship would be to representative institutions. Wright realized
that the community needed leadership, "disciplinary as well as
cultural," and yet his extreme individualism seemed to under-
cut all authority. This was a problem which he faced both in
his theory of Broadacre City and in his own attempts to implement his plans. For the powers he was assigning to the county
architect were precisely those which he longed to be granted
by the American people. The county architect was Wright in
power. How, then, did he conceive the nature and origins of
this power?

The figure of the county architect can best be understood
as an incarnation of a dream of power that had pursued
Wright throughout his career. In the Hull House lecture he
derived the artist's authority from his ability to control the
machine. The Broadacre City plans led him to advance an even
closer link between power and imagination. The creative artist,
he asserted, was the truly representative man. He alone had
both the insight into the true interests of his people and the
ability to express those interests as "prophetic form":

What is it to be an artist? Simply to make objective in form what
was subjective in idea. It is to make things within and yet beyond

the power of the ordinary man. The artist may feel no deeper, may see no further but has the gift that enables him to put that insight into form in whatever medium he uses.[3]

This form was "prophetic" not because the artist could foretell the future but because he could grasp the present. The great artist instinctively penetrates even the society's own myths about itself: "until the artist is more the society he serves than the society is itself, he is not a great artist."[4]

This capacity to understand and objectify the "nature of the people" makes the artist their natural leader. Wright points out that only if the artist is to his people

> as your head is to your body or your mind is to your corporeality, can he do anything at all for them as artist. They see in parts. He must see and grasp the whole. His work is the flower of his race proceeding from that race as seed from the soil, dropping down into it again to germinate and produce other flowering.[5]

The mark of the true artist-leader was his "vision." The forces of technological change were blind; the spirit of a nation inarticulate. The artist, Wright believed, could visualize force and spirit in a plan that would be both truly democratic and truly powerful. The plan was democratic not because it had been debated in a legislature or approved in an election but because it was representative of the nation's deepest feelings as understood by the artist. The plan was powerful because it embodied these feelings and merged them with the current of technological change. All art makes conscious the dreams of the artist's society. The artist-leader's plan objectifies a society's collective dream of justice. It speaks to the people with their own voice and thus commands their allegiance.

Broadacre City was Wright's vision, his chef-d'oeuvre submitted to the American people as evidence of his qualifications as master builder. He directed it to everyone because he believed it derived from the basic truths which the whole nation shared in common. His analysis presupposed that beneath the factional struggles that dominate politics is a realm of shared values from which the artist draws his inspiration. The artist-leader must express the unity of this deeper realm in his plan for social organization. "There must be some way of life where there is no antagonism between the more developed and the less developed—or even between rich and poor if each had a fair chance to be what you call 'rich and poor.'"[6]

Wright's conception of artistic leadership had its origins, I believe, in the aesthetic idea of the "spirit of the age." Victor Hugo's *Notre-Dame de Paris*, a source of so many of Wright's insights, expounded the principle that there was one consistent spirit that informed all aspects of the life of a society, and that the artist best understood and expressed this spirit. Anyone who comprehends the design of an old palace doorknocker, he remarked, will know the features of the king. Wright gave this idea a dynamic turn. The artist, he held, not only comprehends the spirit of his age but also initiates the process of changing it. The principles which enable him to revolutionize his art necessarily apply to the rest of society. If architecture and government are part of the same spirit, then a new kind of architecture implies a new kind of government. Wright proclaimed that "all that Broadacre City needs, in order to come into existence, is the application of the principles of organic architecture to the life of our people, and the interpretation of that life in terms of architecture."[7]

To present his principles to the American people, Wright and his apprentices devoted thousands of hours to the three-dimensional model of Broadacre City which was exhibited at Rockefeller Center and elsewhere in the United States. The model was his way of communicating his vision directly to his fellow citizens: his truth would make them free. The model was exhibited without endorsements from any institution, political party, or interest group. He believed he was revealing the true American city to the American people, and that was power enough.

Wright's conception left him with one great difficulty. He

was so concerned to establish Broadacre City as an ideal city that he could offer no plausible path to reach so exalted a goal. In this respect he was the opposite of Ebenezer Howard, who, as Lewis Mumford has pointed out, often seemed more concerned with the process of creating the Garden City than with its design. Wright offered no "working model" to mediate between reality and his vision. "I have never been more than tolerant of reform," he once said. "It is true form I am seeking."[8] Broadacre City, he emphasized, could not be built piecemeal. It could exist only as the product of the whole nation's conversion to its principles. "Broadacre City is everywhere or nowhere. It is the country itself come alive as a truly great city."[9]

Wright's imagination focused on these two complementary extremes: the present, in which the prophet is wholly isolated, and some distant future, in which the prophecy has been wholly realized. Perhaps Wright knew that there could be no rational connection between these two extremes, that only a mass conversion could unite them. He certainly had only some vague guesses about the future. He occasionally toyed with the idea that a "statesman with the vision and personal responsibility of a Jefferson or a Thomas Paine . . . could in one lifetime lay down the outlines on which we could build the Democratic State. . . ."[10] He wrote in 1940 that "we need only the slight concerted political effort to remove the key-logs from the jam."[11] Usually, however, he emphasized that "organic growth" was "slow growth." He envisioned the steady shrinking of the cities by the migration of "runaways," individuals whose flight from urban life would create the conditions for Broadacre City in "three or four generations."

He completely neglected the work of building small organizations dedicated to his ideas, a tactic which had been the basis of Howard's strategy. Consequently, Wright had no way of collecting or even measuring his support. The opportunities for concerted action were not lacking, since Wright, like Howard, could look to the "Back-to-the-Land" movement as a source of potential supporters. This movement was in-fluential in the United States in the 1930s for much the same reasons it had flourished in England in the 1890s. In both cases there was widespread urban unemployment and un-precedented rural depopulation; resettling the workers on the land seemed a logical solution to the problem. The movement in the United States was often crude in its economics. One agricultural writer complained in 1933 that "hardly a week goes by but some new leader of public opinion discovers the space between the cities as a God-given dump for the unem-ployed."[12] Nevertheless, the Roosevelt administration had been persuaded to set up a Division of Subsistence Home-steads in the Department of the Interior and, in 1935, to create a full-scale Resettlement Administration.

Wright was introduced to prominent "decentralist" intel-lectuals by Baker Brownell, a friend and a professor of philos-ophy at Northwestern University. In 1936, Wright spoke at a conference at Northwestern organized by *Free America*, the leading decentralist journal. He shared the platform with John Crowe Ransom, the poet and critic who was a spokesman for the Southern Agrarians, and Ralph Borsodi, whose books (*This Ugly Civilization* and *Flight from the City*, among others) were the most widely read statements of the decentral-ist position.[13] The decentralists, a loose coalition of individuals and small groups, agreed among themselves only on the need to resettle families on their own homesteads. They were con-cerned to show that this goal did not mean political reaction or a barter economy. Wright's plan for Broadacre City, technologically advanced and as decentralized as the decen-tralists could wish, met with their approval. *Free America* wrote in an editorial that Broadacres was "the only compre-hensive picture we have of the world of the near future."[14]

Howard had been able to use the "Back-to-the-Land" senti-ments for his own ends. Wright, however, received no commissions from the Resettlement Administration and very little support from the decentralists. In 1940 a group in

Detroit sponsoring a plan to resettle auto workers on the land asked him to design a group of homesteads for twenty-five families. This was Wright's first and only opportunity to plan a group of houses whose residents would live according to the principles he advocated for Broadacre City. Each house was surrounded by its own farmland. The workers were to continue part-time employment at a factory 20 miles away, while they gradually brought more and more of the land under cultivation. The houses were designed to permit their owners to perform most of the labor themselves. The foundations were berm-type earthen walls compacted by a bulldozer; in Wright's drawing the community appeared to grow naturally out of its fields.[15]

Construction was never actually begun on this "working model" of Broadacre City. "The times were such," Wright wrote in 1942, "that the group could never get together with much purpose or effect. The affair languished for a year and died." He succinctly summarized the affair in his title for the published plans: "Berm Houses for Cooperative Workers. Failed for Lack of Cooperation."[16]

A full decade of writing and lecturing had produced only this one aborted project. Wright was beginning to be discouraged. Publicly he continued his crusade. When the Broadacre City model was exhibited in Pittsburgh in 1940, he told the citizens that "in all probability" their city would "have to be abandoned, eventually to be a rusty ruin and tumble into the river, staining the waters with oxide of iron for another half-century. . . ."[17] In private he was less certain. He admitted that the model "had not been carried far enough to be easily understood," and although the model had been seen by several hundred thousand people, "by only the Few was the City recognized for what it really was."

Wright's greatest source of discouragement, however, was the coming of war. He recognized that the needs of defense were the greatest spur to centralization. Moreover, he regarded the military mind as the greatest enemy of the individuality on which Broadacre City would have to be built. The army was for him the purest example of the regimented, dependent, vicarious life which the "feudal" economic powers and urban life had forced upon modern man. "Conscription," he proclaimed, was "the ultimate form of Rent."[18]

A decentralized society's weakness in the event of armed conflict with a centralized power was one of the strongest arguments against it. Wright replied simply: if our society was truly decentralized, there would be no war. "Were we ourselves actually to understand Democratic principles and sincerely put them into effect there would be nothing for us to fear," he asserted.[19] Wright had come to believe that nations involved themselves in war because they were overindustrialized, their foreign trade disrupted by the gold standard, their relations with other peoples poisoned by empire and colonies. Broadacre City, however, would have no need for foreign trade or colonies. If other nations quarreled over them, Broadacre City could withdraw into its own agrarian-based economy. "I can look with perfect confidence," Wright said in June 1941, "upon a world entirely undemocratic provided I and my friendly neighbors, if I happen to have any such, are not directly molested."[20]

After the draft was reinstituted in 1940, Wright began publishing his isolationist sentiments in a series of broadsheets he and his apprentices printed. These were called *Taliesin Square Paper: A Nonpolitical Voice From Our Democratic Minority.* The subtitle reflected Wright's growing disdain for the bulk of his fellow citizens.

> The only safe-guard Democracy can ever have is a free, morally enlightened, fearless minority. Unfortunately for our country such enlightenment and courage is (and it may ever be) a minority. But Democracy deprived of either the vote or the voice of that minority will stay in infancy, a pushed, helpless mediocrity. Democracy's very life depends upon entire freedom to continually choose from among its free minority the best and bravest thought.[21]

Fortunately for Wright's reputation, the *Square Paper* circulated among a very small minority. Its contents were a shrill polemic against the English and "that Eastern part of us that is already an out-and-out pseudo-fascist Empire reflecting the great disappearing British Empire."[22] During the Battle of Britain he addressed a "Letter to London" which concluded: "Do not grieve too much—Britain—English culture is safe. Empire is no essential."[23] He was more concerned over what he considered to be the disproportionate influence of the Northeast in the United States, for that region "was never really agrarian" and its foreign trade "remains in power-finance money bags of the power-finance system of New York, an alias of the power-finance system of London."[24] In October 1941 he proposed to curb this influence by re-forming the United States as a tristate confederation. The entire West and Midwest would comprise "Usonia," with its capital in Denver; the South and Border States would form "Usonia South," governed from Atlanta. The Northeast would be called "New England," with Washington, D.C., as its capital. The federation would have its own capital,

> probably placed mid-way on the rolling prairies of the Mid-West beside the Father of the Waters—our Mississippi—there where the amplitude, rectitude and impartiality that might characterize the greater part of our nation, could, unhampered by congenital prejudice or the equivocal influence of foreign powers, be free to initiate and grow the ways and means to live a good life as the independent democracy this country was designed to be.[25]

Pearl Harbor put an abrupt halt to these reflections. In May 1945, however, Wright began publishing the *Square Paper* again with this motto:

> The price for International Peace is fundamental:
> No gold;
> No tariffs;
> No conscription.[26]

In subsequent issues he denounced the Cold Warriors as vigorously as he had the advocates of American involvement in World War II. After the proclamation of the Truman Doctrine, he demanded that

> this whole process of professionalized interference with the lives of the people of other nations should be made liable to the charge of meddling with the private affairs of others. The offending expert should be summarily handed over to the tender mercies of the foreign nations thus offended.[27]

Wright's excursus into foreign policy added little to his reputation as a social thinker. It contributed greatly, however, to his growing discouragement and alienation from his fellow citizens. He began to fear that America was an irredeemably urbanized nation. When Wright was born Chicago was no metropolis; he could believe that before he died it would return to its earlier size. The Great Depression seemed to offer an opportunity for radical decentralization, but the war had imposed its own commanding centralization instead. In 1944, Wright reflected upon some of the hopes he had voiced more than forty years earlier in the Hull House lecture:

> Today, I find it hard to believe that the Machine would go into the Creative Hand even were that magic hand there in its true place.
>   As machine facilities have increased, more inordinate total "Production," more "Total Mechanization," to control foreign markets of the world by Total War, is in sight. The "Machine" has become more and more the Engine of War.[28]

The Cold War and the resumption of conscription seemed to extend this trend into the distant future. Wright had to consider the possibility that he was a prophet scorned not only by his own people but by history as well.

16

The Living City

Genius is a sin against the mob!

FRANK LLOYD WRIGHT,
Genius and the Mobocracy
(1949)[1]

IN 1949, Wright published his angriest book. It was ostensibly a tribute to Louis Sullivan, but Wright's eloquent tribute to the Lieber Meister was overshadowed by his aggrieved reflections on Sullivan's tragic neglect by the American people in the last decades of his life. These reflections impelled him to a more intemperate polemic on the neglect of his own genius by the present "mobocracy."

"A nation industrialized beyond proper balance with its own agronomy is a menace to its own peace and the peace of the world," he began. "It is a house in a chronic state of civil war always divided against itself."[2] To maintain order and to pursue those wars which are "the necessary clearing house" for a society where "head and heart, soul and intellect come in constant conflict," some form of centralized control is necessary. "The artificiality of our mechanized society is helplessly drifting toward a bureaucracy so top-heavy that the bureaucracy of Soviet Russia will seem honest and innocent by comparison."[3]

The structure of centralized authority would necessarily make passivity, conformity, and mediocrity ubiquitous among the American people. Wright never had much faith in the average city dweller's capacity to maintain his individuality. In 1914 he had written, "The 'Democracy' of the man in the American street is no more than the Gospel of Mediocrity."[4] Nevertheless, he maintained that the nation had retained a heritage of genuine ideas on which the artist could base his work. If the artist could penetrate the surface of conformity and touch the bedrock of individualism, the man in the street would recognize works created in this spirit as "prophetic expressions of himself" and would cling to them "for salvation."

In the 1930s, Wright hoped that everyone could perform this act of recognition; by 1949, however, he trusted only an elite, the "democratic minority." For the vast majority, mass conformity and bureaucratic dislike of anything irregular would combine to completely exclude imagination and originality. In the mobocracy the genius is not the natural leader but the natural outcast. "The genius does not 'belong.' He will not 'stay in line.' "[5] If, as Wright believed, the artist needs a healthy "indigenous" culture in which to work, then "demoralization of the creative instinct—O Lord, be merciful —lies in this universalized governmental substitution of a falsely-decorated mobocracy for the thought-built democracy we might have."[6] And if, as Wright also believed, society needs the creative artist if it is ever to attain its proper form, then all hope for significant change must die in the mobocracy.

> So this new democratic architecture we call organic and is original may again be swamped by the same heedless mobocracy or more likely by official statism (the two gangsterisms do work together) and our hope of organic culture will be left to die with principle in this Western Wasteland![7]

Wright, as I have said, thought in terms of complete acceptance or rejection. For all his vaunted democracy, he lacked any conception of a genuinely reciprocal contact between the artist and his people. For him the genius was an individual working alone, true to his own goals and standards. Like an architect presenting his drawings to a design competition, the artist-leader presents his prophetic vision to his people as a completed whole. Wright's "democracy" consisted in his belief that the American nation was capable of living up to his standards.

Having despaired in *Genius and the Mobocracy*, he regained his faith before he died. In one sense this was inevitable, because his harsh judgment of his country implied an equally harsh judgment of himself. Wright was imbued with the idea of a pervasive "spirit of the age"; since the artist could never alienate himself from that spirit, his society's failings inevitably became his own. Wright, finally, could not accept either himself or his country as failures. Moreover, the publication of *Genius and the Mobocracy* coincided, ironically, with a real rebirth of Wright's architectural practice. This new phase in his creative career has been initiated in 1935 by the great Edgar Kaufmann house, "Fallingwater." The commission to build the Johnson Wax Company administration building, awarded the following year, was his first major project since the Imperial Hotel. The fame of these two structures was spread by an influential retrospective of Wright's work at the Museum of Modern Art in New York in 1940. After the war he received commissions from every area of the country. When Wright turned eighty in 1947 he was entering the most productive decade of his life.[8]

He was becoming a national institution; he could hope that Broadacre City would become a national institution as well. In his ninetieth year he completely rewrote (for the fourth time) the book he had published in 1932 as *The Disappearing City*. The city had not disappeared in the intervening twenty-five years: the urban areas and their suburbs had grown, and the countryside had been depopulated. Nevertheless, Wright still asserted that decentralization was "innate necessity." He left the theory virtually unchanged. Even the defense of Henry George was retained. Broadacre City remained one man's vision of the future, unaltered by practice. The vision seemed remote, but Wright was confident that "our nation *is* learning. . . . A new city is as inevitable as sunrise tomorrow though rain may fall."[9] This last affirmation of Broadacres appeared in 1958 as *The Living City*. Wright died April 9, 1959.

17

Summation

AT the beginning of *The Disappearing City*, Wright presented a historical parable. Mankind, he wrote, was once divided into two groups: the "radical" nomad or Wanderer, and the "static," conservative Cave-Dweller.

> The Cave-Dweller became the Cliff-Dweller and began to build cities. Establishment was his. His God was a malicious murderer. His statue . . . he erected into a covenant. When he could he made it of gold.[1]

The Wanderer, however, was an adventurer who found his strength in his mobility and "lived by his freedom and his prowess beneath the stars."

Wright attributed the "Ideal of Freedom which keeps breaking through our present static establishments" to the "survival of the original instincts of the Adventurer." The walled city had supplanted the Wanderer but never conquered him. Now the machine was coming to his aid, undermining the justifica-

tion for static establishments. The city of the future would be
without walls, a city of the Wanderer, where mobility had
brought freedom.

Wright's conscious sympathies in this parable were wholly
with the Wanderer, yet the ideal city he designed had its full
complement of institutions inspired by the Cave-Dweller: the
county architect with his disciplinary powers, the schools, even
a Cathedral towering over the landscape. At the "true center"
of Broadacre City was the homestead, a refuge Wright intended to be as strong as any walled town. Both in his thought
and in his actions, Wright was as strongly attracted to the
values of stability and security as he was to radical change.
Even his most unconventional initiatives were conceived as
attempts to replace corrupted practices with a genuine, lasting
order. If he attacked the American economic system, it was to
open the way to "true capitalism." If he offended the morality
of his time, it was to show the virtues of "true marriage." If he
criticized the architecture of his contemporaries, it was to lead
the fight for true Organic Architecture. The Wanderer and the
Cave-Dweller were in fact personifications of two conflicting
impulses present in all of Wright's work.

The key to this perpetual conflict was Wright's commitment
to his own ideal of individuality. This summum bonum in his
system could exist only in a precarious equilibrium of stability
and change. Wright always emphasized perhaps overem-
phasized—that creative individuality must have its roots in a
stable community whose values the citizen shares and protects.
This is the justification for Broadacre City's schools, churches,
and government. Yet these institutions can have no ultimate
power over the citizen. If individuality is to be preserved,
everyone must be free to pursue his own conception of what
is right, regardless of the consequences for the stability of
society. The individual is thus dependent on a stable community, yet his freedom to question and to negate is always a
potential threat to the society which nurtured him. Hence the
paradox of Wright's individualism: like the serpent eating its

own tail, Wright's individual is always threatening to consume himself.

Wright intended Broadacre City to be the place where this paradox would be overcome. He wanted a city without walls, spiritual or material, which would nonetheless be a stable community. Radical decentralization would finally create an environment in which the freedom of the Wanderer and the conservatism of the Cave-Dweller could coexist. In this organic social order there could be no conflict between what was true in the private heart and what was true for all men. The beauty of Broadacre City, its reconciliation of man and nature, would be the final proof that it was indeed the natural order for the industrial age.

These were Wright's aims, but how well did he succeed even in his own terms? In his ideal city Wright made the family the central institution of his new society. While other institutions led a shadowy existence, the family was the key to the stability of the whole community. Wright had, however, no lasting faith in this all-important institution. Both as a child and as a parent he had intimate experience with the forces that tear families apart. Perhaps because he was so afraid of these forces, he conceived a world in which all structural arrangements combine to bring the individual back to the family. The isolated homesteads of Broadacre City were designed to protect the family from the outside world and, ultimately, from itself.

The family, as Wright well knew, is tragically vulnerable to the disruptive claims of the individual. Stability in Broadacres, therefore, would be uncertain at best. We might also question whether rural decentralization would provide the best environment for the freedom and creativity which Wright also valued so highly. Here he was surely misled by too simplistic an equation of economic and physical independence with individuality. In his search for an alternative to the urban society of his time, he accepted uncritically that aspect of the Jeffersonian tradition which assigns a moral superiority to small-scale agrarian life that neither logic nor historical experience can justify.

To be sure, Wright's homesteader would possess a high degree of independence from outside pressures, but would that independence ever rise above self-seeking acquisitiveness? Despite Wright's expectations, there is little to suggest that a decentralized society would be a free or creative one. The northern United States in the first half of the nineteenth century was as rural, egalitarian, and decentralized as Wright could wish. Nonetheless, its most acute critic, Alexis de Tocqueville, observed that America was already suffering from a deadening conformity of taste and opinion, precisely that "tyranny of the majority" which Wright deplored in the twentieth century and attributed to urbanization.

If anything, the tyranny of the majority has proved stronger on the outskirts than in the centers of industrial society. One need not live on top of one's neighbor to repeat all his ideas. Wright correctly recognized many of the dangers of excessive urbanization, but he refused to acknowledge the power of the big city to foster precisely the values he was espousing. As sociologist Robert Park has convincingly argued, the metropolis—with its freedom born of anonymity, its innumerable juxtapositions of groups with radically different values and experiences, and its limitless range of human contacts—is the natural environment for individualism.

Broadacre City is thus as much an evasion of as it is a solution to its central problem: how can freedom and democracy be preserved in an industrial society? Its lasting value lies less in its specific remedies than in its honest and imaginative embodiment of the contradictory impulses that inspired it. Whatever his other limitations, Wright always took the ideal of democracy seriously. For him it could be nothing less than "the highest form of aristocracy the world has ever known," and he realized that this democracy would require a unique kind of citizen. In practice as well as theory, Wright placed all his trust on an exalted concept of the individual and his capacity to change the world. Wright attempted to speak "prophetically" to individuals, and he resisted group support that might have impaired his independence. Ebenezer Howard, as we have seen, moved easily from his ideal of cooperation to the cooperative efforts to build the Garden City. Le Corbusier, whose ideal city enshrined hierarchy and command, looked to Authority to accomplish his plans. Wright's followers would have to make their own decision to forsake the city, inspired only by Wright's plan itself. Each follower would need sufficient intelligence to comprehend Broadacre City, the initiative to act on it, and most important of all, the vision to see it as the necessary alternative to the centralized society he knew. In his own prophetic mission, Wright assumed that his fellow citizens would share not only his values but also his imagination.

Not surprisingly, this proved to be a vain hope. He gradually narrowed his prophetic appeals from the nation as a whole to the democratic minority capable of understanding him, and finally to that majority of one—the genius—facing a hostile mobocracy. Perhaps it was inevitable that a quest for the ideal city which started from uncompromising individualism would end as it began—in isolation.

III

Le Corbusier

18

Contrasts

WRIGHT and Le Corbusier seem predestined for comparison. Their ideal cities confront each other as two opposing variations on the same utopian theme. Both believed that industrialization had produced the conditions for a new era of justice, harmony, and beauty; that this era would commence with the replacement of all existing cities by new forms of community suited to the new age; and that this physical restructuring of society would be the fundamental revolutionary act separating the past from the future.

Wright, as we have seen, wanted to decentralize society, to abolish existing cities and to replace them with a continuous union of town and country where the individual and his family could flourish. Le Corbusier, like Wright, recognized the city as the natural home of centralized power. For that reason he wished to exalt it. The existing cities, he complained, were not dense enough. They offered too much expression to "anarchic individualism," too little scope for planning. The city of the future would be a Radiant City of glass-and-steel skyscrapers set in parks; it would be an efficient and beautiful center for the great bureaucracies whose total administration of society would bring the order and harmony he sought.

Despite their differences, the two men shared many of the same goals. Both Wright and Le Corbusier had been deeply marked by their exposure to and subsequent reaction against the arts-and-crafts movement. The Radiant City, as much as Broadacre City, was an attempt to revitalize work and reconcile man with nature. It was Le Corbusier, not Wright, who inscribed at the head of his plans: "These studies rest on an inalienable, unquestionable truth that is fundamental to all plans for social organization: individual liberty."[1] That this motto adorns a proposal for a completely planned society provides an important insight into Le Corbusier's way of thinking. He pursued the Holy Grail of "synthesis," the combining of seemingly irreconcilable elements into a logical, coherent, unexpected but inevitable whole. If Howard's deepest value was cooperation and Wright's individualism, Le Corbusier's aim was a society in which both cooperation and individualism could find simultaneous expression.

There is one further comparison with Wright. Both architects began their lives away from the great urban centers, and neither had any formal training in the profession they revolutionized. "Le Corbusier" was the pseudonym of Charles-Édouard Jeanneret, the son of an artisan family from the French-speaking region of Switzerland north of Geneva. Like Wright, he could claim to be his own creation. But the birth of Le Corbusier out of the mind of Charles-Édouard Jeanneret was a long and difficult process.

19

Self-Creation

LE CORBUSIER was born on October 6, 1887 in one of
the most prosperous handicrafts communities left in Europe,
the watchmakers of La Chaux-de-Fonds. His adolescence and
early manhood were dominated by a crisis and decline in that
way of life caused by industrialization. For Le Corbusier, the
Industrial Revolution was a personal experience. As he came
to maturity he was forced to choose between his love for the
values and artistic traditions of the past and his fascination
with the powerful new techniques that were irrevocably
changing his world. His passionate, complex attitude toward
industrialization grew directly out of this conflict. In his ideal
city he would create a vision of a mass industrial society that
would seem to be a defiant rejection of the world of his youth.
Yet even when he was most obsessed with the need for mass
production, large organizations, and control from above, he
always insisted that modern society must ultimately rely on
its own capacity for craftsmanship, cooperation, and self-

discipline. Le Corbusier never stopped searching for an industrial society that would be as harmonious and orderly as an artisan community.

When, in his first book, he depicted the "natural" and "stable" society where "the father watched over his children in the cradle and later in the workshop; effort and gain succeeded each other peacefully within the family order," Le Corbusier was describing the world he had known as a child.[1] The manufacture of watches was then a unique example of order without large-scale organization. Three or four artisans and the *patron* who worked alongside them formed the basic unit of production, the *atelier*. Le Corbusier's father, an engraver, was the master of one such workshop. Each *atelier* had its specialty and each maintained the standards of precision that enabled its products to be assembled with those of other workshops into the watches on whose perfect functioning the prosperity of the whole community depended. Karl Marx, who discussed La Chaux-de-Fonds in *Capital*, called the town "one huge manufactory" and remarked that the citizens had, by their own efforts, achieved a far more efficient and intricate division of labor than any factory owner could have imposed.[2]

In contrast to Wright's unhappy experience, Charles-Édouard's childhood was secure and uneventful. His father was president of the local mountain-climbing club and he bequeathed his love of nature and exercise to his son. His mother was artistic, and when his older brother Albert showed promise on the violin, she encouraged him to pursue his lessons. Charles-Édouard's skills at drawing were noticed early by his parents, so at thirteen they apprenticed him as a watchcase engraver.

The watchcase engravers were the artistic elite of the artisan community. Their elaborately embellished designs provided the final flourish to the heavy time-pieces that hung from every respectable watch-chain. The school that was established primarily for their training, the School of Applied

Art, ranked second only to the academic *Gymnase* in prestige. Le Corbusier once remarked that he would have remained a watchcase engraver all his life were it not for Charles L'Eplattenier, his teacher of drawing. L'Eplattenier was Le Corbusier's first master, and his philosophy of art and society remained a decisive influence in Le Corbusier's life even after he had reacted against it. The drawing instructor was born near La Chaux-de-Fonds, the son of a peasant family. Through incredible effort and complete dedication to art, he managed to enroll in the École des Beaux Arts in Paris. He soon discovered that Paris was the home of decadence and industrialization, and he returned to the Suisse Romande in disgust. He was astute enough to realize that the watchmaking communities were doomed to be supplanted by the industrialization he hated, and he dedicated himself to finding a way out. He had been greatly influenced by the French branch of the arts-and-crafts movement, and he came to believe that the only solution was to revive the old crafts—wood carving, enameling, mural painting—that had been neglected for watchmaking.[3]

As teacher at the School of Applied Art he set himself the task of discovering the most gifted sons of the artisans and training each in a particular forgotten craft. Eventually there would be a whole corps of craftsmen, the nucleus of a movement which would revive the authentic regional style and produce works of art that the machine could never duplicate. The artisans would take up the tools of their ancestors, and the community would be saved.

L'Eplattenier was not slow to recognize the ability of Charles-Édouard Jeanneret. When, in 1902, Jeanneret's skill at watchcase engraving won him a prize at the Turin International Exposition, L'Eplattenier was ready to designate him for the most important position in his future corps of craftsmen. "You shall become an architect," he announced to the apprentice watchcase engraver.[4]

Membership in a corps of craftsmen dedicated to reviving

forgotten techniques might seem an unlikely starting point for
Le Corbusier's career. As we have seen with Wright, however,
the arts-and-crafts movement suggested many of the themes
of the modern aesthetic. L'Eplattenier admired Rodin as well
as the old Jura master masons. He encouraged his students to
disregard the fashionable models and to seek their inspiration
directly from the pattern of forms suggested by nature. More
importantly for our purposes, he impressed on his students a
lesson that Le Corbusier never forgot: all true art must have as
its ultimate aim the regeneration of society. L'Eplattenier gave
special attention to Charles-Édouard's intellectual development. Together they read Ruskin "with reverence." L'Eplattenier also had Jenneret read such works as Henri Provensal's
L'art de demain, which proclaimed that art was "the religious
conscience of nations," and Edouard Schuré's *Les grands
initiés*, which taught that Rama, Krishna, Hermes, Moses,
Orpheus, Pythagoras, and Jesus were all "initiates" who had
penetrated the veil of matter and grasped the truth of the
Spirit.[5]

For L'Eplattenier this truth was summed up as the unity of
man with nature. He emphasized to his students that the
artist must live in the worlds of nature and culture. His
imagination must reconcile the two. "On Sundays," Le
Corbusier recalled,

> a group of us often met on the summit of the highest moun-
> tain. . . . In the midst of peaks and great sweet slopes, bands of
> animals, infinite horizons, flights of crows, we prepared for the
> future. There, the Master said, we shall construct a temple
> dedicated to nature. We shall devote our lives to it. We shall
> leave the city and live in the forest at the foot of the structure
> which we shall slowly fill with our works. The spirit of the entire
> site shall be incarnated there. All the animals, all the plants. Once
> a year there will be a great celebration. At the four corners of the
> temple the ceremonial fires will be lit. . . .[6]

For Le Corbusier, who had little attachment to the Protes-
tantism of his parents, this was the religion of his youth.

And, like most sensitive adolescents, he began to doubt. When Charles-Édouard was seventeen, L'Eplattenier arranged his first commission, the Villa Fallet. The house still stands, a sturdy chalet in the regional style and a loyal application of L'Eplattenier's teachings. (Le Corbusier later described it as "frightful, but free from routine architecture." The house is omitted from his so-called *Complete Works*.) He used his fee to leave on a long journey of travel and self-exploration that lasted more than two years. He told his father as he left, "I haven't asked you for money, don't ask me where I'm going or what I intend to do. I don't know myself!"[7]

His destination, Italy, gives a clue to his hopes, if not to his conscious intentions. Italy was the home of the great tradition in art, the universal tradition that L'Eplattenier had opposed in the name of the region. Jeanneret was declaring his independence. In Italy he traveled, pack on his back, pencil and drawing paper in hand, to the art cities of Tuscany. He then journeyed to Budapest and from there to Vienna, where he spent the winter drawing and going to concerts. He arrived in Paris in the spring of 1908.

Vienna and Paris were the first of the "great brutal cities" he stayed in "to learn, to live, to find a point to apply energies avid to produce." His view of the metropolis always retained something of the poor student's perspective, that combination of constant intellectual excitement and physical discomfort. He did not forget the attic rooms, the *"place des pauvres"* at the concerts, the loneliness. "For youth," he wrote at this time, "the great cities are deserts where you die of hunger in front of thousands of closed doors: inside you can hear the clicking of forks."[8]

Paris was the logical conclusion for a trip undertaken to escape from the provinciality of La Chaux-de-Fonds. It was the capital of a cultural world in which the Suisse Romande was only a remote region. However, Le Corbusier was still sufficiently guided by L'Eplattenier and by his own inclinations to resist any temptation to enroll at the École des Beaux Arts.

(He thus was never entitled to put the letters D.P.L.G.—*diplômé par le gouvernement*—after his name, the mark of an academically trained architect.) Instead, he knocked on the doors of the avant-garde, thet creators of Art Nouveau: Henri Sauvage, Frantz Jourdain, Eugène Grasset. "Where can I find modern architecture?" he asked them. Grasset directed him to the atelier of Charles and Auguste Perret.

Le Corbusier's encounter with Auguste Perret was as important for him as Frank Lloyd Wright's had been with Louis Sullivan. Perret was trained as an engineer and believed in technology as the hope of architecture and society. (Le Corbusier recalled Perret's joyous announcement to his draftsmen, Blériot has flown the Channel! Wars are over! There are no more frontiers!")[9] Perret's particular enthusiasm was reinforced concrete. Although the technique of embedding iron rods in concrete had been known for more than fifty years, Perret was the first to exploit its potential. He believed it would be the basis of a new era in architecture.

Perret gave Le Corbusier a part-time job as a draftsman and guided the studies which Charles-Édouard eagerly pursued in his free time. At Perret's urging he took up advanced mathematics, mechanics, and material sciences, subjects he had neglected at La Chaux-de-Fonds. Perret held that these sciences would be the essential vocabulary for the architect of the future. He also recommended to the young draftsman to purchase and study Viollet-le-duc's multivolume *Architectural Dictionary*. Its author is best known today for his cathedral restorations; as a theorist of architecture, however, he was one of the great precursors of functionalism. He showed how the flying buttresses of Notre-Dame and other much-imitated features of the cathedral were necessary functional parts of the structure. He was among the first to discuss warehouses and ships as architecture and to praise their design. With Perret's guidance, Le Corbusier was thus introduced to technological rationalism: the belief that architecture must be based on a firm knowledge of materials and mathematics, and the hope that it was a science which would necessarily advance as technology had done.

This philosophy was exactly opposed to L'Eplattenier's spiritualized concept of the revival of the ancient arts. Perret's ideas were far closer to the philosophic position Le Corbusier eventually adopted, but his mature thought was not the simple result of rejecting one teacher for another. From his twenty-first to his thirtieth year his mind was continually absorbed in the struggle between the opposing ideals. As always he was seeking a synthesis—a means to realize the values of the old arts with the technology of the future.

His earliest attempts to grapple with the problem were recorded in a series of letters he sent to L'Eplattenier from Paris in 1908. He announced to his teacher that he was seeking a new art in isolation. Paris had become an "arid retreat" for him, but he preferred it to the "affectionate milieu" of La Chaux-de-Fonds. "If I were back home," he asked his teacher, "how could I see for myself? At every moment of doubt I would come running to you, begging you to see for me."[10]

He explained his doubts about L'Eplattenier's movement. "You have stuffed us with ideals," he wrote. The movement was "built on sand." Its members "cover walls with beautiful colors and think that they know how to make everything beautiful. Perhaps their beauty is miserably false. It is facile. A surface beauty. Necessarily, Beauty by chance: to work one must know. . . . Your soldiers have never thought. The art of tomorrow will be an art of thought."[11]

He described his own studies. "With rage and joy I learned about the forces of nature. It's hard but beautiful, so logical, so perfect!" He spoke of his knowledge as "capital" which he was accumulating for a decisive moment—the moment when he could create "the art of tomorrow." This involved not only knowledge but also intense inner conflict. One "battles with oneself," "ties and binds" the "divine self" until it is forced to "speak of the depths of Being: Art is born, and quickly—it flees."[12]

The "art of the future" would be created out of this solitary inner struggle. "Thought unfolds and you must battle with it." This was Le Corbusier's conviction throughout his life. His art and thought proceed from the most disparate elements to final resolution, but even in his most satisfying harmonies there is an unexpected daring, a disturbing sharpness that reveals something of the struggle that preceded it. This, for him, was "living art," the product of the moment when the self discovers the unity in opposites and art is born.

In 1908 he was both frightened and excited by the coming struggle and its almost inevitable consequence, his separation from friends and teachers. "I see conflict ahead with those I love," he wrote to L'Eplattenier. He expressed his feelings in a parable, comparing his teacher to a tree on an arid rock that has struggled to establish itself and then sows its seeds. The saplings

> push their little roots with vivacity! with what joy they point their little leaves at the sun . . . but the sun heats the rock; the sapling looks around with anguish; he feels the pressure of too intense heat; he wants to point his roots toward his great protector. But the large tree has spent twenty years struggling to establish its roots in the fissures of the rock; its roots fill even the smallest crevices. In anguish the sapling accuses the tree that created it. He curses the great tree and dies. He dies of never having lived—for himself.[13]

To create the art of the future: this was to live for himself. This was survival itself. "People talk of the art of tomorrow. This art *will exist*. Because humanity has changed its manner of living, its manner of thinking." Reviving the arts of the past was impossible because creativity depends on the mastery of the most advanced ideals and technology of one's own time.

> These eight months in Paris cry out to me: Logic, truth, away with the dream of the arts of the past. Eyes front, forward! Word for word, with all the meanings of words, Paris tells me: "Burn what you have loved, and love what you once burned."[14]

The new architecture of iron and concrete, he told his teacher, will mark "a highpoint of daring" in the "history of mankind as recorded in its monuments." His principal worry was that he himself would not be among its initiators. He once confessed to L'Eplattenier that he often felt a "great emptiness" and thought to himself, "Poor boy, you still know nothing and, alas, you don't even know what you don't know." In this same letter he wrote, "I have a profound disgust with myself. I can't even draw." Three months later he spoke more confidently. "My idea is larger, it fills me with enthusiasm . . . it drives me on; it transports me; at times when the force is within me I take flight and the voice within cries, 'You can!' " He concluded, "I have forty years to reach what I now see dimly on the horizon."[15]

One might think that these letters were among the last contacts Le Corbusier would have with his old teacher. In fact, they were a prelude to his leaving Paris in 1909 and returning to La Chaux-de-Fonds. He did not retreat to his old home to escape the struggles of Paris but to gain the independence to continue them. His concept of the art of the future remained dim. He needed time to give it substance, to make it his own. Auguste Perret was still a respected and loved teacher, but he was no more anxious to remain Perret's disciple than he was to accept L'Eplattenier's leadership. (Already his friends had begun to call him "le grand Charles.") He was not ready to go as far as Perret in embracing the modern world; at the same time, he wanted to go much further in his designs than Perret's cautious compromise with classicism would allow.

From 1909 to 1916, La Chaux-de-Fonds was the scene of his struggle to create "for himself." He spent the first winter there in an isolated cabin studying mechanics and the use of reinforced concrete. This devotion to Perret's teaching was soon balanced by renewed contact with L'Eplattenier. In 1910, Le Corbusier joined his teacher's "United Arts Workshop," an incipient guild of the craftsmen L'Eplattenier had trained.[16] He also made the acquaintance of many of the most prominent regionalist intellectuals, musicians, and poets who were dedicated to restoring the culture of the Suisse Romande. He kept his own perspective, however, through frequent trips to Paris and Germany and a long journey through the Balkans.

Le Corbusier's attempt to keep his distance from the culture of La Chaux-de-Fonds did not mean that he isolated himself from its problems. At the time of his return from Paris, the artisan-based economy of his native city was in crisis. Mass-produced watches from Germany were flooding the traditional markets. The Workers' Federation of Watch Designers posted placards urging parents not to apprentice their children to this "famine-plagued trade."[17] The situation among engravers was equally severe. On one of his trips to Germany, Le Corbusier saw a machine which aptly symbolized the causes of the trouble. He called it "a horrible hammering machine" because in seconds it turned out a passable imitation of ironwork which required a day's human labor.[18]

Le Corbusier's search for the art of the future was conducted against this background: the destruction of the crafts of the past. The whole social structure that had produced the works of beauty and exactitude—the intricate division of labor, the skills lovingly cultivated and passed down—was in jeopardy. It was threatened, ironically, by the cheap and nasty machine-made imitations of its own work. The crisis which L'Eplattenier had attempted to guard against was now at hand. Le Corbusier was deeply affected by this crisis. He had, however, seen enough of technology to be convinced that it was inevitable.

He summed up his attitude in an image drawn from his trip to the Balkans. He had been joyful at the sight of the simple, harmonious peasant houses of Serbia and the local crafts that combined practicality and beauty in an "instinctive appreciation of the organic line." But he also noticed that even these "unspoiled" peasants were beginning to appropriate the most ugly products of the modern world. Once, at a well, he was grieved to see that only a few women used their beautiful earthen jars to carry water. The rest brought back the water in two empty gasoline cans strung over their shoulders. "The immortal pose of Ruth at the well of Jacob? the truly beautiful craft of the potter that seemed to have always been a part of civilization? *Finished*! Replaced by an iron bucket."

He did not hesitate to draw the moral. "This story from the land of beauty and 'imperishable' works of art is one of the strongest lessons for our time: economic evolution is implacable; nothing can resist it; regrets are useless; a poetry dies that seemed immortal."[19]

A poetry or *all* poetry? Le Corbusier had accepted as inevitable the destruction of the artisan's way of life and his aesthetic. Did this mean the destruction, as L'Eplattenier believed, of all beauty? Le Corbusier's art of the future must be an art of the Machine Age or it would not exist at all.

His first attempt to define the proper relation between art and industry came in a report he wrote for La Chaux-de-Fonds on German industry and art education. The report grew out of L'Eplattenier's efforts to establish a "New Section" in the School of Applied Art which would be the permanent home of his movement. L'Eplattenier had been impressed with the activities of the German arts-and-crafts movement, especially the *Deutscher Werkbund*, where collaboration between artists and craftsmen produced original works of beauty, utility, and fashion. He hoped to use this example to persuade the town fathers of the practicality of his New Section; and Le Corbusier, who was then in Munich, was commissioned to write the report.

Le Corbusier dutifully described the many examples of collaboration between artists and craftsmen, but he realized that the results were necessarily products for the luxury trades. He was more excited by German prowess in production. Germany, he proclaimed, was "organized"; it was the "great workshop of production"; it "must be known." The products of mass production, however, were ugly, while the local

artisans' work "had fallen into a most lamentable state." This
did not surprise him. The era of creative artisans working from
popular tastes was, he believed, a legacy of the ancien régime.
Its doom had been sealed by the French Revolution, even if
its death was a slow one. The artisan tradition, dead in itself,
was powerless to resist the forces of industrialization. Only
the fine arts retained their capacity to humanize and beautify
the world. Like industry, they had "inherited the spirit of the
French Revolution and entered into a new era." In France,
"Cézanne had come like one predestined to open immense
horizons."[20] As yet, these horizons were restricted to the
studio. France had created an aesthetic for the Machine Age,
but this aesthetic had not reached Germany, which possessed
the machines. The opportunity for La Chaux-de-Fonds, midway between Paris and Berlin, was clear: the New Section
must educate designers who could apply the most advanced
French artistic ideas to the most advanced German technology.

This, in Le Corbusier's view, was the great alternative to
ugliness and bankruptcy. It was a view which had important
social implications for a city of artisans like La Chaux-de-
Fonds. He denied that the craftsman "subjected to the taste of
the masses" could create the forms appropriate to a Machine
Age. This could be accomplished only by an elite of trained
designers. Their art must be an art of thought, because the
"instinctive" appreciation of form had died with the old crafts.
Only a reasoned understanding of both advanced technology
and modern art could bring beauty to the products of the
machine. The old workshops must be replaced by factories
where the mass of workers executed the designs of the elite.

Le Corbusier was well aware of the objections that Ruskin
and Morris had raised to the factory. Modern production
methods, he acknowledged, "stole" from the worker the satisfaction of a job completely and individually executed. But the
individual worker could no longer fashion the complete works
of art and utility the modern age demanded. As part of a mass
production team, however, he could share in their production:

Thanks to the rigorous program of the modern factory, the products that are produced are so perfect that they give to teams of workers a collective pride. The worker who does only a part of the job understands the role of his labor; the machines that cover the floor of the factory are examples to him of power and clarity, and make him part of a work of perfection to which his simple spirit never dared to aspire.[21]

Le Corbusier's conception of the New Section was thus very different from L'Eplattenier's. Nevertheless, he joined the faculty in 1912, teaching a course in "the elements of geometry, and their relative values in decoration and building." His fellow instructors, however, remained true to L'Eplattenier's dream of reviving the crafts. Le Corbusier lived with the students in farmhouses they had rented "to be close to nature." He did not enjoy the life. "The young people were too true," he recalled. "They drove themselves crazy."[22]

Both L'Eplattenier's and Le Corbusier's dream of an "art movement at La Chaux-de-Fonds" ended in 1914 when the Socialists won the municipal elections. The artisans who had elected the Socialists distrusted the New Section. Many feared that L'Eplattenier wished to make artists out of the young men whom they had enrolled to learn a trade. (As Le Corbusier commented, the term "artist" at La Chaux-de-Fonds meant someone who was incapable of earning a living.) His own arguments in favor of the New Section did little to win support. L'Eplattenier, in fact, blamed him when the municipal council cut off funds for the New Section in 1914. "It's the ruin of all my teachings," he cried. "You have killed my ten years of accomplishment."[23]

Le Corbusier was especially dismayed that the decision had been made by the Socialists. "It was perhaps my first real surprise as an adult," he recalled. He had expected, it seems, that the self-proclaimed party of the future would rally to his vision of organized mass-production. Instead, their supporters were outraged at his hopes of turning the artisans of La Chaux-de-Fonds into proletarians. It was an important lesson for him. He never again looked to the "people" to take the lead in creating a new industrial order, even though they would reap the ultimate benefits from it. He never believed in an evolutionary democratic socialism. In the course of his career he would espouse views that ranged from technocratic capitalism to revolutionary syndicalism, but he always insisted that the initiative must come from above.

It was in 1914 that Le Corbusier proposed his first plan for the new industrial civilization. It came, ironically, as a response to the mechanized destruction that had marked the first months of World War I. In his shelter in Switzerland, Le Corbusier was convinced that the terrible slaughter could not last more than six months. The rebuilding, he believed, would have to be equally rapid. To meet this need he designed what he called the Dom-Ino house, a plan for mass-manufactured houses based on a reinforced concrete frame. The design marks Le Corbusier's first explicit recognition that a structure could be built without support from its walls. The six reinforced concrete columns hold up the floor and roof. The interior becomes one free space to be divided according to the needs of the inhabitants.[24]

Le Corbusier had studied the problem of housing both at La Chaux-de-Fonds and during his trips to Paris. His major inspiration was the Garden City movement. He meticulously traced illustrations of Hampstead Garden Suburb into his notebooks and even designed a Garden Suburb for La Chaux-de-Fonds, complete with curving roads and picturesque gables.[25] It was Parker and Unwin, rather than Howard, who interested him. He never grasped Howard's theory of decentralization. In the ten years after Letchworth, the city planning principles of the movement had been almost completely divorced from the social concerns that inspired Howard. Georges Benoît-Lévy, the movement's principal exponent in the French-speaking world, wholly neglected Howard's social thought and never distinguished between a true Garden City and a Garden Suburb.

What impressed Le Corbusier was Parker and Unwin's attempt to create an architecture appropriate for a cooperative civilization. Their designs, he acknowledged, were a "manifestation of a collective civilization." He, too, had been raised on William Morris's critique of the anarchic individualism of modern capitalism, its destruction of all sense of communal order, and the consequent ugliness and disorder of the modern city. He, too, wanted to find some architectural expression for a unified, cooperative society.

Although the Hampstead Garden Suburb and the Dom-Ino houses appear to belong to different worlds, they both were intended to express the coming age of cooperation. What separates them is their designers' attitudes toward the machine. Parker and Unwin subscribed at least partially to Morris's rejection of mass production. They consciously went back to the fourteenth century to find an image of cooperative civilization which they hoped Letchworth would shelter.

Le Corbusier, working in the midst of a dying artisan community, rejected any attempt to tie the cooperative ideal to the forms and life-styles of the past. This "revival" would in fact condemn art and cooperation to slow extinction at the hands of inexorable economic forces. The machine must be confronted directly, and its inherent potential for beauty and order discovered.

He believed he had finally begun this task with the Dom-Ino house. This simple design had a special fascination, for it contained in embryo almost all the principles of Le Corbusier's later work in housing. First, he analyzed "the house" into a small number of standardized components, each of which could be manufactured cheaply and in unlimited quantity by mass production. These components were designed to be rapidly assembled on site, using only a few standardized tools and techniques. This was indeed housing for the Machine Age: design and technique were one.

Yet the Dom-Ino house is also an aesthetic breakthrough. Le Corbusier realized that the use of uniform parts imposed a necessary uniformity on the houses, but he believed that this seeming limitation could become the basis of a new beauty. By grouping the individual houses into pleasing and well-proportioned ensembles, the architect could create collective forms of harmony and balance. The details would be uniform, but the planner could achieve variety in the general effect. Each unit would contribute to the beauty and magnificence of the whole. Le Corbusier arranged the Dom-Inos into courtyards similar to those that Raymond Unwin had planned for Letchworth but also reminiscent of the traditional courtyard or *coron* of Flanders, where he hoped the houses would first be constructed.[26] As with these earlier models, the architectural unity of the plan expresses the social unity of the residents.

The Dom-Ino thus represents the "art of thought" that Le Corbusier had been seeking since 1908, an art in which the engineer's calculations and the architect's feelings are perfectly matched, an art in harmony with the reason and power of the machine. This Machine Age architecture is also necessarily a collective architecture. It exists to fulfill mass needs and can find its highest expression only in large-scale enterprises. Where handicraftsmen had worked as individuals for single clients, the Machine Age designer must be part of an organization able to coordinate his plans from drawing board to production line to on-site assembly. The structure of the Dom-Ino house, therefore, has important implications for the structure of the industrial system that Le Corbusier hoped would build it. As Theodor Adorno has observed, "Standardization implies centralization." Le Corbusier came to believe that an authority must exist capable of coordinating all the phases of design and production if the promise of the Machine Age was ever to be fulfilled.

The Dom-Ino house launched him on a lifelong search for such an authority, but he began with the confidence that the solution was near at hand. He thought that a centralized organization appropriate to his plans could already be found in the ministries of war production which were coordinating all the industries of Europe to meet their needs. Le Corbusier's deep horror of war was always accompanied by a fascination with the structure of command that made the battles possible. He was sure that the mobilization that accompanied World War I would have to be continued after it, and that this higher stage of industrial organization forged for destruction could then be turned directly to construction. The same factories that mass-produced munitions for war could be retooled to turn out the thousands of houses Europe would need. All that was required was a plan for the authorities to act upon, and he wanted to be ready to put forward his solution as soon as the war ended.

With the invention of the Dom-Ino house, Le Corbusier reached his artistic maturity. He had resolved architecturally the problems which had concerned him since his first trip to Paris in 1908. Now almost thirty, he was finally ready to leave La Chaux-de-Fonds. He drew up ambitious plans for patenting the Dom-Ino house and for setting up a company to manufacture its parts. In the fall of 1916 he departed La Chaux-de-Fonds for an "unlimited stay" in France.[27]

20

Architecture or Revolution

IN 1916, Le Corbusier became a Parisian; he remained one for the rest of his life. Paris was not just his home but his obsession. It embodied for him the grandeur and the misery of the modern city. His ideal cities were expansions of his ideal of Paris: the center of arts and industry, the locus of decision-making, the home of the elites, the setting for the avant-garde, the place where imagination and power met.

But the real Paris also excited his horror and disgust. It was potentially the site of a magnificent urban civilization for the Machine Age, but in its "pre-mechanical" state the machine was killing the city. The cramped and noisy business center made efficiency impossible; antiquated building codes forbade modern methods of construction; housing was inadequate for all classes; worst of all, the automobile threatened to choke completely the city's arteries and thus to destroy its economy and obliterate its beauty. In the slum districts which the health inspectors termed "unsanitary islands" these deficiencies were more than threats—they were lethal.

Paris was his symbol of a whole civilization in danger of being destroyed by the very tools which might save it. Mechanized power, confined to the irrational structures of an earlier era, had turned cancerous, spread in wild disorder, and poisoned the lives of the people. At La Chaux-de-Fonds Le Corbusier had concluded that the machine, if properly used, could create a society of order, abundance, harmony, and beauty. First, however, it had to be mastered at its controlling point: the great city. He came to Paris like Balzac's Rastignac, who exclaimed after his first sight of Paris from the heights of Montmartre: "At last, face to face!"

Like a man liberated from bondage, Le Corbusier plunged into the life of wartime Paris, both the Paris of the industrialists and war contractors and the Paris of the avant-garde. He settled on the Left Bank and soon found employment as an architect and consultant. He was involved in a number of large-scale projects—hydroelectric plants, arsenals, power stations, refrigeration plants—and even set up his own consulting firm with the high-sounding title of the Society for Industrial Studies and Enterprises. The society made many studies for the Dom-Ino houses but had only one genuine enterprise, a brick factory outside Paris where all Le Corbusier's efforts were focused on the problem of creating bricks that did not crumble after they were produced.[1]

His contact with the avant-garde began when Auguste Perret introduced him to Amédée Ozenfant, a young painter and intellectual who also was fascinated with modern technology. Ozenfant persuaded his new friend to take up painting. The two discovered that they shared a fundamental outlook not only in art but also on social questions. After the Allied victory they collaborated on a manifesto to the avant-garde called *Après le cubisme*. The war, they argued, had opened the way to a new age of synthesis and order. "The war is over," they wrote, "everything is organized, everything is clarified and purified; factories rise, nothing is what it was before the war: the great Contest has called everything into question, it has destroyed all the senile methods and put in their place those that the struggle has proved the best." They were predicting a new classical age in which the order inherent in the scientific revolution would finally become the basis of a whole civilization of harmony and beauty. "Never since the age of Pericles has thought been so lucid."[2]

In industry this meant the mass production of works of increasing utility and perfection of design. In culture it meant an analogous synthesis. *Après le cubisme* was essentially a polemic against the cultural pessimism that the war had engendered, especially the Dadaist attack on all traditional standards. In place of cubism, "the troubled art of a troubled time," they called for a new art, purism. (The term was Ozenfant's.) As both Ozenfant and Le Corbusier practiced it in their paintings, purism was a style that retained the revolutionary innovations of cubism—the flattened perspectives, the multiple points of view, the distortions of familiar objects—but used them for conservative purposes. Their cubism was regulated by the traditional rules of composition. Theirs was an art of harmonious balance, primary colors, pure forms: a classical art for the new industrial era.

Le Corbusier used his business connections to raise money for a journal, *L'esprit nouveau*, which he and Ozenfant edited. First published in 1920, the first issue began with these words: "There is a new spirit: it is a spirit of construction and synthesis guided by a clear conception. . . . A GREAT EPOCH HAS BEGUN."

L'esprit nouveau certainly marked the beginning of a great epoch for Le Corbusier. In a series of articles he put forward a theory of architecture and design which has become the locus classicus of the modern aesthetic. These articles were the first of his works to be signed "Le Corbusier." He had many prosaic reasons for adopting the pseudonym, which was borrowed from a maternal grandfather. Both editors employed pseudonyms, in part to give the impression that the journal had many different contributors. There is, however, a deeper appropriateness in his adoption of this grandiloquent new name, for the articles initiate the mature stage of his creative life. They have a confidence and eloquence worthy of a new era. The ideas, the style, and the typography are original. The arguments are advanced in a series of short declarative sentences, the verbal equivalents of the sketches that illustrate them; repetition and rhythm lend emphasis to the ideas; the page layout juxtaposes words and pictures, giving equal importance to both.

The vigor of the style only underlined the remarkable synthesis that Le Corbusier finally achieved. His lyric celebration of automobiles, airplanes, and grain elevators led many of his readers to believe that he was a functionalist. His real position was more complex.

> When a thing responds to a need, it is not beautiful; it satisfies one part of our mind, the primary part, without which there is no possibility of richer satisfactions; let us recover the right order of events. . . .
>
> ARCHITECTURE is the art above all others which achieves a state of platonic grandeur, mathematical order, speculation, the perception of the harmony that lies in emotional relationships.[3]

Architecture is the "erudite, correct, and magnificent play of forms in light"; it is a "pure act of creation" that puts us "in tune with a universe whose laws we respect, recognize and obey."[4]

It was in this spirit of idealism that he extolled the grain elevator and rejected the prizewinning architecture of his time. The academic architects, "lost in the sterile backwaters of their plans, their foliage, their pilasters," had, in the name of the traditional styles, perverted the laws of harmony and order which were the source of all beauty. Only the humbler engineers had retained some contact with these laws. They had allowed a style for the modern age to emerge spontaneously from their constructions. Like the ancient Greeks building their temples, the modern engineer was always working toward a standard in which "each part is decisive and marks the highest point of perfection and execution." In a caption to a photograph of a frontwheel brake he commented, "This precision, this cleanness in execution go farther back than our reborn mechanical sense. Phidias felt the same way: the entablature of the Parthenon is a witness."[5]

It was in this context that Le Corbusier made his most famous (or notorious) pronouncement: "A house is a machine to live in."[6] The modern house, he proclaimed, must be as functional, as orderly, as precise, and as perfectly executed as a modern machine. It was a high ideal indeed. Le Corbusier did not, however, believe that the architect of a house or any other structure could merely imitate the engineer. His work must be "a pure creation of the spirit," a work of imagination that is both functional and uplifting. The engineer's achievement only points the way. "We claim, in the name of the steamship, the airplane, and the automobile, the right to health, logic, daring, harmony, perfection."[7]

The distinction that L'Eplattenier had taught him between the world of art and the soulless domain of the machine had been entirely transcended. He had not forgotten, however, his teacher's fears of the disruptive influences of technological change. Le Corbusier's descriptions of the unrest caused by industrialization were reminiscent of William Morris:

> The tools of the past were always *in man's hands*; today they have been entirely refashioned and for the time being are out of our grasp. The human animal stands breathless and panting before the tool he cannot take hold of; progress appears to him as hateful as it is praiseworthy; all is confusion within his mind; he feels himself to be the slave of a frantic state of things and experiences no sense of liberation or comfort or amelioration. This is a great but critical period, above all a moral crisis.[8]

The root of this crisis was that society was "profoundly *out of gear.*" The average citizen "is conscious, on the one hand, of a new world which is forming itself regularly, logically and clearly, which produces in a straightforward way things that are useful and useable, and on the other hand he finds himself, to his surprise, living in an old and hostile environment." His house and his city are relics of an old order which "crush us in our daily contact with them."[9]

The workers who produce the equipment for the modern age are thus deprived of its benefits. They are forced to live in the debris and the disorder of the modern city. "The modern age is spread before them, sparkling and radiant . . . on the far side of the barrier!" This is the essence of modern exploitation: the workers at the factory "each day make use of the brilliant and effective tools that the age has provided, but they are not permitted to use them for themselves."[10] This exploitation, he believed, was the cause of the disorder that plagued industrial society, the perpetual crises, perhaps even revolutions, which Le Corbusier then regarded with abhorrence. But mankind could not turn back.

The architect must create a new social harmony. This was his special mission. The engineer and the businessman had pioneered new forms of production. Now the architect must design the mass-produced houses and radiant cities that will extend the "essential joys" of the new era to everyone. He must create a whole new environment in which the techniques of industrialization serve the citizen in his daily life. Then disorder will cease. The worker will see that "things have changed; and changed *for the better.*" The harmony of society thus becomes "a question of building." Le Corbusier concluded his series of articles with a call to action.

> Architecture or Revolution.
> Revolution can be avoided.[11]

21

The Contemporary City

LE CORBUSIER has recounted the origin of his first plan
for an ideal city, the "Contemporary City for Three Million
People." In 1922 he was asked by the organizers of the Salon
d'Automne to prepare an exhibition on urbanism. "What do
you mean by urbanism?" Le Corbusier asked the salon's director. "Well, it's a sort of street art," the man replied, "for
stores, signs, and the like; it includes such things as the orna-
mental glass knobs on railings." "Fine," said Le Corbusier, "I
shall design a great fountain and behind it place a city for
three million people."[1]

This "Just So" story contains at least one element of truth.
The 100-square-meter diorama depicting the Contemporary
City which he prepared for the salon reflected his own grand
conception of urbanism. The Contemporary City was the
answer to the social problems which he had raised in the
Esprit nouveau articles. If, as he had argued, these problems
require for their solution the rebuilding of industrial society,

then the urbanist must forsake mere decoration and prepare to undertake "great works." His task was to create a complete environment in which man, nature, and the machine would be reconciled. The Contemporary City was Le Corbusier's first systematic attempt to envision such an environment and to put forward the general principles of its design.

The ideas for the Contemporary City can be traced back to sketches Le Corbusier made at La Chaux-de-Fonds in 1914–1915 while he was working on the Dom-Ino houses.[2] He continued to develop the plans after he moved to Paris, but turned to the ideal city in earnest only after his brick factory had gone bankrupt in the recession of 1921, dragging down with it the Society for Industrial Enterprises. His architectural practice was meager; his small income came almost entirely from the sale of his paintings. Like Howard and Wright, he undertook to plan the society of the future at a time when he was isolated, unheeded, without influence, and certainly without power. Le Corbusier's position sharply contrasts with that of the Bauhaus theorists—Gropius, Mies, Hilberseimer—who shared many of his ideas. Their ties to the Socialist parties encouraged them to think in pragmatic terms. They produced many partial plans but no ideal cities. Le Corbusier, however, could rely only on the inherent persuasiveness of his vision. His plans therefore took the form of a complete alternative society which would take power first in the imagination and then in fact.

The title of this plan, "A Contemporary City for Three Million People," was a proclamation that this was not an exercise in science fiction but "the city for our times." It was, he wrote, "an act of faith in favor of the present." He believed the time had come for a series of "great works" which would sweep away the "leavings of a dead era" and inaugurate the age of "collective spirit" and "civic pride." The decision to build the new city would mean that the "radiant hour of harmony, construction, and enthusiasm" had finally arrived. It would be the crucial *act* separating the past from the future;

it would restore order to industrial society and make the world safe for beauty.

Le Corbusier was explicitly scientific in his approach. He wished to portray the "ideal type" of an industrial city, to formulate an image which would express in graphic terms the general truths which he believed were applicable to all modern societies. To "separate himself from all contingent circumstances" he placed his ideal city on a perfectly flat plain, a tabula rasa unmarked by nature or by man. He compared his task to that of a "scientist in his laboratory . . . constructing a rigorous theoretical structure." His aim was to formulate "the fundamental principles of urbanism," to create "the *rule* according to which the game can be played."[3]

City planning, he believed, must take its place as one of the applied sciences, the province of specially trained theorists and technicians. The design of cities was too important to be left to the citizens. The organic city, the city that emerged slowly as the result of many individual decisions, was a thing of the past. It belonged to the age when carpenters built their own houses and artisans created their own handicrafts. In the Machine Age, however, a rigorous theory implemented from above was necessary if the city were ever to display the harmony that is the basis of efficiency and beauty.

For Le Corbusier, order is expressed by pure forms. The Contemporary City is a perfectly symmetrical grid of streets. The right angle reigns supreme. Two great superhighways (one running east-west, the other north-south) form the central axes; they intersect at the exact center of the city. This triumph of geometry had much the same meaning for Le Corbusier that perfect circles had for Ebenezer Howard. The fearful symmetry of the Contemporary City symbolized the victory of reason over chance, of planning over anarchic individualism, of social order over discord.

"To order is to classify," Le Corbusier once observed.[4] In the Contemporary City everything is classified by function. Industry, housing, and offices each occupy a separate sector.

As in a well-run factory, the various functions are first separated analytically, then assigned to different areas, and finally connected with each other in the most efficient manner possible. The transportation system preserves the very life of the city. As Le Corbusier realized, the health of the city is its capacity for speed. Speed is freedom, the freedom to exchange, to meet, to trade, to coordinate. "The city that achieves speed," he wrote, "achieves success."[5]

He strove to build speed into the very structure of the Contemporary City. He designed an elaborately coordinated system of transportation: superhighways, subways, access roads, even bicycle paths and pedestrian walks. Fittingly, the very center of the city is a multilevel interchange for the whole system. The two great superhighways cross there; below them is the station where all the subway lines intersect; above the highways, mounted on great steel pillars, is the main railroad terminal; the roof of this huge structure is a runway where planes can land.

The exact center of the Contemporary City, though eminently functional, lacks the symbolic value one might expect. Le Corbusier has placed no cathedral or civic monument there. The center serves people going somewhere else—people in motion. There is perhaps a deeper meaning in his choice. Le Corbusier believed that the city existed for interchange: the most rapid possible exchange of ideas, information, talents, joys. Only the concentration of a metropolis could provide the multitude of creative juxtapositions which is the special joy of urban life. The central terminal and interchange is thus an appropriate symbol of the Contemporary City. Where everything is in motion, speed becomes the only constant.

Surrounding the central terminal are twenty-four glass-and-steel skyscrapers, each sixty stories high. They house the business center of the Contemporary City, the "brain" of the whole region. The symmetrically organized skyscrapers represent Le Corbusier's most daring and original contribution to urbanism. Each stands completely free in the midst of a great park. There are no more "corridor streets," as he called them—no more narrow roadways filled with traffic, completely lined with five- or ten-story buildings. Instead, the "streets" are elevators, rising straight up instead of spreading out over a whole district. One skyscraper might have more usable space than a neighborhood, but it occupies only a little more ground than an older building. Thus, the business center is far more concentrated than the most crowded sections of Paris but incomparably less congested. Work takes place in an atmosphere of sunlight and quiet; every window looks out upon a magnificent view. Although 500 to 800 thousand people could work in the twenty-four skyscrapers, these towers cover less than 15 percent of the ground in the business center. The rest is devoted to parks and gardens. Sir John Summerson caught the spirit of Le Corbusier's design when he observed of this Central Park (which is also the business center): the park is not in the city; the city is in the park.[6]

The skyscraper, this tool given by the engineer to the architect, permitted Le Corbusier to reconcile the seeming opposites of urban design: density and open space. Like all of Le Corbusier's great syntheses, it was not a compromise between two opposites but a triumphant affirmation of both. The skyscrapers free the ground for greenery; they also are a fitting symbol for the grandeur of the functions they house. The central towers serve as the headquarters of bureaucracies that administer whole nations. For Le Corbusier, the industrial era would be an age of triumphant rationality, and as Max Weber had already observed, the rule of reason in Western society meant the dominance of bureaucracy. Le Corbusier did not shrink from this conclusion: he embraced it. The Contemporary City is above all a city of administration:

> From its offices come the commands that put the world in order. In fact, the skyscrapers are the brain of the City, the brain of the whole country. They embody the work of elaboration and command on which all activities depend. Everything is concentrated

there: the tools that conquer time and space—telephones, tele-
graphs, radios; the banks, trading houses, the organs of decision
for the factories: finance, technology, commerce.[7]

Le Corbusier thus embraced and idealized precisely what
most repelled Howard and Wright in the modern city: its contribution to the centralization of society. He believed since his
experiences at La Chaux-de-Fonds that society must be guided
from above. In the Contemporary City he proclaimed his faith
in large organizations to "put the world in order." The
business center would be the headquarters of headquarters. It
would provide conditions of efficient coordination which the
elite would need to create harmony throughout society. It was
the natural "seat of power." Le Corbusier emphasized that he
meant "power" in the "widest sense of the word." The great
towers would be the headquarters of the intellect as well as
industry. He listed among their occupants "captains of business, of industry, of finance, of politics, masters of science, of
pedagogy, of thought, the spokesmen of the heart, the artists,
poets, musicians."[8]

Were the great towers the headquarters for private enterprise or for socialism? Le Corbusier maintained that the plan
was addressed neither to bourgeois capitalism nor to communism—because it applied to both. When a writer for the
Communist paper *L'Humanité* reproached him for not specifying whether the proletariat or the ruling class would control
the great organs of administration, Le Corbusier replied, "On
my plan I wrote *Administrative Services, Public Services.*
That will suffice."[9] He believed the task of the great bureaucracies was essentially the same, regardless of their formal
control. Any industrial society must be hierarchically organized, administered from above, with the best qualified people
in the most responsible positions. Capitalism or communism
might make these conditions easier to attain, but both must
submit to the requirements of industrial society or risk chaos.

In putting forward this position Le Corbusier believed he

was speaking as an objective "technician," above partisan struggles. In fact he was continuing a tradition of social thought that goes back to Henri de Saint-Simon. In such works as *The Industrial System* (1821–1822) and *On Social Organization*, Saint-Simon had maintained that society was evolving a new order based on the organization of industry. The future, he predicted, would see the triumph of large-scale enterprises—the great factories, banks, and trading houses. In these organizations men would "henceforth do consciously, and with better directed and more useful effort, what they have hitherto done unconsciously, slowly, indecisively, and too ineffectively."[10] These organizations would bring not only prosperity but also order to society. They were imposing a hierarchy of authority on all workers and had brought an elite of proved ability and knowledge into the commanding positions. This elite was already taking the most important decisions into its hands: the exploitation of natural resources, the development of inventions, the administration of production and distribution.

Saint-Simon looked forward to the time when the men he called *industriels*, the elite of industrialists, scientists, and artists, would, in their capacities as heads of the great organizations of production and learning, take over all the functions of government. The repressive powers of the state would wither away. The elite would not have to fear disorders arising from the class struggle because, in Saint-Simon's view, the proletariat was fundamentally indifferent to questions of ownership and equality. The masses wanted jobs and prosperity. If the great organizations gave them both, they would accept the *industriels* as their natural leaders.

Le Corbusier's Contemporary City was a twentieth-century incarnation of the society Saint-Simon had foreseen in the nineteenth. There, in Saint-Simon's famous formula, the "administration of goods" had replaced the "government of men." In the Contemporary City the structures devoted to government had literally withered away. They stood on the outskirts of the business center, in the shadow of the great towers of administration. These towers were the headquarters of Le Corbusier's elite of industrialists, scientists, and artists—the exact same three categories that constituted Saint-Simon's *industriels*. Like the *industriels*, Le Corbusier's elite was to include the most gifted members of the work force. They would bring prosperity, order, and beauty to society through the beneficent act of administration.

Le Corbusier probably never read Saint-Simon. He was, however, an avid follower of the intellectual movement sometimes called neo-Saint-Simonianism. Many of the writings of this school were self-proclaimed "technical" works on industrial efficiency or modern organization whose authors more readily acknowledged their debt to Henry Ford than to Henri de Saint-Simon. Nevertheless, their message was clear. The elite of technically trained managers must be allowed to rationalize production and distribution; this alone would end social disorder by satisfying working-class demands for higher wages and better living conditions.

In France in the 1920s this current of thought—which would soon be labeled "technocratic"—was an ideology frequently invoked to defend the interests of larger, more efficient firms over smaller ones. Ernest Mercier, the head of a great utilities combine and the most influential advocate of technocratic thought, sought to overcome the opposition of the conservative middle class to large-scale enterprise by presenting the modern corporation as the only alternative to revolution. Its methods, he argued, must be universally adopted; its managers must assume power in the government.[11]

Le Corbusier's thought often shared this perspective. "Big business," he declared in 1923, "is today a healthy and moral organism."[12] His motto, as we have seen, was "Architecture or Revolution." To avoid the latter he would soon join Mercier as an active member of the Redressement français, an organization dedicated to "the awakening of the elites."[13] The aspiring technocrats, however, prided themselves upon being "social engineers" firmly grounded in the realities of the present. Le Corbusier's concern was the ideal city, and he used the technocrats' ideas the way a great architect uses an engineer's inventions—as starting points for a work of humane imagination. In constructing a complete alternative society he took the technocrats' ideas much further than they dared to carry them. This, ironically, brought Le Corbusier closer to Saint-Simon. Without conscious intent, he revived precisely those utopian elements in Saint-Simon's thought that the technocrats had been careful to neglect.

It was in his designs for housing in the Contemporary City that Le Corbusier showed most clearly his particular interpretation of the Saint-Simonian tradition. Throughout his life he sought to create the proper dwellings for an industrial age. As we have seen, he believed that the well-being of the whole society depended on whether the architect could bring the techniques of mass production to bear in creating functional and beautiful dwellings for everyone. Only then would the citizen "suddenly understand that society has at last grasped its new and proper objectives." Thus, "the problem of the mass-produced house" was for him "the problem of our time."[14]

In the Contemporary City all dwellings are mass-produced, but they are not all alike. One's house and its location depend upon one's position in the hierarchy of production and administration. The elite of *industriels* live in luxurious high-rise apartments within the city; their subordinates occupy more modest garden apartments in the satellite towns on the outskirts. The structure of the residential areas—the elite in the center, the workers at the outskirts—corresponds to the hierarchy of functions in the great organizations. As Saint-Simon had recommended, the industrial hierarchy provides the model for the organization of the whole society.

The Villa-Apartment Blocks in which the elite reside follow the same architectural principle as the towers in which they work. The buildings' height permits a very high density while leaving at least 85 percent of the ground free for parks, gardens, tennis courts, and other recreational facilities. The structure of the apartment blocks, however, represents an important innovation. They are "apartment houses" in a literal sense, for they are made up of separate two-story mass-produced houses which are then mounted in the reinforced concrete frame of the apartment block as one would put a bottle into a wine rack. This gives the residents the spaciousness, privacy, and absolute silence of a separate dwelling with the convenience of an apartment. Each unit has a large terrace (or "hanging garden," as Le Corbusier called it); the top story of the apartment block has a gymnasium for indoor sports, and the roof boasts a 300-yard track.

Le Corbusier dwelled lovingly on the communal services that each apartment block would provide the *industriels* who lived there. There would be twenty-four-hour maid service and a private laundry. A special purchasing service buys the residents' food; a gourmet kitchen staff is available to cook it; and waiters will serve it at any hour to any number of guests either in the resident's apartment or in a communal dining room. Le Corbusier compared these apartment houses to an ocean liner in which a whole staff made possible a far greater degree of luxury than any individual could command.

The many communal comforts of these apartment blocks led one scholar to describe them as Le Corbusier's modern version of Fourier's phalanstery.[15] Another influence, I believe, was Ebenezer Howard's cooperative housekeeping scheme, which Le Corbusier studied while he was living in La Chaux-de-Fonds.[16] Like Howard's plan, Le Corbusier's was put forward as the ultimate solution to the servant problem. It extended community services into the domestic economy while maintaining the privacy and autonomy of the family unit on which Howard had insisted. Each apartment block in the Contemporary City is ten times larger than the cooperative quadrangle and immeasurably more luxurious, but both Howard's and Le Corbusier's ideal dwellings were to be owned jointly by their residents and run as nonprofit cooperatives.

Howard, however, had seen his quadrangles as centers of neighborly life. Le Corbusier did not believe that his elite wanted or needed a refuge from the "impersonality" of city life. The *industriels* were natural city dwellers who delighted in the immense range of possible encounters that the Contemporary City provided. The services of the apartment blocks existed to free the residents from the more mundane ties of family and neighborhood life. Their social circle was the entire community of the elite. The same qualities of rapid interchange, communication, and juxtaposition that brought efficiency to the business center would bring a uniquely rich and varied social life to its leaders. Every taste and talent could find its counterparts, and the groups would inevitably collide and mix.

To provide an appropriate setting for the public gatherings of the elite, Le Corbusier violated his own rule of relegating different functions to different sections of the city. He made the administrative center also the cultural and entertainment center. In the midst of the greenery at the center of the city, in the shadow of the "majestic crystal and pure prisms" of the skyscrapers, Le Corbusier placed sweeping terraces at treetop level. These were the sites of the fashionable shops, cafes, restaurants, and art galleries. Adjacent to them were the great theaters and concert halls. The flat roofs of the administrative towers were transformed into hanging gardens which after dark become elegant nightclubs. These establishments are the salons of the new society. The elite gather to talk and dance in the "profound calm 600 feet above the ground." The other roof gardens appear as "slivers of gold suspended in the distance." The Contemporary City falls away beneath them, a pattern of order stretching into the distance.

The proletariat and the subordinate office workers who lived in the satellite towns did not share in this luxury. Le Corbusier assumed at this time that the hierarchy of functions in society implied a hierarchy of privileges. This assumption often makes the Contemporary City seem as deeply marked by class division as was France in the 1920s. Le Corbusier's social hierarchy, however, has little if any linkage to property, the basis of class divisions. The individual and his property are dwarfed by the great organizations. Members of the elite cannot inherit their positions at the top; they are "nomads" who move through the ranks according to merit. Their dwellings never belong to them in the sense that a Frank Lloyd Wright house belongs to its owner. Wright's emphasis on the completely detached house standing on its owner's ground derived from his belief in a society where the individual would enjoy the independence that comes from self-sufficiency. The apartment blocks of the Contemporary City stand for an opposite principle. No one in the city can build his own house or buy the land it occupies. Each apartment is only one element in a great architectural and social complex that together forms a unified structure of beauty and grandeur. The individual's privilege exists only as part of a collective order.

The proletarians in their satellite cities have none of the special privileges of the elite, but they too are part of a collective order that furnishes what Le Corbusier called "the essential joys" to everyone. These were not a matter of size or expense but of proper planning. He was fond of pointing to the staterooms of luxury liners, which, though smaller than a rich man's closet, served his needs far better than his own bedroom because they were meticulously organized. Mass production had made the material basis for a new way of life available to the workers, and architecture must embody it in design.

As in the central city, the basic principle of the satellite town was to achieve economy and aesthetic effect by grouping the separate residences into larger units. Instead of isolated cottages, each surrounded by its own tiny lawn and garden, there would be garden apartments built from mass-produced components designed for "unity in detail and variety in general effect." The ground would be left free for rolling lawns, playing fields, and gardens—all directly in front of the apartments.

In the satellite towns the workers would "live in full sunshine." Since the walls no longer supported the structure, they could be opened with broad bands of windows. Inside, Le Corbusier strove to create a sense of spaciousness consistent with economy. The ocean liner and the railway coach had taught him that rooms need not conform to their accepted dimensions. "It is a crime," he once exclaimed, "to make WC's thirty-six square feet!"[17] He made the small rooms as small as possible and used the space he saved to create a "family center"—a combination living room, dining room, and kitchen —of generous proportions.

This workers' housing he believed "worthy of the new era." It made a clean break with the past: the endless streets in cities or factory towns without greenery or any facilities for recreation; the interior courts of five or six story walk-ups where the sun never penetrated; the confusion of airless rooms within. This dark and damp unhealthiness was for him the most potent symbol of the slums and the most telling sign of the rottenness of the society that built them. The sunshine that fills every house and field in the satellite towns represented an equally potent symbol of the beneficent power of planning and the fundamental soundness of the new social order.

The satellite towns, like the central city, emphasize in their design the collective nature of the new order. Le Corbusier's row houses and shared facilities were radical departures from the "cottage" philosophy of workers' housing that was written into French legislation governing state subsidies to homeowners. From the Siegfried Laws of the 1890s to the Loucheur Law of 1928, the official purpose of state intervention was to enable the worker to own his own property.[18] It was hoped that this would turn a member of the proletariat into a loyal defender of property and the established order.

Le Corbusier believed in using more modern methods to secure the stability of society. He had, moreover, great contempt for the view that the worker and his family, once settled on a tiny plot on the outskirts of the city, would be "re-attached to the soil" and lose those rebellious qualities which the bourgeois legislators associated with the urban proletariat.

He had no desire to pretend that the proletarian was anything but an industrial worker. Eight hours of factory labor, he maintained, was a necessity for most of the population if the living standards of a modern civilization were ever to be attained. It was not, he admitted, a pleasant necessity. Although he often glorified the production line, he realized that a full day's work there was physically and mentally debilitating. It gave the worker no opportunity for creativity or initiative.

Nevertheless, he was opposed to all proposals to make the factory laborer a part-time farmer or artisan. Industrial work is so damaging to the laborer, he argued, only because the worker's leisure time is lost in commuting and then wasted in a slum or dreary suburb. In the Contemporary City the dehumanizing effects of eight hours of work would be overcome by eight hours of productive leisure. The satellite towns were leisure cities, where hard work would be rewarded by comfort and abundance. They provided a cheerful setting for the worker's family life; abundant opportunities for sports and other physical recreation; facilities for crafts and other hobbies; clubhouses, dance halls, and cafes. They were the realms of freedom and creativity for those who spent their working hours taking orders.

The problems of work are thus solved in the realm of leisure. Out of the materials provided by disciplined labor the planner creates a world of play, and this world restores to the worker his creative independence. This solution is the opposite of the one Frank Lloyd Wright had proposed. Wright wanted to merge the two worlds until work and leisure became one. Le Corbusier wished to sharpen the distinction between the two. Characteristically, he attempted to resolve the problem by juxtaposing the two extremes: eight hours of intensive labor bring eight hours of joyful leisure. "Modern organization," he concluded, "must, by the rational arrangement of the collectivity, redeem, *liberate the individual.*"[19]

Although such concern for the individual seems out of place in the Contemporary City, it is in fact central to the architectural and social synthesis which Le Corbusier was attempting. In describing this design one inevitably overemphasizes the relentless ordering, the symmetry, the overwhelming structures which seem to swallow up all individuality. Pierre Francastel even described it as a "univers concentrationnaire."[20] This drastically distorts Le Corbusier's achievement. When considering, for example, the rigid and symmetrical ground plan of the city, one must remember that the streets and buildings cover only 15 percent of the land; the rest is devoted to winding footpaths, trees, grass, flowers, and playing fields. This duality, I believe, is symbolic of Le Corbusier's larger intentions. The city of administration is also the "Green City." The symmetrically constructed realm of order and collectivity is at the same time the realm of nature and play. This latter realm of individuality and freedom exists *inside* the Contemporary City. The ground plan of the city is like a cubist painting in which the same object is viewed from two perspectives simultaneously. Collective order and individual freedom are the two perspectives, and their juxtaposition defines the Contemporary City.

In the clearest statement of his aims, Le Corbusier put forward his belief that

> life flows between two powers each capable of attaining the sublime. One of these poles represents what man does alone: the exceptional, the moving, the holy act of individual creation.
>
> The other represents what men undertake when organized in groups, cities or nations: those forces, those great movements of the collectivity.
>
> Here, individual grandeur, the scope of genius.

There, administration, order, direction, leadership, civic action.[21]

In planning the Contemporary City, Le Corbusier attempted to combine as completely as possible both poles of the sublime. When trying to define his ideal human environment, he was fond of recalling an experience from his first trip to Italy in 1907. "I saw a *modern city*, crowning the hillside in the harmonious landscape of Tuscany." It was the monastery of Ema, a medieval structure which houses an order of Carthusian monks. "I thought I would never again encounter so joyous an interpretation of habitation."[22] The joy came from the structural combination of an intensely private life of meditation and an intensely ordered life of communal work and prayer. Each monk had an apartment of two rooms with a view over the valley. This was the realm of the individual alone with nature and with God. The cells were structurally connected by the cloisters to the realm of "communal services: prayers, visits, eating, burial."

Le Corbusier's conceptions of individual and community life in the modern world had the same intense purity as the monastic ideals. Both are paths to the sublime. Organization is the sign of a harmonious society where men labor together to create works of logic, clarity, and power. The greatest of these works is the city. "In a chaotic nature man creates, for his security, a protected zone which is in accordance with what he is and what he thinks." The city is "the grip of man upon nature"; its geometrical form is the expression of a society liberated from the constraints of ignorance and conflict, a society which has organized itself according to the *human* laws of reason. "Free, man tends to geometry," he wrote. "The work of man is to put things in order."[23]

Although the city began in the struggle against the chaotic forces of nature, its highest aim is to reconcile man with these forces. Geometrical order, triumphant, no longer needs to exclude nature as an alien presence; rather, it seeks out the

Green City as the necessary counterpart to itself. Similarly, the triumph of the world of administration means that it no longer need engross man's whole life. The triumph of administration is the *liberation* of man from its clutches, the liberation of man to live another life of individual creativity in the midst of his family.

The Contemporary City is thus a city of leisure as well as order, a city of meditation as well as production. To the man at work, the city is one great organization; after work he sees it from a very different perspective. His family life exists outside the hierarchy of authority. Le Corbusier designed each apartment to be as private as a monk's cell at Ema. Each is an independent home, a site of abundance and love. Outside is the garden of delights, the Green City, the realm of art and play. The apartments and their surroundings form a coherent environment, a world of individual fulfillment and creation.

Le Corbusier's two paths to the sublime meet at the Contemporary City.

22

Plan Voisin

THE Contemporary City had no history. It sprang full-
grown from one man's imagination. In planning his ideal city,
Le Corbusier had absolute freedom to create the rules of
urban design and to apply them without exception. Within
his realm he was, as he put it, an absolute sovereign who could
"organize the world on his drawing board." No intractable
subjects—not even time itself—disturbed his perfect sym-
metries.

When he attempted to move from theory to practice he was
immediately dethroned. He was forced to confront the limitations which particular sites and particular societies imposed.
Le Corbusier dealt effectively with nature's constraints; his
most imaginative plans, e.g., those for Algiers and Rio de
Janeiro, were brilliant applications of his principles to challenging terrains. His responses to social limitations were less
serene. He became obsessed with the many obstacles to large-
scale planning: the laws of property that divided the city into

thousands of tiny independent holdings; the fragmentation of governmental authority; the forms that the city of the past had imposed on the present; the citizens who clung to their old cities and refused to make way for the "era of great works."

For Le Corbusier did not believe in piecemeal planning. The great urban harmony he developed in the Contemporary City required the coordination of many different elements if its principles were ever to be realized in any existing metropolis. The planner needed open spaces in which he was free to create his own urban order. He must be master of the whole environment. "Nothing can be undertaken properly without a view of the whole." The "rules" he had laid down in the Contemporary City made urban planning a highly complex problem of organization. Skyscrapers required a system of transportation to support them; the transportation system had to be efficient and yet not intrude on the 85 percent of the land given over to parks; and thousands of similar problems would have to be resolved in advance. Only then could a collective order—beautiful and efficient, "worthy of the age"—emerge.

The planner needed the power and the resources to carry out his solutions. Le Corbusier realized that the urban transformation he sought would require a concentration of efforts analogous to the military mobilization of the Great War. The grandeur of the prospect excited him. He believed that rebuilding the cities was the proper task of the great organizations that would have their headquarters there. Their readiness to undertake the task would be proof of their maturity, proof that the new era had indeed begun. His quest for the ideal city resolved itself into a search for an authority that had the power and the imagination to implement his plans.

The search started in 1925 with his Plan Voisin for Paris. It was not a modest beginning. He proposed that the crowded Right Bank business district opposite the Cité—an area of almost two square miles in the heart of Paris—be completely demolished. Eighteen skyscrapers would rise in its place, surrounded by luxury apartments and gardens, and bisected

by a great highway. The skyscrapers would become the headquarters for the great international corporations, making Paris
a world center for administration.

Not surprisingly, the plan was attacked: first, for its seemingly perverse concentration on the center of the city, where
land values were highest and dislocations most difficult;
second, for its inhuman scale, its vast empty spaces, and its
elimination of the close-knit old streets with their rich and
varied public life; and finally, for its radical destruction of
Paris's architectural heritage of the past. Although most of
Le Corbusier's work from the 1920s has mellowed into
respectability, the Plan Voisin still arouses the same horror
it did at its original showing. It has to bear not only the burden
of its own audacity but also its status as the archetype for so
many disastrous plans that others subsequently carried out.
For better or worse, the concepts embodied in the Plan Voisin
represent Le Corbusier's contribution to the practice of urban
planning. It is important, therefore, to understand his reasons
for prescribing such drastic change.

First, the plan addresses itself to the central city because Le
Corbusier believed that the center was the heart of the problem. Undeveloped areas at the outskirts of old cities might
seem more appropriate locales for the new order he wished to
establish, but Le Corbusier was wary of creating regions that
lacked a clear focus. He had great respect for the idea of the
center, the one area consecrated by history and geography
to be the capital of a region or nation. This center must be
attacked head on, for victory there would decide the issue.

> The great city commands everything: peace, war, work. The
> great cities are the spiritual workshops where the work of the
> world is turned out.

> The solutions found in the great city are those which will be
> followed in the provinces: fashions, styles, intellectual move-
> ments, technology. This is why, once the urbanization of the
> great city has been achieved, the whole country will at once be
> won.[1]

Le Corbusier was thus committed to transforming the area most resistant to change, the place where population was greatest, property values highest, and tradition most firmly entrenched. He was committed, moreover, not merely to modifying the center but to destroying its network of narrow streets, knocking down almost all the buildings that lined them, opening vast spaces crisscrossed by superhighways in the middle of Paris, and erecting freestanding skyscrapers on a scale that dwarfed all other structures in the city. This dramatic rending of the older urban texture has convinced many critics that Le Corbusier was a misdirected formalist who understood nothing of the real sources of urban beauty and urban vitality. His attempt to "destroy" the street—and, consequently, urban streetlife—lies at the heart of the critics' case. Here, however, it is important to distinguish between the Plan Voisin and subsequent projects which superficially resemble it. Le Corbusier, to be sure, wanted to destroy the street—but only to save it.

He was well aware of the value of what he called the "Balzacian drama" of urban life. "There is so much to enjoy in the street if we know how to see it; it is better than the theater, better than a novel: the faces and the emotions."[2] Yet he believed that the traditional "corridor street" had become an impossible setting for the urban drama. These dark canyons clogged with heavy traffic (with was still an offensive novelty in the 1920s)—these "streets without joy," as he called them— could neither "create in us the joy which is the effect of architecture, nor the pride which is the effect of order; nor the spirit of enterprise which is at home in large spaces. . . . Only pity and commiseration at the shock of seeing other people's faces and the hard labor of the lives."[3]

In the age of the automobile and the skyscraper, the corridor street had become a "dead organ" incapable of fulfilling its function. In the Plan Voisin, Le Corbusier analyzed this function into two parts, transportation and sociability, and created two new urban forms to deal with them. Transportation is provided by the superhighways, avenues of unobstructed motion. And, in the midst of the skyscrapers, rising from the parks, are elevated pedestrian malls, "streets of repose" wholly separate from automobile traffic, "tucked in among the foliage of the trees." These "streets of repose" have three levels. The first is a broad mall punctuated by fountains and sidewalk cafes; gently sloping ramps lead to two upper promenades which are lined with an array of shops, clubs, and restaurants. At the top level, as Le Corbusier enthusiastically pictured the scene, "one is almost on top of the greenery: one sees a sea of trees; and here and there are those majestic crystals, pure prisms, limpid and gigantic [the skyscrapers]. Majesty, serenity, joy."[4] These "gardens of Semiramis" in the middle of Paris would become the most attractive district for shopping and strolling—the counterparts in the realm of leisure to the crystalline towers of administration.

Finally, to those who charged that he was a barbarian whose plan was a futurist assault on Paris and her heritage, Le Corbusier replied that his plan was "wholly in accord with tradition." The monuments of the past would be saved from destruction and preserved like museum pieces in the parks that surround the skyscrapers. More importantly, he could consider himself a "traditionalist" because tradition for him meant a series of revolutionary breaks with custom. The Gothic of Notre-Dame was a startling repudiation of Romanesque; the Pont Neuf discarded the Gothic. Consciousness unfolds in history; no one can stop it without exalting imitation and risking decay. For Le Corbusier, being true to the monuments of the past meant continuing in their revolutionary spirit. "At certain times man begins again to create; and those are the happy times."[5] The Plan Voisin announced that a new era was at hand; only a sterile antiquarianism could deny it. "In the name of the past: the present."

He believed that the Plan Voisin was particularly appropriate to the urban planning traditions of Paris. The men he admired—Louis XIV and his Place Vendôme and Invalides,

Napoleon and his rue de Rivoli, above all Baron Haussmann—
were those who tried to bring a measure of geometrical order
to Paris. The Plan Voisin would be the necessary sequel to
this tradition, bringing the quest for order into the age of the
automobile and the skyscraper.

Le Corbusier also admired the elite positions occupied by
these *grands seigneurs* of Parisian planning. Their status made
them worthy models for the modern planner, who must have
the authority to create order. The planner must stand above
the accidental configurations of the city and deal with them
"without remorse." Le Corbusier once described his feelings
when visiting the statistical bureau of the Paris city government. He was impressed by the labors of the "modest workers
of precision" he found there, but he confessed to a deeper
horror at their direct contact with the details of the city he
wished to transform. They were immersed in a multitude of
complicated facts from which no grand pattern could emerge.
They could discern the complex web of human relationships
that made each street unique. From their perspective, Le
Corbusier observed, "one is afraid to propose even the smallest
changes: one can already hear the cracking and the upsets."[6]

The planner, he concluded, must detach himself from the
actual life of the empirical city, for only then can he realize
the harmony and beauty of the ideal type. He must not be
tempted by or restricted to palliatives. Only "urban surgery"
can create urban order. Like a surgeon cutting into a patient,
the planner violently rends the tissues of urban life. Painfully,
he restores the city to health.

Le Corbusier's concept of the planner combines two distinct
images. One is the planner as scientist, surgeon, "technician"
—the man of reason, a disinterested lover of humanity who
studies the problems of the city, formulates clear solutions,
and carries them out with an unswerving will. The second is
the planner as artist, the isolated man of vision whose insights
are the most profound record of his nation's spiritual life.

The planner shares the detachment which is common to the

artist and the scientist. His loyalty is to society as a whole, and to the ideal of order. Planners form a special corps within the elite. Their calling includes skills from the three categories—industrialists, scientists, and artists—that comprise the *industriels*. They are, therefore, uniquely qualified to coordinate the goals of the great organizations. They must provide both the vision and the technical expertise to guide society toward harmony. Their task is to "pose the problem, arrange, organize, take hold, and create that indispensable lyricism that, in the last analysis, alone raises our hearts and moves us to action."[7]

Le Corbusier, like Wright, arrived at the conclusion that the architect-planner was the natural leader of society. He had, however, a very different conception of that leadership from Wright's broad appeals to unorganized individuals. Le Corbusier believed his mission was to convert the elite. His plans must reach the heads of the French organizations he then respected most—the large corporations—and inspire the key decision-makers. He began by presenting the plan for Paris to the chief executives of the major automobile companies. "The automobile has killed the great city," he announced to André Citroën, "the automobile must now save the city"—i.e., the Citroën Company must sponsor his plan.[8] M. Citroën did not take up this opportunity, but Le Corbusier managed to persuade the automobile division of the Voisin Aircraft Company to pay for printing and exhibitions. With the newly christened "Plan Voisin," he set out to persuade the industrial magnates to reconstruct Paris.

He believed the profit motive alone would be enough to recommend his plan. "Urbanization makes money" was his motto.[9] He proposed that a private consortium, operating with capital furnished by banks and corporations, buy all the property within the area designated by the plan, level the buildings, and construct the eighteen skyscrapers to replace them. Each skyscraper would provide as much rentable space as a whole neighborhood; even with most of the land given over to parks, there would be five times as much space available for offices as in the old business district. It would, moreover, be efficient, beautiful, orderly space—fitting for the modern age of business. Land values would at least quadruple. Le Corbusier advanced an elaborate formula reminiscent of Ebenezer Howard's imaginary accounting to prove—to his own satisfaction, at least—that the whole operation would be marvelously profitable.

The Plan Voisin was the culmination of Le Corbusier's period of infatuation with big business. He envisioned the international corporations beginning the "era of great works" on their own initiative. Government's role would be limited to clearing away the archaic building codes and thus allowing construction to proceed. As in Saint-Simon's theory, the great private organizations would take over the functions of government; the plan their leaders adopted would determine the form of the city for everyone. Le Corbusier was confident that the top executives would implement his proposal. When they turned him down, he was forced to reexamine not only his tactics but the view of society on which they were based.

23

The Ghost of Colbert

LE CORBUSIER'S gradual realization that the capitalist magnates were unwilling and unable to carry out the Plan Voisin did not affect his confidence in the plan. It destroyed his faith in capitalism. The plan, he believed, defined the steps which any society must take in order to fulfill the promise of the Machine Age. If private enterprise, even with government assistance, was not equal to the task, then it was unworthy of the new era. It must be replaced by a system capable of great works; otherwise, "the lifeblood of the new era will be squandered by obsolete, cruel and inhuman organizations."[1] In the late 1920s he searched among increasingly radical alternatives. He finally settled upon a doctrine that combined elements of the extreme right and extreme left: revolutionary syndicalism.

Unlike Wright's radicalization, Le Corbusier's came at a time when his career was advancing. His paintings, writing, and architecture had won him a secure place within the

Parisian avant-garde. His circle of friends included artists like Fernand Léger and rich patrons of the arts like Raoul la Roche and Henri Frugès. These latter were also his principal clients. La Roche, heir of a Swiss banking family, commissioned the villa which is now the home of the Fondation Le Corbusier. Frugès, whose family ran a sugar processing plant in Bordeaux, assigned Le Corbusier the task of building housing for his workers. The group of houses at Pessac, a suburb of Bordeaux, gave Le Corbusier his first opportunity to put into practice the plans for low-cost housing he had outlined for the Contemporary City. He did not have many clients, but almost all of them belonged to a select group: men and women of independent wealth, sympathetic to the avant-garde, often creative artists themselves.

Le Corbusier's reputation in France was limited to this elite, but his reputation was not limited to France. When the first International Congress of Modern Architecture was convened in Switzerland in 1928, Le Corbusier made himself a leader and virtual spokesman for a group which included J. J. P. Oud, Marcel Breuer, Mies, and Gropius. His standing among his fellow modernists was a personal achievement, for he alone had no institutional base like the Bauhaus on which to found his reputation. His architectural offices consisted of two small rooms in a former Jesuit monastery. He had no following in schools of architecture or in professional organizations. Although he was a great theoretician on the virtues of organization, he was virtually incapable of working in one. He could never accommodate himself to any hierarchy of authority, except perhaps to one in which he was at the top.

What Le Corbusier lacked in organized support he easily made up for with his unceasing energy. He was continuously productive: painting in the morning, designing in the afternoon, writing at night. He was witty, eloquent, and fervent. One conservative banker refused to listen to his appeal for the Plan Voisin—but only out of fear that Le Corbusier might persuade him.[2]

Le Corbusier had enthusiasm, but he also had a leader's distance and sense of self-importance. When, in 1927, Mies van der Rohe invited him to build two houses for a Werkbund exhibition at Stuttgart and politely offered him the first choice of sites, Le Corbusier unhesitatingly chose the two most prominent. He could be—and often was—lofty and severe. He affected a gravity that was half instinctive, half ironic. Léger has recalled his first meeting with Le Corbusier. The artist was sitting at an outdoor cafe in Montparnasse when a friend remarked, "Just wait, you are going to see an odd specimen. He goes bicycling in a derby hat."

> A few minutes later I saw coming along, very stiff, completely in silhouette, an extraordinarily mobile object under the derby hat, with spectacles and in a dark suit. It was the outfit of a clergyman and of an Englishman on a weekend. He advanced quietly, scrupulously obeying the laws of perspective.[3]

In his dress as in his art, he was fond of putting the conventional in an unexpected context, thus creating his own sort of originality.

A friend from the 1920s remembered his "clean-shaven face, thin, almost like the blade of a knife, with a pinched mouth that made a sharp incision, a face whose eyes were by turn piercing and absent, dominated by a large, high forehead from which the hair was carefully combed straight back. A large, thin body, slightly bent as if on stilts, but well-coordinated, deliberate in its movements, almost nonchalant."[4] He often seemed to wish to escape the image of the artist, to become a responsible "technician," to wear his dark suits and leave behind the derby and the bicycle. But an equally strong desire for what he called "lyricism" drew him back. During a visit to Prague in 1928 he spent a night drinking with the poet Nezval. In the early morning, after the two had exchanged confessions of faith, Nezval struggled to his feet. "Le Corbusier is a poet!" he exclaimed, and roused the remaining patrons at the bar to join him in a toast. The newly christened poet was deeply moved. "That night," he recalled, "I received my first profound reward."[5]

He wished to be both a leader and an independent artist, a poet and a technician, a man of both imagination and power. Within the charmed circle of the avant-garde he succeeded. But once he attempted to step outside it—to design cities, not villas—he was frustrated. At a lecture in the late 1920s he drew a pyramid which was supposed to represent the French people. The lower 90 percent of the pyramid represented that part of the population immured in "academicism," conventional ideas about houses and cities. The top 10 percent—the elite—was receptive to the new age.[6] It was not a wholly pessimistic appraisal. He still believed the people at the top were potentially his allies, but his faith was beginning to crumble when he saw "academicism" take the offensive and win important victories. His first exposure to the reaction against modernism came in 1927 when the German Heimatschutz League accused him and his fellow contributors to the Stuttgart exhibition of *Kulturbolschewismus*. "The protectors of the homeland are those who create it," he succinctly replied.[7] In France he was accused of fostering alien "Germanic" styles of art.

The polemics did not worry him. "Invective makes me happy," he had written to L'Eplattenier in 1908.[8] He was, however, deeply hurt when the self-proclaimed foes of "barbarism in architecture" robbed him of the commission to design the Palace of the League of Nations. The award was to be decided by a public competition. Le Corbusier submitted a magnificent plan for the great assembly hall and the surrounding administration buildings. All the columns, pilasters, and statues which traditionally clung to important structures were omitted from his elegant, horizontal, glass-walled palace. His was the only design that met all the requirements and still stayed within the stipulated budget. A plurality of the international selection committee approved it, but Le Corbusier's opponents used a technicality to upset that judgment. The selection was referred to another committee, where pressure from the architectural and diplomatic establishment was brought to bear. In 1927 the second committee completely rejected Le Corbusier's plans and commissioned instead the elephantine structures that now stand in Geneva.[9]

Le Corbusier had hoped that the Palace of the League of Nations would mark a crucial stage toward the "era of great works." An organization which represented the hopes of its time would adopt a design that embodied the beauty of its time. Instead, he was forced to confront the deep-seated opposition to the modern which even the leaders of the most technologically advanced states still harbored. His former optimism rested on the conviction that the elite, if presented with good design, would recognize it and choose it. Now he had begun to fear that the leaders of a bourgeois democracy would never appreciate his work and were incapable of carrying out his plans.

Their incapacity disturbed him more than their unwillingness. Le Corbusier had concluded that the problems of industrial society must be solved through the creation of a new urban environment. This involved the concentration and coordination of resources on a grand scale—the Plan Voisin. But the urban landscape was divided among thousands of landlords, each with an absolute veto on progress. Even if a consortium could be organized to undertake the plan, the profit would go to the land speculators, who could withhold key tracts until offered exorbitant prices. The Plan Voisin could not be undertaken unless the system of landholding was altered.

If Le Corbusier's disillusionment with the bourgeois elite began with the League of Nations rejection, his disillusionment with capitalism arose from his frustration with property rights. He arrived independently at many of the same positions that Howard and Wright had learned from Henry George. Capitalism, he believed, was essentially healthy, but the landlord's greed and inertia were preventing the system from operating productively. "Although every other sort of human enterprise is subject to the rough warfare of competition," he wrote, "the landlord, ensconced in his property, escapes the common law in a princely fashion: he is a king. On the existing principle of property, it is impossible to establish a program for construction that will hold together."[10]

Le Corbusier's first call for change was directed, therefore, not against all property but against property in land. In 1928 he published a pamphlet under the auspices of the Redressement français, which, though explicitly antirevolutionary in tone, anticipated many of his most radical positions. He was arguing for what he called "the mobilization of the soil," a striking term for the right of eminent domain. He wanted the government to "mobilize" real estate by purchasing all the land within a given tract at its assessed value and delivering the tract to builders who would undertake projects like the Plan Voisin.

It was not a subversive proposal. The Redressement français was explicitly capitalist, dedicated to the revitalization of France through the efforts of an "industrial elite of intelligence, talent, and character." Ernest Mercier, the organization's leader, and Lucien Romier, its leading intellectual, tended to identify this elite with the managers of large corporations. Le Corbusier's call for government intervention was an important feature of their own ideology. They advocated a strong state which would use its power to favor large, efficient organizations.

The principal interest of this pamphlet lies in the means that Le Corbusier outlined to implement his proposal. He had believed when he first formulated the Plan Voisin that the international corporations had the power and will to accomplish it. Now he saw that some higher authority was needed, an authority that could overcome all weaknesses and divisions that prevented action. The power to mobilize the soil would therefore be vested in one man, the Minister of Public Works.

He would not be responsible to Parliament; he would stand above politics. He would have the power to oversee projects from beginning to end, to override all opposition which might deform them, and to ensure the triumph of order.

"For many years," Le Corbusier remarked in 1929, "I have been haunted by the ghost of Colbert."[11] Louis XIV's greatest minister, the tireless reformer of taxes, laws, and industry, Jean-Baptiste Colbert (1619–1683) symbolized for Le Corbusier the heroic, all-powerful administrator: rational, indefatigible, authoritative. The new Minister must be a modern Colbert. "The scope of his vision will be the greatness of his country."[12]

The modern Colbert would be above day-to-day politics because Le Corbusier had little faith in the capacity of parliamentary democracy to rise to the present crisis. The task of authority, he wrote, was to "put ourselves in accord with a situation that has been revolutionized. If this accord is not reached quickly, the sickness that already threatens society will disorganize social life and produce these evils: confusion, incoherence, chaos, all leading to mental disarray and panic: the revolution."[13] Parliamentary politics could not evade this revolution of panic. It did not solve problems; it "devoured energy." The disorder at the top was fatal to the whole society. "Harmony is as necessary to us as our daily bread," Le Corbusier remarked. Only imagination applied on a grand scale—as a series of coordinated efforts—could bring harmony. This task would be the responsibility of the Minister of Public Works and the source of his extraordinary powers.

Le Corbusier concluded the pamphlet with four sentences that summed up his beliefs.

A machine age is born.
We act under the authority of a pre-mechanical age.
This leadership destroys all our initiatives.
We must create the leadership of a machine age.[14]

In 1928 he still believed that bourgeois democracy was capable of mobilizing its efforts to create the strong authority he believed the times demanded. This position, however, was more a pious wish than a reasoned conclusion. It did not survive very long after the stock market crash in the United States. The crash discredited those Frenchmen like Mercier who held up a glorified image of American capitalism as a model for France. For Le Corbusier it was proof that capitalism was too chaotic to serve as a basis for order. In an article published in 1931 he placed this caption under a photograph of Wall Street: "All is paradox, disorder; the liberty of each destroys the liberty of all. Indiscipline."[15] He regretfully concluded that capitalism and parliamentary democracy had failed the new era. They were incapable of forming an elite fit for leadership or of providing the authority that the Machine Age needed. The system that he had once concluded was destined to initiate a new Periclean epoch was now his symbol for confusion. He still recoiled at social upheaval, but he was even more afraid that the "established disorder" was allowing society to drift toward a catastrophe. Le Corbusier became a revolutionary out of fear of something worse.

At the same time, he retained his ideal of order. By invoking the name of Colbert he consciously identified himself with that tradition in French thought which always disdained capitalist individualism and its liberties. The orderly and harmonious masterpieces of French classical design had been created at the command of an absolute sovereign. Le Corbusier was convinced that the masterpieces of the Machine Age would require a similar exercise of authority to be born. He fervently hoped that the present crisis could be turned into an opportunity to create a new leadership and a new social structure which would have the strength to begin the era of great works.

Coincidentally, he suddenly received an opportunity to observe the workings of a strong regime at close hand. In 1928, when the Soviet Union was still encouraging avant-garde design, he had been chosen to build a headquarters for trade unions in Moscow. In that year and in 1929 he traveled to Russia to lecture and to supervise construction. He was impressed by the determination of the Soviet leaders and their commitment to industrialize their country. He even tried to adapt his Contemporary City plans for use in Russian urbanization, and this initial attempt to plan for a "classless" society became the starting-point for much of his work during the 1930s.[16] Nevertheless, he rejected communism even before the communists rejected him (and all other modernists). Their authoritarianism was too crude for his complex ideal of a strong authority that still left scope for individual freedom. He also discerned that Leninist ideology and Stalinist practice rigorously subordinated the planner to the Party. Le Corbusier could never be part of someone else's orthodoxy.

He turned instead to an indigenous French doctrine, a doctrine he believed would guide the society of the future: syndicalism. This ideology grew out of the French trade-union movement of the 1880s and 1890s. Its fundamental tenet was that independent groups of workers—the *syndicats* —must own and manage the means of production. But history added many conflicting, even contradictory, ideas to that basic idea. In the 1920s and 1930s, syndicalism offered many intellectuals a radical perspective which seemed to transcend the orthodoxies of right and left. The movement also provided a political vocabulary in which opponents of liberalism from both ends of the political spectrum could find a common ground and express their hopes for a new order.

Le Corbusier was attracted to syndicalism in part because it was undefined. The disparate elements of syndicalism were the raw materials out of which he created his own synthesis. He shaped the doctrines to fit the requirements of urban planning; and, as we shall see, syndicalist ideas inspired him to alter fundamentally the form of his ideal city.

The major conflict in syndicalist thought—and the one that

became the center of Le Corbusier's concerns—was between authority and participation. Syndicalism began as a quasi-anarchist doctrine. After the revolution, each *syndicat* would run its own factory; each member would participate equally, and there would be a minimum of organization. The syndicalist leaders were hostile to the state, and they were especially hostile to all attempts to subordinate the trade unions to a parliamentary party. Their concept of revolution was a spontaneous mass rising—the general strike.[17]

If syndicalism originated as a participatory movement of the extreme left, it was soon modified by authoritarian elements of the extreme right. The agent of this modification was Georges Sorel, the movement's first intellectual advocate. Sorel portrayed syndicalism as the great rejection of bourgeois civilization: its individualism, its parliamentarianism, its reformism, even its rationalism. The essence of the movement, he believed, was its irrational myth of the general strike. When, however, the trade-union leaders showed signs of allying with the parliamentary Socialists, Sorel angrily repudiated them and turned to the extreme right. In 1910 he declared himself a reactionary and published his attacks on the bourgeoisie in that last stronghold of hatred for the Third Estate, the monarchist Action française.[18]

The more thoughtful monarchists noticed a strong resemblance between Sorel's syndicalism and the reactionary doctrine of corporatism. The corporatists wished to revive the old guild system as the answer to capitalism and its class struggle. Employers, workers, and managers in a given industry would all be enrolled in a guild which would have the power to regulate wages, profits, and competition. Disciples of the monarchist leader Charles Maurras met with Sorel's students in an attempt to create a union of reactionary and socialist ideas.[19]

The members of this group, called the Cercle Proudhon, were agreed primarily on their hatred of parliamentary democracy. The fusion of their thought led to an odd hybrid, the syndicalist state, which combined workers' organizations with the hierarchical structures of the medieval guild. As Hubert Lagardelle, Sorel's disciple, explained it, parliamentary democracy started from the "abstract" citizen who was expected to take an interest in everything in the republic. The result was that citizens were manipulated by special interests or by demogogues who stirred up class conflict. The syndicalist state however, would be based on man as a member of his trade. The "real man," the man at work, knew his fellow workers and his immediate interests. He would vote as a member of the *syndicat*; his representative would meet with others from the same trade and elect a master. A council of masters drawn from each trade would govern the country.[20]

This form of representation, it was hoped, would restore the sense of hierarchy and order that the guilds once possessed. Each trade would have complete authority to regulate itself, and considerable judicial authority over its members. The reactionaries assumed that the "natural" leader of the factory—the *patron*—would assume command at each level, and the government would become a glorified employers' council. Sorel's followers hoped that a new elite of talent would emerge. In any case, the flaccid compromises of the parliamentary era would be over.

This plan had one special merit: it could mean anything. It could be the basis for anarchy or dictatorship; it was either the victory of the proletariat or the final end of the workers' movement. For a generation that distrusted all the old ideologies, its ambiguities were its attraction. Syndicalism was a radical doctrine for workers who had lost faith in the proletariat, for sons of the bourgeoisie who hated the middle class, and for all those who knew only that the parliamentary regime must go. Seen from any perspective, it appeared to promise a new order.

After World War I, Georges Valois, a disciple of both Sorel and Maurras, began a campaign sponsored by the Action française to win the workers to syndicalism. The campaign was financed by industrialists who wished to weaken Marxist unions, and it gave wide publicity to the new doctrine. Valois favored the ideology's authoritarian elements and fancied himself the French Mussolini. In 1925 he founded his own party, the Faisceau, which called for the abdication of Parliament, a "national dictatorship above parties and classes, under the command of a Leader," and the formation of syndicalist assemblies.[21] Among his supporters was a young doctor, Pierre Winter, who was also a friend of Le Corbusier. Both men were physical fitness enthusiasts who played basketball together each week. Le Corbusier absorbed many of Winter's ideas on public health, and Winter was soon converted to Le Corbusier's town planning theories, which he expounded in Valois's daily newspaper. In 1926, Winter concluded an article on the Plan Voisin with his own commentary: "Only a strong program of urbanism—the program of a fascist government—is capable of adapting the modern city to the needs of all."[22]

Le Corbusier was not ready to embrace this opinion himself in 1926. Through Winter, however, he was introduced to the syndicalist doctrines and to the leading syndicalist intellectuals. By 1930, Le Corbusier was a convert. At that time the Faisceau no longer existed. Valois had grown disillusioned with Mussolini, and the syndicalists were now anxious to dissociate themselves from fascism. Syndicalism was now expounded not through a political party but in many "little reviews," each claiming to be the nucleus of a movement. In 1930, Philippe Lamour, a young lawyer and former associate of Valois, proposed to Le Corbusier that they found their own review, devoted equally to syndicalist politics and to the arts. The first issue of *Plans* appeared in January 1931.

The years 1929–1931 mark a decisive change in Le Corbusier's thought and life. In 1930 he married Yvonne Gallis, his wife until her death in 1957. In 1930 he also officially renounced his old identity—Charles-Édouard Jeanneret, Swiss citizen—and became Charles-Édouard Le Corbusier, citizen of

France. He abandoned the "purist" style in his paintings; the human figure made its first appearances on his canvases. In his architecture he departed from the smooth white "purist" facades which had been his style, and incorporated rough stonework and textured concrete into his designs.

Finally, he rejected the dream of a smoothly functioning capitalist elite and entered into the rough world of political activism. To his careers as architect, painter, and theorist he added one more: editor and spokesman for syndicalism. This new vocation was not a romantic rush for the barricades. He did not lose contact with old associates like Mercier. He was reluctant to call himself a revolutionary. "Nothing is more dangerous," he observed in 1932, "than the revolutionary with beak and claws, the negator, the destroyer, the scoffer."[23] "Bloody revolution" was "not obligatory." The leaders of the future were men who had sufficient strength to "take charge over every dangerous minute that passed during the battles of the great transformation."[24] His concept of his own role was to imagine "a complete system, coherent, just and indisputable."[25] This system, he declared, would be "nothing more or less than a revolutionary event." This system took the form of an ideal city for a syndicalist society: the Radiant City.

24

The Radiant City

THE Radiant City retained the most important principle of the Contemporary City: the juxtaposition of a collective realm of order and administration with an individualistic realm of family life and participation. This juxtaposition became the key to Le Corbusier's attempt to resolve the syndicalist dilemma of authority and participation. Both elements of the doctrine receive intense expression in their respective spheres. Harmony is in the structure of the whole city and in the complete life of its citizens.

The Radiant City was a more daring and difficult synthesis than the Contemporary City. In his effort to realize the contradictory elements of syndicalism, Le Corbusier made the Radiant City at once more authoritarian and more libertarian than its predecessor. Within the sphere of collective life, authority has become absolute. The Contemporary City had lacked any single power to regulate all the separate private corporations which accomplished the essential work of society; Le Corbusier had then believed that the invisible hand of free competition would create the most efficient coordination. The Great Depression robbed him of his faith. He now held that organization must extend beyond the large corporations. They had rationalized their own organizations, but the economy as a whole remained wasteful, anarchic, irrational. The planned allocation of manpower and resources which had taken place within each corporation must now be accomplished for society. In the Radiant City every aspect of productive life is administered from above according to one plan. This plan replaces the marketplace with total administration; experts match society's needs to its productive capacities.

The preordained harmony which Le Corbusier had called for in urban reconstruction would now be imposed on all productive life. The great works of construction would become only one element in the plan. This was a crucial extension of the concept of planning. Ebenezer Howard and Frank Lloyd Wright had believed that once the environment had been designed, the sources of disorder in society would be minimized and individuals could be left to pursue their own initiatives. This belief rested on a faith in a "natural economic order," a faith which Le Corbusier no longer shared. He confronted a world threatened by chaos and collapse. It seemed that only discipline could create the order he sought so ardently. Coordination must become conscious and total. Above all, society needed authority and a plan.

Syndicalism, Le Corbusier believed, would provide a "pyramid of natural hierarchies" on which order and planning could be based. The bottom of this pyramid is the *syndicat*, the group of workers, white-collar employees, and engineers who run their own factory. The workers have the responsibility of choosing their most able colleague to be their manager and to represent them at the regional trade council. Le Corbusier believed that although citizens would usually find it impossible to identify the most able man among a host of politicians, each worker is normally able to choose his natural leader. "Every man is capable of judging the facts of his trade," he observed.[1]

The regional council of plant managers represents the first step in the hierarchy. Each level corresponds to a level of administrative responsibility. The manager runs his factory; the regional leaders administer the plants in their region. The regional council sends its most able members to a national council, which is responsible for the overall control of the trade. The leader of this council meets with his fellow leaders to administer the national plan. This highest group is responsible for coordinating the entire production of the country. If, for example, the national plan calls for mass housing, they allot the capital needed for each region and set the goals for production. The order is passed down to the regional council, which assigns tasks to individual factories and contractors. The elected representative of the *syndicat* returns from the regional council with instructions that determine his factory's role in the national productive effort.

This hierarchy of administration has replaced the state. As Saint-Simon had urged, a man's power corresponds exactly to his responsibilities in the structure of production. He issues the orders necessary for fulfilling his quotas, and these orders provide the direction that society needs. The divisive issues of parliamentary politics cannot arise, for everyone shares a common concern that the resources of society be administered as efficiently as possible. Even the tasks of the national council are administrative rather than political. The members do not apportion wealth and power among competing interests groups. Their task, like that of all the other functionaries, is a "technical" one: they carry out the plan.

"Plans are not political," Le Corbusier wrote.[2] The plan's complex provisions, covering every aspect of production, distribution, and construction, represent a necessary and objective ordering of society. The plan is necessary because the Machine Age requires conscious control. It is objective because the Machine Age imposes essentially the same discipline on all societies. Planning involves the rational mastery of industrial process and the application of that mastery to the specific conditions of each nation. The plan is a "rational and lyric monument" to man's capacity to organize.

The plan is formulated by an elite of experts detached from all social pressure. They work "outside the fevers of mayors' and prefects' offices," away from the "cries of electors and the cries of victims." Their plans are "established serenely, lucidly. They take account only of human truths."[3] In the planner's formulations, "the motive forces of a civilization pass from the subjective realm of consciousness to the objective realm of facts." His plans are "just, long-term, established on the realities of the century, imagined by a creative passion."[4]

This plan for Le Corbusier was more than a collection of statistics and instructions; it was a social work of art. It brought to consciousness the complex yet satisfying harmonies of an orderly productive world. It was the score for the great industrial orchestra. The plan summed up the unity that underlay the division of labor in society; it expressed the full range of exchange and cooperation which is necessary to an advanced economy.

Le Corbusier used the vocabulary and structures of syndicalism to advance his own vision of a beautifully organized world. His "pyramid of natural hierarchies" was intended to give the human structure of organization the same clarity and order as the great skyscrapers of the business center. The beauty of the organization was the product of the perfect cooperation of everyone in the hierarchy. It was the expression of human solidarity in creating a civilization in the midst of the hostile forces of nature. The natural hierarchy was one means of attaining the sublime.

Man at work creates a world which is truly human. But that world, once created, is a realm of freedom where man lives in accord with nature, not in opposition to it. Like the Contemporary City, the Radiant City identifies the realm of freedom with the residential district. As if in recognition of the need to counterbalance the industrial realm's increased emphasis on organization, Le Corbusier has displaced the towers of administration from the central position they occupied in the earlier plan. The residential district stands in the place of honor in the Radiant City.

It is, moreover, a transformed residential district. Le Corbusier had lost the enthusiasm for capitalism which had led him originally to segregate housing in the Contemporary City according to class—elite in the center, proletariat at the outskirts. Now he was a revolutionary syndicalist, with a new appreciation of workers' rights. When he visited the United States in 1935, he found much to admire in the luxury apartment houses that lined Central Park and Lake Shore Drive, but he added, "My own thinking is directed toward the crowds in the subway who come home at night to dismal dwellings. The millions of beings sacrificed to a life without hope, without rest—without sky, sun, greenery."[5] Housing in the Radiant City is designed for them. The residential district embodies Le Corbusier's new conviction that the world of freedom must be egalitarian. "If the city were to become a human city," he proclaimed, "it would be a city without classes."[6]

No longer does the residential district simply mirror the inequalities in the realm of production. Instead, the relation between the two is more complex, reflecting Le Corbusier's resolve to make the Radiant City a city of organization *and* freedom. The realm of production in the Radiant City is even more tightly organized, its hierarchies of command and subordination even stricter than in the Contemporary City. At the same time, the residential district—the realm of leisure and self-fulfillment—is radically libertarian, its principles of equality and cooperation standing in stark opposition to the hierarchy of the industrial world. The citizen in Le Corbusier's syndicalist society thus experiences both organization and freedom as part of his daily life.

The centers of life in the Radiant City are the great high-rise apartment blocks, which Le Corbusier calls "Unités." These structures, each of which is a neighborhood with 2,700 residents, mark the culmination of the principles of housing that he had been expounding since the Dom-Inos of 1914. Like the Dom-Ino house, the Unité represents the application of mass-production techniques; but where the Dom-Ino represents the principle in its most basic form, the Unité is a masterful expression of scale, complexity, and sophistication. The disappointments of the 1920s and the upheavals of the 1930s had only strengthened Le Corbusier in his faith that a great new age of the machine was about to dawn. In the plans for the Unité he realized that promise of a *collective* beauty which had been his aim in the Dom-Ino design; he achieved a collective grandeur which the Dom-Ino houses had only hinted at; and finally, he foresaw for all the residents of the Unité a freedom and abundance beyond even that which he had planned for the elite of the Contemporary City. The apartments in the Unité are not assigned on the basis of a worker's position in the industrial hierarchy but according to the size of his family and their needs. In designing these apartments, Le Corbusier remarked that he "thought neither of rich nor of poor but of man."[7] He wanted to get away both from the concept of luxury housing, in which the wasteful consumption of space becomes a sign of status, and from the concept of *Existenzminimum*, the design of workers' housing based on the absolute hygienic minimums. He believed that housing could be made to the "human scale," right in its proportions for everyone, neither cramped nor wasteful. No one would want anything larger nor get anything smaller.

The emphasis in the Unité, however, is not on the individual apartment but on the collective services provided to all the residents. As in the Villa-Apartment Blocks of the Contemporary City, Le Corbusier followed the principle that the cooperative sharing of leisure facilities could give to each family a far more varied and beautiful environment than even the richest individual could afford in a single-family house.

These facilities, moreover, take on a clear social function as the reward and recompense for the eight hours of disciplined labor in a factory or office which are required of all citizens in a syndicalist society. The Unité, for example, has a full range of workshops for traditional handicrafts whose techniques can no longer be practiced in industries devoted to mass production. Here are meeting rooms of all sizes for participatory activities that have no place in the hierarchical sphere of production. There are cafes, restaurants, and shops where sociability can be cultivated for its own sake. Most importantly in Le Corbusier's own estimation, the Unité provides the opportunity for a full range of physical activities that are severely curtailed during working hours in an industrial society. Within each Unité there is a full-scale gymnasium; on the roof are tennis courts, swimming pools, and even sand beaches. Once again, the high-rise buildings cover only 15 percent of the land, and the open space around them is elaborately landscaped into playing fields, gardens, and parkland.

The most basic services which the Unité provides are those which make possible a new concept of the family. Le Corbusier envisioned a society in which men and women would work full-time as equals. He therefore presumed the end of the family as an economic unit in which women were responsible for domestic services while men worked for wages. In the Unité, cooking, cleaning, and child raising are services provided by society. Each building has its day-care center, nursery and primary school, cooperative laundry, cleaning service, and food store. In the Radiant City the family no longer has an economic function to perform. It exists as an end in itself.

Le Corbusier and Frank Lloyd Wright were both intensely concerned with the preservation of the family in an industrial society, but here as elsewhere they adopted diametrically opposite strategies. Wright wished to revive and strengthen the traditional economic role of the family, to ensure its survival by making it the center both of the society's work and of its leisure. Wright believed in a life in which labor and leisure would be one, whereas Le Corbusier subjected even the family to that stark division between work and play which marks the Radiant City. The family belongs to the realm of play. Indeed, it virtually ceases to exist during the working day. When mother and father leave their apartment in the morning for their jobs, their children accompany them down on the elevator. The parents drop them off at the floor where the school or day-care center is located and pick them up after work. The family reassembles in the afternoon, perhaps around the pool or at the gym, and when the family members return to their apartment they find it already cleaned, the laundry done and returned, the food ordered in the morning already delivered and prepared for serving. Individual families might still choose to cook their own food, do their own laundry, raise vegetables on their balconies, or even raise their own children. In the Radiant City, however, these activities have become leisure-time hobbies like woodworking or weaving, quaint relics of the pre-mechanical age.

The Unité is thus high-rise architecture for a new civilization, and Le Corbusier was careful to emphasize that its design could only be truly realized after society had been revolutionized. He therefore never concerned himself with such problems as muggings in the parks or vandalism in the elevators. In the Radiant City, crime and poverty no longer exist.

But if the Unité looks to the future, its roots are in the nineteenth-century utopian hopes for a perfect cooperative society, the same hopes that inspired Ebenezer Howard's cooperative quadrangles. Peter Serenyi has aptly compared the Unité to that French utopian palace of communal pleasures, the phalanstery of Charles Fourier.[8] An early nineteenth-century rival of Saint-Simon, Fourier envisioned a structure resembling the château of Versailles to house the 1,600 members of his "phalanx" or rural utopian community. "We have no conception of the compound or collective forms of luxury,"

Fourier complained, and the phalanstery was designed to make up that lack.[9] He believed that in a properly run society all man's desires could find their appropriate gratification. The phalanstery, therefore, contains an elaborate series of lavish public rooms: theaters, libraries, ballrooms, and Fourier's special pride, the dining rooms where "exquisite food and a piquant selection of dining companions" can always be found.

The phalanstery can be seen as the nineteenth-century anticipation and the Unité as the twentieth-century realization of architecture in the service of collective pleasure. Both designs represent what Le Corbusier termed "the architecture of happiness," architecture created to deliver what he was fond of calling "the essential joys." Fourier, however, could only express his vision in the anachronistic image of the baroque palace. Le Corbusier finds the forms of collective pleasure in the most advanced techniques of mass production. For him, the architecture of happiness is also the architecture for the industrial era.

The comparison of the phalanstery and the Unité suggests, finally, the complexity of Le Corbusier's ideal city. For Fourier was the bitter antagonist of Saint-Simon, whose philosophy is so central to Le Corbusier's social thought. The rivalry of the two nineteenth-century prophets was more than personal. Since their time, French utopian thought has been divided into two distinct traditions. The Saint-Simonian tradition is the dream of society as the perfect industrial hierarchy. Its setting is urban, its thought technological, its goal production, and its highest value organization. Fourier and his followers have envisioned society as the perfect community: rural, small-scaled, egalitarian, dedicated to pleasure and self-fulfillment. In the Radiant City, Le Corbusier combines these two traditions into an original synthesis. He places a Fourierist phalanstery in the center of a Saint-Simonian industrial society. Community and organization thus find intense and appropriate expression: both are integral parts of Le Corbusier's ideal city for the Machine Age.

25

Quest for Authority

L E CORBUSIER perfected his vision of the ideal industrial
society precisely when the Great Depression was reaching
its depths. Like Wright, he saw this economic disaster as a
vindication of his criticisms of the old order and proof that a
new order must be at hand. The Depression, he declared,
was an industrial "time of troubles" which would lead to the
"Second Machine Age." In the "First Machine Age" (1830–
1930) the machine had oppressed man. It was the age of greed,
ugliness, conflict, and oppression. The Second Machine Age
about to dawn would be an age of harmony, in which the
machine's potential for liberation would be realized—the age
of the Radiant City.[1] He spoke of the Radiant City as if it had
already solved the problems of the Depression. "The Radiant
City is on paper," he announced. "When a technical work is
drawn up (figures and proofs), it *exists*. Only spectators,
gapers, impotents, need the certainty that comes from execution. The Radiant City that will dissipate our anguish, that will

succeed the reigning darkness—it exists on paper. We await the OK from an Authority that will come and will prevail."[2]

Yet beneath this confident optimism there flowed a deeper current of fear. The fervor with which he advanced his visions of future harmony reflected this growing anxiety at the disorder he saw around him. For Le Corbusier was well aware that the Machine Age could destroy as well as create. He himself had experienced at La Chaux-de-Fonds the "crisis of the artisans," in which a stable, productive community had been swept away ruthlessly by the unrestricted play of economic forces. Now this disease seemed to be reappearing in a more virulent form, bringing with it the same unemployment, hardships, and bewildered anger, but on a global scale. Le Corbusier was afraid that the Second Machine Age might never be reached. This time of troubles could prove fatal to civilization.

As the crisis continued, his anxieties turned to panic. The incapacity of the Western democracies to deal with the Depression intensified his disdain for parliamentary methods. When he published the *La ville radieuse* in 1935 he began the text with the following words: "These studies rest on an inalienable, unquestionable truth that is fundamental to all plans for social organization: individual liberty."[3] The book, however, is dedicated "To Authority." As the decade wore on, Le Corbusier first questioned and then abandoned the "unquestionable truth" of individual liberty and allied himself with the opponents of democracy. He came to believe that only a government equipped with dictatorial powers could inaugurate the age of harmony. His whole approach to politics resolved itself into a desperate search for the absolute authority that would say Yes to his plans.

Le Corbusier's growing interest in authoritarianism must be seen in the context of a revulsion from liberal democracy so widespread in the 1930s that it was almost the spirit of that troubled age. The Western democracies appeared paralyzed by the Depression, and their impotence was taken as proof that a pluralistic society could never cope with the demands of the modern era. While production in the West was falling to half its pre-Depression level and unemployment approached 25 percent, Stalin's Five-Year Plan was doubling Soviet production, Hitler was restoring full employment to Germany, and Mussolini's posturings managed to convince the credulous that Italy too was forging ahead. Even the New Deal was seen in Europe as a presidential dictatorship over the legislative branch. Intellectuals in all parties were fascinated with the idea of a charismatic leader whose unquestioned personal authority would suppress the interest-politics of the parliaments and unite the masses behind a positive program. Le Corbusier included a photograph of a fascist rally in Venice in *La ville radieuse* and put this caption underneath: "Little by little the world approaches its destiny. In Moscow, in Berlin, in Rome, and in the United States, the masses gather around a strong idea."[4] This "strong idea" was not a doctrine but the respect for authority—any authority that seemed capable of building the new age.

The syndicalist movement, which could agree on virtually nothing else, was united in its repugnance for parliamentary democracy. In their eagerness to reject party politics and the shibboleths of right and left, the syndicalists endorsed repression and exploitation; they glorified the élan and the mass rallies of the antidemocratic parties; they "went beyond" democracy and civil liberties. These ideas remained in the realm of theory for the French syndicalists (who had no mass following), at least until 1940, when many joined the Vichy regime. In the 1930s their program remained largely negative: denunciations of democracy in general and the Third Republic in particular. "France needs a Father," Le Corbusier proclaimed. "It doesn't matter who."[5]

If Le Corbusier's quest for authority reflected the spirit of the age, it also reflected ideas and preoccupations which date back to his call for a "modern Colbert" a decade earlier. His whole analysis of industrial society and his conception of planning predisposed him to authoritarian methods. This can be seen even in the synthesis of liberty and order which he offers in the Radiant City.

This synthesis is possible only because Le Corbusier has excluded politics from his ideal city. The individual's liberty is absolute, but only within the sphere of private life. He can organize leisure activities among his neighbors, but he cannot change the system itself. The great questions of the divisions of the society's resources are never put to a vote. They are prescribed in the plan, which has been promulgated "objectively" by experts. The citizen does have a voice in choosing the member of his trade who he feels is most qualified to administer the plan, but he can only vote for his immediate superior. The heights of the natural hierarchy are not subject to direct democratic control.

Le Corbusier had a Platonic suspicion of "opinion." He shared Plato's belief that social order must depend upon truth, not the shifting will of the majority. For Le Corbusier, this "truth" lay in the structure and functions which the Machine age imposes on all industrial societies. The expert planners, who understand the objective needs of the structure, formulate efficient and imaginative ways of meeting them. Once the principle of equal compensation has been accepted, however, there can be no fundamental disagreement on values. Everyone's interest is to have the system function as well as possible. To that end, the workers choose their most able colleagues as their managers, and each level of the hierarchy has men and women who are the best qualified for their posts.

The sociologist Michel Crozier has called attention to what he calls "l'horreur du face-à-face" in French life: the inability of groups in their perpetually conflict-ridden society to bear the strains of genuinely cooperative efforts, and the consequent eagerness to turn to some higher authority who would impose order without the groups having to experience the "horror" of face-to-face compromises among themselves.[6] The system of the Radiant City is a reflection, indeed an intensification, of these attitudes. Each level in the syndicalist hierarchy relies on the higher-ups for basic decisions, which are then executed without further discussion. Even the leaders of the various trades, meeting in the highest councils, do not work out the national priorities through discussion and compromise. Instead, they turn to the planners and defer to their apolitical deductions from "the objective realm of facts."

Politics, therefore, had no role in the running of the Radiant City, and Le Corbusier did not expect that parliamentary democracy would ever be able to create it. A city for the Machine Age could never emerge from discussion and compromise: that was the path to chaos. The harmonious city must first be planned by experts who understand the science of urbanism. They work out their plans in total freedom from partisan pressures and special interests; once their plans are formulated, they must be implemented without opposition. Governmental authority in the Radiant City must be absolute within its sphere. If not, the planners' solutions would be mangled in execution. Le Corbusier's concept of a rational, technically objective plan drawn up by experts thus implies the existence of an absolute authority to carry it out. Only power can make the plan a reality, and only unobstructed power can realize a work of perfect order and truth.

Le Corbusier decisively rejected both Frank Lloyd Wright's faith in the capacity of individuals to create the new industrial society and Ebenezer Howard's trust in small-scale cooperation. As an ardent syndicalist, he worked to make the concept of absolute authority a reality. In 1932, Le Corbusier broke with Philippe Lamour and *Plans* and became a member of the Central Committee for Regionalist and Syndicalist Action and an editor of its journal, *Prélude*. The best-known member of the committee—which was more impressive in name than in fact—was Hubert Lagardelle, by this time the Grand Old Man of French syndicalism. Lagardelle had close ties with the left wing of Italian fascism, those followers of the Duce who still held to the young Mussolini's revolutionary syndicalist pronouncements long after he himself had abandoned them. *Prélude,* whose editors included Lagardelle and Pierre Winter, was cautiously pro-fascist. Fascism was "worthy to be studied very closely," even though "the financial ties which ensnare the fascist government prevent it from attempting to resolve the problem of capitalism."[7]

Le Corbusier at first had little respect for fascism. In a 1933 article in *Prélude* he attacked both "Mussolini modern" architecture and the regime itself: "Rome imitating Rome: a foolish redundancy."[8] In 1934, however, Mussolini began to encourage progressive architecture. Le Corbusier was invited to go to Italy and was enthusiastically received; his view of fascism changed immediately. In Marinetti's pro-fascist *Stile futurista* he wrote:

> The present spectacle of Italy, the state of her spiritual powers, announces the imminent dawn of the modern spirit. Her shining purity and force illumine the paths which had been obscured by the cowardly and the profiteers.[9]

As the language clearly indicates, Le Corbusier was hoping that Mussolini would be the authority who would decree the Radiant City. But the "imminent dawn" refused to shine. Mussolini lost interest in modern architecture, and Le Corbusier returned to France empty-handed.

This foreign adventure only emphasized the difficulties of building a syndicalist movement at home. The raw materials were there: the bankruptcy of the parliamentary system was evident; the trade unions had made syndicalist ideas widely familiar among the working class; and "little journals" like *Plans* and *Prélude* had spread syndicalism among the intellectuals. Le Corbusier plunged into the work, spending almost every evening writing, editing, or at meetings. His associates at the Central Committee were men like Norbert Bézard, a peasant turned syndicalist activist who persuaded Le Corbusier to design a "radiant farm"; François de Pierrefeu, an engineer and fervent advocate of the Radiant City; and Father Borda-char, a priest sympathetic to syndicalism who was a leader in Catholic veterans' organizations. With these modest associates he shared his surprisingly elitist hopes for revolution. "It may entail the most violent struggles," he confided, "but the conflict will never exceed its proper limits and spread outside the official decision-making groups."[10]

These groups, however, were not to be won over by the Central Committee. The era of authority and mass enthusiasm seemed a distant goal indeed. The only authorities that existed ignored the syndicalists, and the masses were equally apathetic. In these circumstances Le Corbusier designed a "National Center of Collective Festivals for 100,000 People," his attempt to imagine the spirit of the collective regime he was seeking so earnestly. This center is a huge sports stadium, a "civic tool for the modern age," at which the mass rallies of the future would also be held. A great arc of concrete where the spectators sit is focused upon a speakers' platform. There the leader would inspire his people, speaking directly to all and receiving approval directly from all.[11]

Yet Le Corbusier did not intend the spectators to be passive. Even in his most authoritarian stage he believed that a true revolution must create a collective consciousness, a spontaneous sense of participation and union. This great transformation cannot be imposed from above. It arises from the individual's feeling of belonging to "a world reborn." The collective consciousness is the highest achievement of the new order. The conclusion of every rally, therefore, would be a parade of the masses. The spectators would stream down and occupy the field. They would become the actors in their own pageant. Men and women in work clothes would group themselves spontaneously into columns, still carrying their tools. There would be marching, perhaps dancing.[12]

What is the relationship between the leader on the platform

and the masses on the field? How can a regime of authority create a feeling of participation? Le Corbusier could never say. He knew only that both must be present in his ideal city. They were the two elements in a synthesis which he sought but could never really define. In his many drawings and plans for the "National Center," the great stadium is always empty.

26

Vichy

LE CORBUSIER'S career as an editor and political activist extended from 1931 to 1935. These were the years of syndicalism's greatest influence among the intellectuals. The movement's call for an alternative to parliamentary democracy seemed logical and necessary at a time when the political parties were paralyzed by the economic crisis. The coming of the Popular Front, however, revived hopes for change through political action. The syndicalists, who claimed that elections were a snare and a delusion, now seemed increasingly irrelevant. *Prélude*, never robust, had to suspend publication in 1935, and the "movement" that supported the journal dispersed. Nevertheless, Le Corbusier maintained his private efforts. "With obstinacy and tenderness, we continue to *make Plans.*"[1] He submitted urban renewal proposals to Stockholm, Zürich, Algiers, Antwerp, and Geneva; none was implemented. He suggested that the government build a Unité for

5,400 people as part of the Paris Exposition of 1937. The suggestion was tentatively adopted and then rejected.[2]

The threat of war was another blow to his hopes. After the Great War, Le Corbusier had suggested that the heavy war industries be retooled for making houses. The "era of great works," the alternative to the era of great wars, never took place. Now the factories were retooling—but to make new munitions. In 1938 he published a book whose title can be translated "Cannons? Bombs? No thanks. Housing please!!" His request was not followed. When the war broke out, he received his first major commission of the decade: to build a munitions factory.

The factory was still uncompleted when the armistice was signed. There was no work or food for him in Paris; he and his wife left for Ozon, a small town in the south of France. There he attempted to evaluate the new regime of Marshal Pétain. As an opponent of parliamentary democracy, Le Corbusier had no regrets over the fall of the Third Republic. The Vichy regime, moreover, seemed to promise the authority that Le Corbusier and his fellow syndicalists had been advocating in the 1930s. In *La ville radieuse* he had quoted with approval Pétain's statement that "the leader must have three qualities: imagination, will, and technical knowledge . . . and in that order."[3] In 1940, Le Corbusier permitted himself to hope that the old general himself might become the leader who would implement his plans.

From his remote place of refuge Le Corbusier set out to gain a position with the new regime. He discovered he knew Marcel Peyrouton, the Minister of the Interior. Peyrouton had been Governor-General in Algiers when Le Corbusier had presented his plans for that city, and had presided at the public lecture in 1934 at which Le Corbusier had expounded his theories.[4] Through Peyrouton he sought a position as commissioner for the rebuilding of devastated areas.[5]

In January 1941 he arrived at Vichy. "I enter into the tumult," he wrote to a friend, "after six months of doing nothing and equipped with twenty years of hopes."⁶ Thus began eighteen months of fruitless attempts to persuade authority. It was not his finest hour. There is something both comic and frightening in the spectacle of the greatest architect of his time currying favor with decaying notables of the past; presenting plans for social harmony to the ministers of repression; begging—in vain—for an interview with Pétain; intriguing to keep the tiny room which the regime had allotted him.

One is tempted to explain the episode as an artist's total misapprehension of the politicians he was dealing with. Le Corbusier, however, understood very well at least one aspect of Vichy, and wholly approved of it. A powerful faction of the regime wished to use the Marshal's autocratic power to control and rationalize French industry, to organize the trades into self-regulating "corporations," and to institute planning from above. In this group were many of Le Corbusier's associates from the 1930s, including Lagardelle. The Redressement français was represented by its former director, Lucien Romier, whom Le Corbusier had known since the 1920s.

Both the syndicalists and the technocrats were enthusiastic supporters of the idea of national planning, an idea which was also of vital interest to Le Corbusier. François Lehideux, a nephew of the automobile magnate Louis Renault, had been chosen to formulate a "Directive Plan for National Equipment" which would govern the allocation of French capital investments. The official in charge of construction for the plan was Robert Latournerie, a leading jurist and member of the *conseil d'État*. Latournerie was also a good friend of the playwright Jean Giraudoux, an enthusiastic admirer of Le Corbusier. With Giraudoux's assistance, Le Corbusier applied to be a consultant on architecture.⁷ Giraudoux then introduced Le Corbusier to the man who was to become his most powerful backer within the regime, Henry du Moulin de Labarthète, a member of the elite Inspectorate of Finance then serving as chief of Pétain's civil cabinet.⁸

These efforts bore fruit. On May 27, 1941 Le Corbusier was appointed to head a "Study Commission for Questions relating to Housing and Building." The commission was charged with advising Latournerie and Lehideux and with "proposing measures necessary to begin and to put into effect a national policy" for building. The commission could embark upon "all inquiries or missions which it judges useful, in France, in the Empire, or in foreign countries." The members of the commission were Le Corbusier and two close associates, François de Pierrefeu and André Boll.[9]

Le Corbusier believed that authority was about to act, and, more importantly, to act on his plans. These early days at Vichy, he later recalled, were the first time that men in power ever took him seriously.[10] Le Corbusier deserved this warm welcome. The Vichy of the technocrats was the embodiment of the darker side of his social thought: the contempt for democracy, the eagerness to accept authoritarian solutions, the awe of power. His had been one of the leading voices arguing for a rapprochement between technological rationalism and autocratic government. The journals he edited had anticipated virtually all the technocrats' programs. Vichy was the end of a road he had been traveling for more than a decade.

The Vichy of the technocrats was not the only Vichy. Of equal influence with the Marshal were the more traditional authoritarians who argued that industry and cities had been the cause of France's downfall, that France must be made a primarily agricultural country, and that the local elites must be restored to power. Although Le Corbusier believed he was on the verge of power, he was in fact a minor member of an embattled faction. His study commission was one of a score of competing groups, each with its own plan, each struggling to impose its views on a grand plan that was, in fact, never implemented. He never understood—or refused to understand—his real position. The phantasmagoric atmosphere of Vichy, the absence of real power combined with the illusion of omnipotence, encouraged his wildest speculations. His theory of planning was transformed into an authoritarian fantasy.

Le Corbusier did not doubt that Lehideux would accept his proposals. His concern was to make his concept of architecture and city planning the official one for France. As chief of construction for the national plan, he would have a decisive voice in the Corporation of Architects that Vichy had already created. This corporation was part of the regime's attempt to organize each profession into a self-regulating guild. Le Corbusier proposed that a new elite be created within the Corporation of Architects: the master builders. These men would be the town planners and industrial designers of France. They would head large offices of architects and engineers which would undertake mass housing and urban reconstruction. They would have the power to override local building codes and to overrule opposition from local authorities.[11]

The principal task of the master builders would be to carry out the instructions of the national plan. The chief planners would define the basic methods of construction; they would set up factories in which the components of buildings could be prefabricated; and they would allocate these and other materials to the master builders for use in the projects they would specify.

At the head of the whole structure of authority was a man Le Corbusier called the "regulator." He was the last and most grandiose of the modern Colberts that Le Corbusier devised. The regulator was both an architect and an administrator, and he was supremely powerful in both fields. He was the natural leader of the master builders; by example and by command, his doctrine of construction would become theirs. He formulated the national plan for building, and thus had responsibility for the structure of the whole country. He could "zone" the nation, reserving some areas for cities, others for agriculture, others for wilderness. He determined the equilibrium between industry and agriculture. If the regulator believed that the growth of a city threatened its surrounding agricultural region, he could stop that growth or even reverse it. His control over the location of industries gave him a decisive voice in the distribution of population. If a region seemed overly concentrated, he could forbid new factories and homes there, assigning construction to less crowded areas.[12]

In Le Corbusier's proposal, the regulator has supreme power over the enviromnent. The chief of state must secure his approval before any legislation affecting the environment can be approved. Aided by a staff of experts, the regulator "serenely, lucidly puts the word in order."[13] Le Corbusier never named his nominee for so august a post. To have named someone else would have ruined the fantasy. By now it seems apparent that the "specter of Colbert" which had been pursuing him was always his own shadow.

The regulator was a hope for the future. Le Corbusier also had plans for the present. He wished to begin building immediately a series of "exemplary works" which would reveal the grandeur of his conceptions and demonstrate his power within the regime. His attention was focused first on Algiers. He had executed three remarkable plans for that city during the 1930s; they had earned him a place on the Algiers Planning Commission, where he was completely ignored. Shortly after he arrived in Vichy in 1941, he received a letter from a friend in Algiers, Pierre-Auguste Emery, informing him that the Planning Commission was about to approve a rival plan.[14] Le Corbusier soon convinced himself that he now had the influence to impose his will on the Planning Commission and make Algiers an "exemplary" city "guiding the future of architecture in metropolitan France and in the rest of Europe."[15]

Le Corbusier's efforts to secure the implementation of his plan for Algiers showed how clearly his practice followed his theories. He assumed from the first that the plan would have to be imposed from above. Although he frequently traveled to Algiers and gave public lectures to arouse "collective enthusiasm," his relations with the local authorities were distant and hostile. His aim was to persuade the authorities in Vichy to "delegate to Le Corbusier the mandate to give orders."[16] As he explained to General Maxime Weygand, then Vichy's highest representative in North Africa, "In the present administrative state, only the highest authorities of the country can permit the necessary innovations, create the useful precedents, authorize the ignoring of old regulations, permit the Plan to enter into life."[17] With support from du Moulin, he called upon Weygand to suspend the local commission and give control over planning to Le Corbusier and his associates:

> By an order from above the local plan must be interrupted and its continuance forbidden. This gesture of authority will have a decisive effect on Algerian opinion, showing that the government of Marshal Pétain has taken into consideration the most pressing problems of urbanism and that in fact from now on it intends to impose a new orientation.[18]

Unfortunately for Le Corbusier, the intentions of the Vichy regime were subject to rapid change. After he went to Algiers for three weeks in June, presenting himself in public lectures and private meetings as a spokesman for Vichy, he found his mandate abruptly rescinded. Lehideux, the Plan's Director, grew annoyed at Le Corbusier's pretensions. On July 14, 1941—Bastille Day was not celebrated at Vichy—Le Corbusier received official notification that "The Minister sees no possibility of working with Le Corbusier, François de Pierrefeu and André Boll in any way."[19]

This notice was the "decree of death," as Le Corbusier put it, for the study commission.[20] Nevertheless, continued support from du Moulin and the general confusion permitted the committee to maintain a posthumous existence. Le Corbusier convinced himself that all his problems would be solved if Pétain gave his personal blessing to the Algiers plan. As he wrote to du Moulin, "You must be there to realize what the name of the Marshal means in Algiers and the least of the opinions he voices."[21] All his efforts were directed to securing an interview with Pétain. "I'm down on my hands and knees doing everything to get results," he wrote to Emery. "But, my dear friends, it's really *tough* to preach in the desert and make others act!!!"[22] The interview was never granted. The most he obtained was a letter from Pétain's personal secretary, Dr. Bernard Ménétrel, acknowledging that *Sur les 4 routes*, a book which Le Corbusier published in 1941 and sent to the Marshall, contained "many suggestions for the regeneration of urban life, often happy ones."[23]

Writing to Emery in January 1942, he remarked that he found only "mediocrity, hostility, cliques" at Vichy. "Is this a reason for surrender? Never."[24] From his tiny hotel room he plotted a spring offensive. He never considered offering a compromise plan to the Algiers authorities. Instead he applied directly to the Governor-General of Algeria, A. R. Chatel, to create a Committee for the Study of Housing and Urbanism for Algeria.[25] The committee was to be advisory, but Le Corbusier's real aim was to turn it into a superagency which would have power over all the local bodies.[26]

In April 1942, Le Corbusier again went to Algiers to make his final effort to get his way. He brought with him his last and most ambitious plan for Algiers, covering seventy-five years of urban development.[27] To the leaders of Algiers he declared, "I give you my help; the least you can think of it is that it represents the result in ideas of courage, tenacity, and an unshakable confidence in the possibilities of our time."[28]

This, it seems, was insufficient. The new plan soon provoked even more opposition than the old. The municipal officials were hostile to modern architecture and unwilling to risk the capital investment that Le Corbusier's plan required. They objected in particular to Le Corbusier's provision for preserving the Casbah untouched. The municipality wished to demolish a large section of it and replace the "slum" with housing for Europeans.[29]

If Le Corbusier had been in Vichy working through his remaining friends in power, he might have saved the situation. Unfortunately, he was in Algiers, the worst position for him, for he lost no time in antagonizing his enemies and exasperating his friends. The Mayor of Algiers denounced him to the Prefect as a Communist and (according to Le Corbusier) demanded his arrest.[30] He returned to Vichy on May 22, and on June 12 the Algerian City Council voted definitively and unanimously to reject his plans.[31] The authorities in Vichy were unwilling to reverse the decision. He conceded defeat and left Vichy for Paris on July 1, 1942. "Adieux, cher merdeux Vichy!" was his parting judgment.[32]

Le Corbusier was deeply disappointed by his Vichy experience, but never deeply troubled. One more regime had proved its unworthiness by rejecting him and his plans; that was his final judgment of Vichy. What seems worst about this episode in his life is that he never seems to have realized its meaning.[33] He never acknowledged the link between his plans and the authoritarian nature of the regime. Even while at Vichy he was fond of calling himself a nonpolitical "technician" who dealt objectively with problems of technology and design. There was a certain truth in this assertion. He never modified his plans to suit the tastes of his superiors. The designs he attempted to force on Algiers in the name of the Marshal were among his most joyous conceptions of the potentials for modern life. But in his anxiety to build he failed to distinguish between coercive and noncoercive authority, exploitative and nonexploitative hierarchies. In his concern for the *administrative state* he had lost touch with the *just state*.

Although he was neither racist nor collaborationist, he gave his best talents to a regime that was both, and turned against it only after it had failed to support him. This was a personal as well as doctrinal failure. He had spent eighteen months in daily and demeaning contact with the powerful at Vichy before he finally cried *merde*, eighteen months of self-deception and willing blindness. His was a failure of imagination, a failure to perceive.

Le Corbusier never apologized for his role at Vichy, but his social thought was irrevocably changed by it. The fascination with authority disappeared. His search for a movement that combined extremes of leadership and mass enthusiasm was over. These phenomena now frightened him. His constant adage became "The river flows between two banks; there is no truth in the extremes."[34] This moderation was perhaps admirable in itself, but it jarred with his plans for the future. His ideal city was based on the belief that the polar opposites of authority and participation could be joined in the building of a new society. Where could the Radiant City be found, if not at the extremes?

27

Triumph and Disillusionment

IN 1937, Le Corbusier published *Quand les cathédrales étaient blanches* ("When the Cathedrals Were White"), a book whose title expressed his faith that the modern age was about to enter a great age of synthesis comparable to the burst of creativity that built the medieval cathedrals. Our age was as young and as promising as the early Middle Ages. "I feel young as well," he added. "Before I die I hope to participate in great transformations."[1] He had just turned fifty. When he turned sixty in 1947, his attitude had changed. He no longer hoped for a great wave of enthusiasm and authority to sweep Europe; the prospect scared him. He realized that the great transformation he had wished for would have to occur slowly, if at all. "The dreams of my twenties," he predicted in 1964, "will be realized in three hundred years."[2]

Ironically, he lost faith in his great mission precisely when his own reputation as a father of modern architecture was finally established, when he became an inspiration in the academies instead of an enemy, and when authority finally permitted him to build on an urban scale. In 1945 the French Ministry of Reconstruction commissioned Le Corbusier to build a Unité for Marseilles. In 1950 the state of Punjab in India appointed him architectural adviser for its new capital, Chandigarh.

The Unité and Chandigarh were the crowning achievements of Le Corbusier's career as a city planner, but also the crowning ironies. In both cases he created masterpieces of design appropriate for the Radiant City, but not for the societies in which they were actually built. Le Corbusier had hoped that the Unité would prove that Machine Age construction had now put modern housing within the reach of all classes. Unfortunately, in his anxiety to make the Unité the model of all his theories, he failed to adapt his design to the limitations of French postwar industry. The Unité was an architectural triumph, but one so costly that it discouraged the emulation Le Corbusier had wished to promote.

In Chandigarh the opposition between the city and the society in which it existed reached the level of the absurd. He was finally given the opportunity to shape a city according to his principles, but these principles had been devised to express the life of the most advanced industrial civilizations. The great highways of Chandigarh are empty of traffic; the city itself has become a group of almost isolated villages which occupy odd corners in the ground plan. Only the government center —a magnificent ensemble of Palace of Justice, Assembly Hall, and Secretariat—functions as planned.[3]

The Unité and Chandigarh stand as monuments to an industrial society that does not yet exist, and perhaps never will. Le Corbusier always assumed that his architecture was a response to the great new era; and indeed, its magnificent new forms derived their élan from his conviction that they were part of a still greater transformation. When the revolution he expected did not occur, he did not abandon his architecture.

He ignored the social context and created isolated monuments to his own genius.

In his architecture he continued to grow and change as he explored new forms and the expressive use of color and natural materials. In such masterpieces as the chapel at Ronchamp (1950–1955) and the monastery of La Tourette(1956–1959) he revived or adapted the handicrafts techniques of his youth to create a synthesis of the natural and the mechanical within the design itself. This final synthesis was not, however, reflected in his urbanism. There his plans stayed within the categories he had established in the 1920s and 1930s. Perhaps his last significant innovation for our purposes was the linear city. The great urban centers, he argued, must be connected by transportation corridors along which new factories and housing could be built. The factories would receive their raw materials and ship their finished goods along the corridor; the housing would be convenient to the factories and at the same time border on the open countryside that everywhere surrounds the corridor. He envisioned Europe spanned by a great east-west linear city that stretched from the Atlantic to the Urals. Other linear cities would link the North Sea to the Mediterranean.[4]

Le Corbusier's drawings of this linear city system ignore national boundaries and even the post-war division between East and West. This was the last embodiment of his Saint-Simonian hopes for a Europe beyond politics, devoid of ideological or national barriers, united by the objective logic of technology and geography. Yet the implicit denial of political and ideological realities also expressed his loss of faith in positive action. He saw no hope in any political system. They were all run by "bureaucrats closed in on themselves," incapable of new initiatives, "*Messieurs les Non*," as he called them.[5] These bureaucrats were especially incapable of understanding his work. His many achievements were overshadowed in his own mind by the commissions he wanted desperately but failed to receive: the United Nations Building in New York, the UNESCO Building in Paris, the rebuilding of the center of West Berlin. Siegfried Giedion, a close friend, recalled that "a profound bitterness was etched into Le Corbusier's features . . ." because he had convinced himself that "it was his fate to be obstructed and misunderstood in the realization of his work, always to be mistrusted and pushed aside."[6]

Le Corbusier was forced to the conclusion that his imagination would inevitably separate him from those who held power, and that his efforts were doomed to frustration. In 1952 he told a group of notables who had assembled for the dedication of the Unité, "You realize that imagination is not the strong-point of ministers, or mayors, or municipal councils, or associations of veterans, or trade unions of all kinds. Imagination is a gift of the gods to a very few, and it earns them innumerable kicks in the ass for the whole of their life."[7]

Although he continued to pursue his architectural practice with vigor, he turned away from the realm of collective fulfillment. After the death of his wife in 1957, he increasingly lived alone. He built a small cabin in the south of France near Cap Martin; there he escaped for long periods of meditation. The cabin and an even smaller workroom 6 feet by 12 feet were like monks' cells, planned down to the smallest detail to eliminate the superfluous. It was there, perhaps, that he wrote the words that can serve as his final evaluation of his efforts to create a new world. "My absorption in the preparation of plans," he observed, "is no unpleasant task. It is the most magnificent work there is. It's not the putterings of an eccentric but a daily act of joy. In front of us is light and free spaces. One moves from solution to solution." He compared planning to a "vast symphonic sport that creates cities by the force of the imagination, a game of chess that profoundly, silently—yes, even for forty years of a man's life— absorbs all the resources of his mind, all the feelings of his heart, in sculpting urban and rural splendors." The capacity to plan, he concluded, is a "gift from the most beautiful side of life."[8]

Still healthy and active after seventy-five years, Le Corbusier seemed capable of rivaling Frank Lloyd Wright even in longevity. But he died suddenly on August 27, 1965 after suffering a heart attack while swimming alone near his cabin. He was 77. In honor of his contributions to French culture, the Ministry of Cultural Affairs paid an elaborate homage to his memory. The Cour Carrée of the Louvre was filled with all the pomp and eloquence that André Malraux could muster. There was an element of hypocrisy in the ceremony, for the Ministry had persistently vetoed Le Corbusier's dream of crowning his career with the first high-rise structure in central Paris. Nevertheless, this posthumous tribute from authority, held amid the baroque splendors of Louis XIV's palace, had an ironic appropriateness. It was a funeral worthy of a modern Colbert.

28

Summation

L E CORBUSIER defies summation. He escapes like Houdini from even the most ingenious interpretation. Lewis Mumford, one of his most perceptive and persistent critics, has tried for more than forty years to give a definitive account of Le Corbusier's triumphs and failings. An admirer of Ebenezer Howard, Mumford usually emphasizes the failings. "From the time I read the first edition of his *Vers une architecture*," he once remarked, "I knew we were . . . predestined enemies."[1]

Mumford, an admirer of Ebenezer Howard and the Garden City movement, has consistently rejected Le Corbusier's glorification of the centralized metropolis. In an article published in 1962 titled "Yesterday's City of Tomorrow," he argued that Le Corbusier, in putting forward an ideal city for the twentieth century, was in fact reviving and glorifying the most pernicious practices of the nineteenth. The whole city, he wrote, was inspired by that great nineteenth-century pseudo-religion, the worship of science and technology. Its size reflected the Victorian love of bigness for its own sake. Wrapped in twentieth-century glass and steel, the design embodied the Napoleonic dream of absolute, centralized power which haunted the nineteenth century.[2]

Today, Mumford's view of Le Corbusier has become almost standard. His Le Corbusier is an elitist technocrat, an authoritarian classicist, a sociologically naïve formalist with his grand design, "his Cartesian clarity and his Cartesian elegance but also—alas!—with his Baroque insensitiveness to time, change, organic adaptation, functional fitness, ecological complexity."[3] The portrait is at once perceptive and wholly misleading. It captures the detached, gem-hard, purist side of him, but does not even hint at the Le Corbusier who designed the Chapel at Ronchamp; the self-proclaimed poet who declared that all planning must begin from the premise of individual liberty; the creator of the Unités, the realm of equality, family, leisure, and self-fulfillment. If, as Mumford asserts, Le Corbusier was the twentieth-century champion of the spirit of triumphant industrialization, he was also an heir to the movement which sought to eliminate the barbarisms of the Machine Age.

Victor Prouvé, the founder of an arts-and-crafts school at Nancy which greatly influenced the young Le Corbusier and his teacher L'Eplattenier, once painted a picture which showed workers streaming out of a grimy factory town. They were accompanied by their wives and children, who were strewing them with flowers and leading them toward the open countryside. Prouvé called the painting *The General Strike*.[4] Le Corbusier never discarded the critique of nineteenth-cenutry industrialization which he had learned from the arts-and-crafts movement. He did reject the idea that the problem could be solved by fleeing into a world of trees, grass, flowers, and handicrafts. His experience of the "crisis of the artisans" at La Chaux-de-Fonds convinced him that large-scale production and its consequences—great cities and bureaucracies—were inevitable in the modern world. To stake art or freedom on the survival of the preindustrial style of life was to risk the loss of both. The "Green City" must be found *within* the "City of Towers" or not at all.

Le Corbusier faced, as neither Wright nor Howard had done, the scale of modern life and the problems of order and authority which this scale raised. The great city was unavoidable; it must be mastered, its potential for beauty and freedom exploited. For Le Corbusier, as Mumford correctly observed, mastering the city meant intensifying the elements of centralized organization within it. He was afraid above all of the disorder of great cities, that "cancer" which made both organization and liberty impossible. Yet this was never organization for its own sake. Prouvé and L'Eplattenier find their place in Le Corbusier's plans along with Colbert and Haussmann. The administrative city, as we have seen, exists to create its counterpart: the world of leisure, craftsmanship, and the family, the Green City. Both make up the Radiant City.

Le Corbusier's social thought is thus a play of opposites: authority and freedom, organization and individuality, mechanization and craftsmanship, planning and spontaneity. He held tenaciously to all these opposites and, if his efforts make him difficult to summarize, they also make him the most complex and fascinating figure in modern design. As a social thinker he can perhaps be best compared with another Swiss watchmaker's son who continues to perplex commentators, Jean-Jacques Rousseau. Both men organized their thought around the polarity of absolute union with the community and detached, spiritually self-sufficient individuality. Rousseau's "two paths to the sublime" were that of the citizen of the *Social Contract*, in wholehearted identification with the "general will," and that of the "solitary Walker," the isolated individual who finds the sublime through identification with all nature. Le Corbusier's two analogous paths were that of the worker, who forms an integral part of an organization dedicated to "great works," and that of the artist or craftsman, who creates the "indispensable poetry" of life. Both men sought to reconcile these opposites in a single figure who combined the social authority of the community with the spiritual authority of the individual. Rousseau most clearly depicted this figure as the Tutor in *Émile*; Le Corbusier presented him as the modern Colbert, the planner who merges imagination with power. Both men combined an attitude of reverence toward an imagined authority with an almost paranoid suspiciousness of actual authorities. As they grew older, both grew increasingly bitter toward those whom they saw as irrationally rejecting their ideas and themselves. Both died alone.

This comparison of Rousseau and Le Corbusier suggests a further problem. Several critics have attempted to isolate an authoritarian or even totalitarian element in Rousseau's thought. They focus on Rousseau's idea that there is a general will which expresses the true interests of all the citizens. To dissent from the general will is to act against one's own interests; any citizen who acts so irrationally must be "forced to be free." The analogue in Le Corbusier's thought is the plan, the general will of an industrial society. It expresses everyone's true interests in the form of a comprehensive directive for production and construction.

Just as Rousseau was unable to formulate the rights of individuals to resist the general will, so Le Corbusier makes no provision for legitimate opposition to the plan. Here his synthesis of authority and participation seems to break down. He was unable even to conceive of an approach to action which combines the two in a meaningful way. His view of the planner as the artist of society—the "symphonic sportsman" who creates a vast social harmony—carries with it the implication that the planner must have the same freedom to manipulate his materials that the artist has with his. The experts who draw up the plans act beyond the reach of elections or parliaments. They consult only their own understanding of society's needs, resources, and values. They act from above through the medium of the great administrative hierarchies. The plans, with their principles of standardization, rationalization, and classification, are designed to mesh with the needs of the large organizations which must carry them out; they make no provision for individual exceptions. In such a system there is no room even for a "loyal opposition"; administration has indeed replaced politics. There is diversity —each society, each city has its own industrial symphony— but dissent within the system can only mean disorder.

One need not draw out the relationship oí these ideas to modern authoritarian movements. Le Corbusier made the connection himself at Vichy. We must recognize, however, that his search for a perfectly administered social order was more than a reflection of the antidemocratic spirit so prevalent in Europe between the wars. Le Corbusier's hostility to democracy was closer to Plato's than to Pétain's. The details of social planning and syndicalist organization in the Radiant City are used to express an ideal as old as the *Republic*: the ideal of a society ruled not by "opinion" but by truth. For Le Corbusier the rule of a worthy elite is the opposite of authoritarian domination by force. It reflects the natural hierarchy in society. The planner's authority rests on his ability to discern and promote the well-being of the whole, to guide self-seeking individuals into accord with the larger order. For Le Corbusier, urban design—indeed, the planning of a whole society—was in the realm of truth, not politics.

His concept of authority thus has little in common with the ideologies of the dictatorships or democracies of his time. Its roots are in classical political thought, the tradition to which Le Corbusier, with his "Cartesian clarity" and rigor, instinctively returned. His ideas, however, differ from the Platonic tradition in one crucial respect. The authority of the philosophers in the *Republic* was rational and verbal; there the artist was a potentially subversive figure to be kept under strict discipline. For Le Corbusier, however, the power of the elite was primarily imaginative. The fundamental task of the planners was to make the harmony of the whole real and active through design.

Le Corbusier once called the Unité a "vertical community without politics."[5] He meant that the design itself brings the residents together into a community and directs their relationships into cooperative channels. Politics, by which he meant unproductive conflict, no longer exists. For him, the plan of the city is its real constitution. It not only symbolizes the harmony of society, it also creates harmony. It is the fundamental level of social organization. In the Radiant City, therefore, the planner plays the role of philosopher-king. Only he can bring society into accord with the "cosmic laws" of order and create that healthy social equilibrium which Le Corbusier called harmony and Plato called justice.

CONCLUSION

THE URBAN THEORIES of Le Corbusier were intended as a refutation of Frank Lloyd Wright and especially Ebenezer Howard, yet they embody a conception of the ideal city which goes back to that morning in 1888 when Howard, inspired by his reading of *Looking Backward*, walked through the dark crowded streets of the London slums. As Howard meditated on Bellamy's demonstration of the "absolute unsoundness of our economic system," he was suddenly struck by "an overwhelming sense of the temporary nature" of the urban environment that surrounded him and of its "entire unsuitability for the working life of the new order—the order of justice, unity and friendliness."[1] However much Wright and Le Corbusier were to differ with Howard, they came to share his perception that the nineteenth-century metropolis, so deeply bound up with an unjust social order, was necessarily "unsuitable" for the social reconstruction all three believed to be inevitable. The new order would need new cities.

At the heart of the three planners' theory of the ideal city lay a contrast between the dying old cities and the new. For all three, the old cities had become self-consuming cancers because they had degenerated into a means of exploitation. The capitalist system had given control over the environment to thousands of speculators and landlords, each seeking to increase his profits. Since the individual landowners' decisions were necessarily shortsighted and uncoordinated, they could result only in destructive disorder. Laissez-faire had thus created the metropolis in its own image: chaotic, ugly, inhuman. For Howard, Wright, and Le Corbusier, the great city represented the landscape of selfishness, a whole environment built by greed.

Their ideal cities were to be planned cities. This meant that human rationality would take control from the blind operation of economic forces. Profitability would no longer determine a city's structure; the community would assert its mastery over self-seeking individuals. The common good would be embodied in every detail of the city's plan. In such a setting the harmony inherent in industrial society would finally be achieved. This harmony would find its physical expression in the logic and efficiency of the urban plan; its social expression in first-rate housing available to all and in magnificent public facilities for everyone's use; and its aesthetic realization in the beauty of the city as a whole.

Between the old city and the new stands the planner. He sees beyond the social conflicts of his time to the true order of industrial society. His imagination is the first to comprehend the common good and give it form as a design for a new kind of community. This is the source of his authority, an authority that Howard, Wright, and Le Corbusier believed to be deeper and truer than that of any political leader. For the planner does not sponsor the goals of any single group. Rather, he works to create a society in which all social differences would be reconciled. His plans do not mirror public opinion—which in any case is divided and uncertain—but instead reflect an understanding of the course which must be followed for a just and beautiful society to emerge. The planner must therefore unite imagination with power. This is the path to the ideal city.

These are the assumptions that guided the work of Howard, Wright, and Le Corbusier. But what, finally, are we to think of their audacious hopes? What meaning, if any, can their quest have for us? Like so many other confident predictions of the future, their ideas now seem firmly circumscribed by the limited perspectives of their own time. In particular, their uncritical faith in the power of planning to solve society's ills appears as quaint to us as the "rugged individualism" it was meant to replace. For all three were optimists about the future of industrial society, and the twentieth century has not been kind to optimists. We have seen too many well-intentioned plans defeated by the unexpected complexity of the task, too many triumphs of technology turned to inhuman ends, too many well-organized institutions used not for liberation but for repression, too much conflict, irrationality, hatred, blood-shed, and sheer barbarism among even the most advanced nations for us to believe that industrial society is headed inevitably toward brotherhood and harmony. The ideal cities of Howard, Wright, and Le Corbusier have not been pushed aside by more up-to-date solutions. They have been super-seded by the belief that no such "solution" exists.

There is now a widespread reaction against the idea of large-scale planning. Its most profound source, I believe, is the loss of confidence in the reality of a common good or pur-pose which can become the basis of city life. The planner's claim to be serving the interests of all—the basis of his authority—is now seen as either a foolish delusion or, worse, a hypocritical attempt to impose his own limited values on everyone else. In the recent literature on urban problems, planners have been pictured as arrogant, undemocratic ma-nipulators bent on clamping a sterile uniformity over the diversity of modern life. In these analyses the characteristic values of Howard, Wright, and Le Corbusier are completely and ironically reversed. The three planners saw the chaos and diversity of the great city as a kind of disease and the worst enemy of social harmony. Their critics have no desire to conform to an all-embracing harmony that leaves people unable to plan for themselves. They put their trust in diversity and see in urban disorder the last, best hope for individual freedom and self-realization.

Conclusion

The best way to define these attitudes is to consider the arguments of what is surely the most influential work on planning in recent years, *The Death and Life of Great American Cities* (1961), by Jane Jacobs. The book is remarkable for its refreshing freedom from pseudo-scientific jargon and for its beautifully rendered observations of the mundane but all-important details of urban life. She sees with a novelist's eye the complex web of behavior that makes one street lively, prosperous, and safe, and another a frightening desert; one park a cherished resource of the people who live around it, and another a wasteland to be shunned; one neighborhood a community spontaneously regenerating itself, and so many others dismal, decaying slums. She has taught a whole generation of planners how to look at the city.

Her individual observations, moreover, lead directly to a tightly reasoned argument about the limitations of planning. She begins from the conviction that the characteristic values of cities—and the qualities that keep them prosperous and healthy—are intensity and diversity. What cities need most, she writes, is a "most intricate and close-grained diversity of uses that give each other constant mutual support."[2] These "uses" (i.e., the thousands of services, skills, and entertainments a great city offers) form a pattern of urban life that is far too complicated to be anticipated or created by even the most powerful planner working from outside. Big cities, observes Jacobs, are "just too big and too complex to be comprehended in detail from any vantage point—even if this vantage point is at the top—or to be comprehended by any human; yet detail is of the essence."[3]

What the most powerful planner cannot accomplish, however, thousands of individuals and small groups can. Their independent, unpredictable choices create precisely the vitality the city needs most. Operating without guidance or approval from above, individuals decide to open a restaurant in an abandoned storefront; to convert a loft into a ballet school or a judo academy; to offer a service or product never before

268

needed. Jacobs cites the example of an old building in Louisville which had housed, among other things, an athletic club, a riding academy, an artist's studio, a blacksmith's forge, and a warehouse, and was currently a flourishing center for the arts. "Who could anticipate or provide for such a succession of hopes and schemes?" she asks. "Only an unimaginative man would think he could; only an arrogant man would want to."[4] She concludes that "most city diversity is the creation of incredible numbers of different people and different private organizations, with vastly differing ideas and purposes, planning and contriving outside the formal framework of public action."[5]

The implications for the planner are clear. He must work as modestly and unobtrusively as possible to develop "cities that are congenial places for this vast range of unofficial plans, ideas and opportunities to flourish."[6] Jacobs angrily rejects Le Corbusier's concept of "urban surgery," for it means imposing his one plan over everyone else's. His neatly arranged skyscrapers-in-the-park, she argues, are a terrible oversimplification of urban order. Their rigid separation of functions makes a true diversity impossible; their inhuman scale and vast empty spaces kill off the close-knit vitality of an attractive city. She neatly turns Le Corbusier's biological analogies on their head. For her, the high-rise housing projects and business districts are the dying "unsanitary islands" of the modern city, and the dense, complex districts that Le Corbusier wanted to level are the true sources of urban health.

Above all, Jacobs believes that the planner must no longer try, as Howard, Wright, and Le Corbusier once tried, to define the central goals of his society and offer a unified plan for attaining them. One sees this most vividly in the polemic against Ebenezer Howard that runs through her book. She chose Howard as her target because he seemed to her to be the source of so many of the attitudes toward planning she opposes. Howard, Jacobs claims, "conceived of good planning as a series of static acts; in each case the plan must anticipate all that is needed and be protected, after it is built, against any but the most minor subsequent changes. He conceived of planning also as essentially paternalistic, if not authoritarian."[7] This is, of course, a caricature of Howard's real views. As we have seen, he was a flexible and modest man who was very much concerned with allowing the residents of the Garden City to shape their own future.

Nevertheless, it is certainly true that the Garden City, like Broadacre City and the Radiant City, was not conceived as a neutral environment. Howard designed it to promote the values he believed in—small-scale cooperation, family life, contact with nature—and to discourage those practices he abhorred: large-scale industry, land speculation, accumulations of power. For Howard these were not merely personal preferences but embodiments of the era of cooperation and brotherhood toward which mankind was evolving. Jacobs, however, regards this attitude as "paternalistic" or worse. She disagrees not so much with his particular choice of values as with his right to make a choice; for he was necessarily restricting the options of others. The Garden Cities, she comments pointedly, were "really very nice towns if you were docile and had no plans of your own and did not mind spending your life among others with no plans of their own. As in all Utopias, the right to have plans of any significance belonged only to the planners in charge."[8] In Jacob's ideal city it is the planners who have no significant plans of their own. The common good is served through maximizing the individual's opportunity to pursue his own ends.

Jacobs wanted to shake up a planning profession which was all too complacent in its conviction that "urban renewal" —more slum clearance, more high-rise housing projects, more highways—held the answer to all urban problems. She wrote, moreover, when it was all too easy for politicians and planners to override citizens' objections and to impose their own values on people who had neither the opportunity nor the desire to practice them. In this context, Jacobs's theories were a genuinely liberating force. One can only regret that her ideas could not do more to stop the many disastrous projects which still disfigure the cities.

Yet, for all her enthusiasm for cities, Jacobs's message is an essentially negative one. Her faith in individual action is more than counterbalanced by an overwhelming skepticism about what people can accomplish together. To go from Howard to Jacobs is to go from a world that can still be radically re-formed to one whose physical and social foundations cannot be moved. For Jacobs, the cities are already built. They can be renovated but never transformed. To expect citizens to agree on a better kind of city and unite together for its construction is either a delusion or the self-serving illusion of the "new aristocracy of altruistic planning experts." Nor does her very real concern for the urban poor imply a commitment to any economic or social reforms. Indeed, the logic of her argument calls for even greater freedom for the capitalist entrepreneur.

Jacobs is especially skeptical about government. We see in her work nothing of Le Corbusier's hopes for a corps of expert administrators who bring order and beauty to the urban environment. Government for her creates more problems than it solves. She depicts a bureaucracy composed of mazes

> too labyrinthine even to be kept mapped and open, let alone to serve as reliable and sensitive channels . . . of action for getting things done. Citizens and officials both can wander indefinitely in these labyrinths, passing here and there the bones of many an old hope, dead of exhaustion.[9]

She recommends that planners be confined to local administrative units where, if the mazes are no less labyrinthine, they are necessarily smaller. At the local level, moreover, planners can be carefully watched by the citizens. Jacobs's most enthusiastic renderings of civic action are always reserved for those occasions when people join together to resist a highway or some other project being forced on them by their own officials.

Even while glorifying the "intricate and close-knit" city, Jacobs communicates a disquieting sense of an environment out of control, of complexities beyond human capacity to deal with, of systems so huge and unwieldy as to defy any radical attempt at change. In such a world the individual might succeed at creating for himself a comfortable niche, but the planner with great expectations must fail out of ignorance or oversimplification. Her critique of large-scale planning is reminiscent of the works of Joseph de Maistre and other conservatives of the early nineteenth century who damned the insolence of the American and French revolutionaries for presuming to write their own constitutions. Such works, they claimed, were too complex for the human mind. It is no doubt significant that our twentieth-century de Maistre, William F. Buckley, Jr., has included a long section from Jacobs's work in his anthology of American conservative thought.[10]

We must not suppose, however, that Jacobs's conclusions are held exclusively, or even predominantly, on the right. Her work has had a significant impact on the left, perhaps most notably in a book by the sociologist and urban historian Richard Sennett, *The Uses of Disorder* (1970). Sennett, who identifies himself with the anarchist tradition, accepts almost all of Jacobs's premises and carries them even further. He believes the planners' search for harmony is not only bad urban policy but even worse psychology. For him, this goal stems not from altruism but from a "fear of the sources of human diversity."[11] It is a refusal to accept the unpleasant truth that conflict and disorder are inevitable in any society. To evade this truth, planners unconsciously try to simplify the world and to mold it in their own image. Sennett compares the planner to an adolescent who avoids the pain of growing up by rigidly confining himself within a safe and familiar world.

To the extent that planners actually succeed in homogenizing the environment, they keep not only themselves but also the rest of society in a state of prolonged adolescence. Sennett holds that the only path to adulthood lies "in the acceptance of disorder and painful dislocation."[12] And this can best be achieved in what he calls "a dense, uncontrollable human settlement," his phrase for Jacobs's "intricate and close-knit" city. In such an area there are too many different groups in too small a space for any one group to enforce its values. No one can isolate himself from conflict. Everyone, therefore, is forced to become an adult.

Sennett fears that the municipal authorities in this dense, uncontrollable human settlement might nevertheless try to impose their own version of order. To counter this, he recommends that not only planning but virtually all other city services be either eliminated or controlled locally. His aim is to promote what he calls "a disordered, unstable, direct social life." Land-use laws would be repealed, and "if a bar down the street were too noisy for the children of the neighborhood to sleep, the parents would have to squeeze the bar owner themselves, by picketing or informal pressure, for no zoning laws would apply throughout the city."[13] Police control of civil disorder would be sharply reduced, so that neighborhoods would be responsible for keeping the peace themselves. Schools would be under direct local control.

Sennett admits that the citizens in such neighborhoods would experience a "high level of tension and unease," but he adds that "it would be better in the end if they did feel uncomfortable, and began to experience a sense of dislocation in their lives."[14] For their discontents would lead them to confront their problems directly. Without a professional bureaucracy to mediate for them, they would be forced to deal with people different from themselves and to experience in their own lives the movement from conflict to agreement. A disorder that brings freedom, diversity, and maturity is thus preferable to the bland, deceptive pleasures of harmony. With

Conclusion

Sennett we have come full circle: Howard looked at the "dense, uncontrollable human settlement" of contemporary London and resolved that mankind must be taken away from such environs; Sennett wants to put us back.

Whatever the limitations or extravagances of Sennett's arguments, he and Jane Jacobs speak far more directly to the concerns of our time than do those who still urge large-scale planning. At "Habitat,' the United Nations Conference on Human Settlements held June 1976 in Vancouver, Le Corbusier and his ideas of urban surgery were repeatedly attacked. The conference recommended renovating the decaying stock of housing and factories in old neighborhoods rather than striking out in any radically new directions.[15] To be sure, a loss in funding has dramatically spurred the loss of faith in the old projects, yet this loss reflects a larger shift in priorities.

The technology for an "era of great works" exists, more powerful now than even Le Corbusier imagined it would be. What is lacking is the confidence that we know how to use it. Only the New Towns program in Europe and the United States still survives as an active force. The first of the three planners' programs to be implemented, it may also prove to be the last. A more fitting symbol for our present paralysis is the fate of the Pruitt-Igoe Towers in St. Louis. When constructed as part of an urban renewal project begun in 1954, these welfare Unités were conceived as a union of high-rise technology and beneficent public administration. Like so many other projects, the Towers fell victim to poor design and inadequate maintenance; at the same time, the "parks" between them turned into no-man's-lands. In desperation the city authorities decided in 1972 to abandon and then to destroy most of Pruitt-Igoe. This once-promising new environment met its ultimate critic—the wrecker—and in minutes there was nothing left but rubble.[16]

One might conclude that Lewis Mumford's phrase "Yesterday's City of Tomorrow" applies to all three ideal cities, though in a broader sense than Mumford intended it. The difficulty is not with the details of the plans; rather, the very concept of the ideal city appears to belong to the past. As we have seen, the plans of Wright, Howard, and Le Corbusier assume that disorder and conflict will eventually be overcome in a harmonious industrial society; that human understanding can grasp and human will can solve the problems of society; and that reason, imagination, and social concern can come together in a unified design. They hold that the planner can successfully look beyond the limitations of particular issues and concern himself with larger questions, even (perhaps especially) the good of the whole. Once these assumptions fade, the ideal city becomes a mere fantasy—the planner's vain attempt to mold society in his own image.

There is, however, one significant trend that points to the productive survival of the habits of thought embodied in the ideal city. If the energy crisis of the 1970s has diminished our resources for dealing with social problems, it has at least stimulated new interest in the larger issues of social policy. In particular, planners have been examining the implications of the overall structure of American metropolitan areas. They discern an "order" very different from anything Howard, Wright, or Le Corbusier foresaw, and one which Jacobs and Sennett could never endorse. In the center of the typical metropolitan area is a business, administrative, and cultural "core", with its complement of expensive apartments and town houses. Surrounding this core, however, is a decaying "inner belt" of substandard and abandoned housing, low-wage jobs, high crime, and inadequate city services. This inner belt is continually threatening to encroach upon the adjacent communities of the "outer ring" of suburbs, which form the furthest limits of the metropolitan area. As the inner belt deteriorates, those who can do so flee further and further into suburbia, and the suburbs expand inexorably along the superhighways into what had been open farmland.

The result is an absurd and expensive dispersion. Convenient locations in the inner belt that are minutes away from the central core degenerate into wastelands, while people laboriously commute from the remote outskirts of the region. Solidly built homes, schools, and other facilities in the inner belt are allowed to deteriorate until they have to be abandoned, while comparable facilities are being constructed at great cost in former orchards and cornfields. The pattern is wasteful, divisive, and culturally debilitating. Even the United States may not be able to support it indefinitely.

Jacobs and Sennett have argued that this dispersion is far from "unplanned," and they correctly point to government highway and mortgage policies as prime causes of our present problems. Yet precisely because the crisis has grown in large part out of past mistakes in policy, it is unlikely that Jacobs's or Sennett's anti-planning strategies will ever be effective in solving it. "A region," says Jacobs, "is an area safely larger than the last one to which we found no solution"[17]; but only coordinated action on a regional scale can hope to be effective. Already there is wide agreement among planners and citizens alike that further suburban expansion into the countryside must be restricted, and that this negative measure must be combined with positive efforts to revive the inner belt.

These efforts necessarily raise anew the larger questions to which Howard, Wright, and Le Corbusier addressed themselves: What is the proper relationship between the central city and its region? How large can an urban area grow before it loses coherence and efficiency? Which design best embodies modern techniques of transportation? Which design best serves social justice? Planners confront these questions not out of a desire to be paternalistic dictators but in order to comprehend the full implications of their actions and thus work more effectively to achieve their goals. And they confront the question of values not as a search for some utopian harmony or in order to impose their self-image on others, but because planning can never be separated from consideration of the common good.

At the moment, however, these tentative efforts at large-scale planning are dwarfed by the still larger scale of the problem. We cannot know whether even the best plan will win enough support to have a significant impact. We are left, finally, with this dilemma: if the need for large-scale planning has been growing more acute, the resistance to it is also gaining strength.

"Tomorrow," observed Samuel Johnson, "is an old deceiver, and his cheat never grows stale."[18] Howard, Wright, and Le Corbusier believed that the twentieth century would be a period of social reconstruction crowned by the creation of magnificent new cities. They were wrong, but who can say that their critics might not also be surprised? For, in spite of all the controversies and changing perspectives, their ideal cities still defy time. They exist—preserved in the blueprints, drawings, books, articles, and letters on which their creators lavished so much hope and genius. There, at least, we can always find the cooperative quadrangles and quiet shops of the Garden City; the Usonian farms, roadside markets, and unspoiled landscape of Broadacre City; and the great, orderly skyscrapers and superhighways of the Radiant City. The plans endure, unchanging and unconsummated.

NOTES

Introduction

1. Joseph Conrad, *The Secret Agent* (New York, 1953), p. 11. The quotation is drawn from the Preface, first published in 1921.

2. For statistics of urban growth, see Adna Ferrin Weber, *The Growth of Cities in the Nineteenth Century* (Ithaca, N.Y., 1899).

3. Hsi-Huey Liang, "Lower-class Immigrants in Wilhelmine Berlin," In *The Urbanization of European Society in the Nineteenth Century*, eds. Andrew Lees and Lynn Lees (Lexington, Mass. 1976), p. 223.

4. Le Corbusier, *La ville radieuse* (Boulogne-Seine, 1935), p. 181.

5. For Owen, see J. F. C. Harrison, *Quest for the New Moral World* (New York, 1969).

6. For Fourier, see Jonathan Beecher and Richard Bienvenu, eds., *The Utopian Vision of Charles Fourier* (Boston, 1971).

7. For Haussmann and his influence see David H. Pinkney, *Napoleon III and the Rebuilding of Paris* (Princeton, N.J., 1958); Howard Saalman, *Haussmann: Paris Transformed* (New York, 1971); and Anthony Sutcliffe, *The Autumn of Central Paris* (London, 1970).

8. Peter H. Mann, "Octavia Hill: An Appraisal," *Town Planning Review* 23, no. 3 (Oct. 1953): 223–237.

9. Friedrich Engels, *Zur Wohnungsfrage*, 2d ed. (Leipzig, 1887).

10. See Barbara Miller Lane, *Architecture and Politics in Germany, 1918–1945* (Cambridge, Mass., 1968).

11. Le Corbusier, *Urbanisme* (Paris, 1925), p. 135.

Notes

Chapter One

1. Lewis Mumford, "The Garden City Idea and Modern Planning," introductory essay to F. J. Osborn's edition of *Garden Cities of To-morrow* (Cambridge, Mass., 1965), p. 29. Although Osborn's edition bears the title of the 1902 edition, his text restores portions of the 1898 text that were cut in 1902. Osborn's is therefore a "definitive" text and I follow his usage in always referring to Howard's book as *Garden Cities of To-morrow*. All further references will come from Osborn's edition, abbreviated *GCT*.

2. See Donald Canty, ed., *The New City* (New York, 1969) for the details of this recommendation.

3. The New Towns, however, have had their problems. See " 'New Towns' Face Growing Pains," *New York Times*, June 13, 1976. p. 26.

4. F. J. Osborn, Preface to *GCT*, p. 22.

5. Ibid., pp. 22–23.

Chapter Two

1. Ebenezer Howard Papers, Hertfordshire County Archives, Hertford, England. Draft of an Unfinished Autobiography, Folio 17.

2. C. C. R., "The Evolution of Ebenezer Howard," *Garden Cities and Town Planning* 2, no. 3 (Mar. 1912): 46.

3. Howard Papers, Folio 17.

4. J. Bruce Wallace, *Towards Fraternal Organization* (London, 1894), p. 19.

5. Ibid., p. 19.

6. Howard Papers, Folio 17.

7. For Bellamy's influence, see Sylvia E. Bowman, *The Year 2000: A Critical Biography of Edward Bellamy* (New York, 1958).

8. E. Howard, "Spiritual Influences Toward Social Progress," *Light*, April 30, 1910, p. 195.

9. E. Howard, "Ebenezer Howard, the Originator of the Garden City Idea," *Garden Cities and Town Planning* 16, no. 6 (July 1926): 133.

10. An account of the Nationalisation of Labour Society can be found in Peter Marshall, "A British Sensation," in Sylvia Bowman, ed., *Edward Bellamy Abroad* (New York, 1962), pp. 86–118.

11. Howard, "Ebenezer Howard, the Originator of the Garden City Idea," p. 133.

12. Edward Bellamy, *Looking Backward* (New York, 1960), p. 127.

13. Peter Kropotkin, *Fields, Factories, and Workshops* (London, 1899).

14. Howard Papers, Draft of an Autobiography, Folio 10.

15. E. Howard, *Garden Cities of To-morrow*, ed. F. J. Osborn (Cambridge, Mass., 1965), p. 131. Hereafter, *GCT*.

16. Howard Papers, Folio 10.

17. *GCT*, p. 47.

18. Ibid., p. 145.

19. Ibid., p. 146.

20. Ibid., p. 48.

Chapter Three

1. James Silk Buckingham, *National Evils and Practical Remedies, with the Plan of a Model Town* (London, 1849). Although Howard mentions the utopian city of Buckingham in the text of *GCT* as one of the proposals he combined into the Garden City, he states in a footnote that in fact he had not seen Buckingham's plan until he had "got far on" with his project. E. Howard, *Garden Cities of To-morrow*, ed. F. J. Osborn (Cambridge, Mass., 1965), p. 119. Hereafter, *GCT*.

2. Howard Papers. Early draft of GCT, Folio 3.

3. Ibid.

4. E. Howard, "Spiritual Influences Toward Social Progress," *Light*, April 30, 1910, p. 196. *Hygeia* was published in London in 1876.

5. Benjamin Ward Richardson, *Hygeia, A City of Health* (London, 1876), p. 21.

6. *GCT*, p. 76.

7. Ibid., pp. 50–56 and 71. Placing the churches along Grand Avenue means that no single church occupies the center of town. Howard's religious upbringing was Non-conformist.

8. *GCT*, p. 53.

9. Ibid., p. 54.

10. *GCT*, Diagram #2. The diagram also shows such institutions as "convalescent homes" and the "asylums for blind and deaf" in

the green belt. In an earlier version of his plan Howard wanted the Agricultural Belt to cover 8,000 acres. See his "Summary of E. Howard's proposals for a Home Colony," *The Nationalisation News* 3, no. 29 (Feb. 1893): 20.

11. Howard Papers, Common Sense Socialism, Folio 10.

12. Alfred Marshall, "The Housing of the London Poor," *Contemporary Review* 45, no. 2 (Feb. 1884): 224–231.

13. Howard Papers, Folio 10. Howard recalled meeting Marshall in connection with stenography work he did for parliamentary commissions and discussing the Garden City idea with him. In a note added to *GCT* he claimed that he had not seen Marshall's article when he first formulated his ideas. *GCT*, p. 119.

14. *GCT*, pp. 58–88.

15. Howard Papers. Quoted by Howard in an early draft of *GCT*, Folio 3.

16. *GCT*, pp. 89–111.

17. Ibid, p. 136.

18. "Return of Owners of Land Survey," analyzed in F. M. L. Thompson, *English Landed Society in the Nineteenth Century* (London, 1963), pp. 317–319.

19. Henry George, *Progress and Poverty* (New York, 1911), p. 201.

20. Howard, quoted in W. H. Brown's interview with him. "Ebenezer Howard, A Modern Influence," *Garden Cities and Town Planning* 7, no. 30 (Sept. 1908): 116.

21. *GCT*, p. 131.

22. Ibid., pp. 96–111.

23. Howard Papers, Lecture to a Fabian Society, January 11, 1901, Folio 3.

24. *GCT*, p. 104.

25. Ibid., p. 139.

26. I suspect the population of the Central City was put at 58,000 so that the whole complex would attain a population of exactly 250,000.

27. *GCT*, p. 142.

28. Ibid.

29. Ibid. Spencer held that public libraries in themselves were only "mildly communistic." See his "The New Toryism," *Contemporary Review*, 45, no. 2 (Feb. 1884): 153–167. These of course were Spencer's later views. A younger Spencer in *Social Statics* had called for the nationalization of the land. This permitted Howard to refer to Spencer as one of his influences. *GCT*, pp. 123–125.

Chapter Four

1. A handwritten text for a lecture titled "Common Sense Socialism," which can be found in the Howard Papers, summarizes all the essential parts of the Garden City idea. It is dated 1892 in the author's own hand, but the dating appears to be written many years later and may not be accurate. There is, however, a letter from Harry C. Howard to Ebenezer Howard dated 9 October 1892 (Howard Papers, Folio 25) that refers to the manuscript of Ebenezer Howard's book. This, I believe, is the early manuscript of *To-morrow* now in the Howard Papers, Folio 3. This tends to confirm that Howard had indeed formulated his ideas by 1892.

2. E. Howard, *Garden Cities of To-morrow*, ed. F. J. Osborn (Cambridge, Mass., 1965), p. 117. Hereafter, *GCT*.

3. Howard Papers, Lecture to a Fabian Society, January 11, 1901, Folio 3.

4. John Orme and J. Bruce Wallace, "A Proposed Voluntary Cooperative Commonwealth," *The Nationalisation News* 2, no. 317 (Feb. 1892): 43.

5. E. Howard, "Summary of E. Howard's Proposals for a Home Colony," *The Nationalisation News* 3, no. 29 (Feb. 1893): 20.

6. Howard was evidently deeply disappointed by this failure, because he never referred to the incident in his subsequent and frequent accounts of the history of the Garden City ideal. It was first discussed by Peter Marshall in his essay on the Bellamy movement in England already cited. The first student of the Garden City movement to draw attention to it was Stanley Buder, "Ebenezer Howard: The Genesis of a Town Planning Movement," *Journal of the American Institute of Planners* 35, no. 6 (Nov. 1969): 390–397.

7. Howard Papers, Draft of an Unfinished Autobiography, Folio 17.

8. Ibid.

9. *Times* (London), October 19, 1898. Howard's scrapbook, in which this and many other reviews and articles concerning the Garden City can be found, is now in the possession of the Welwyn Garden City Public Library.

10. Phyllis Deane and W. A. Cole, *British Economic Growth 1688–1959* (Cambridge, 1964), p. 261.

11. T. W. Fletcher, "The Great Depression in English Agriculture," *Economic History Review*, second series, 13, no. 3 (Apr. 1961): 417–432.

12. The full range of proposals can be found in J. A. Hobson, ed., *Co-operative Labour Upon the Soil* (London, 1895).

13. Alfred Russel Wallace, *Land Nationalisation* (London, 1882). Wallace is best known as the man who formulated the theory of evolution independently of Darwin.

14. *GCT*, pp. 58–65.

15. A. R. Wallace, *Land and Labour* (May 1899).

16. Ibid.

17. My own count, based on a comparison of the list of vice-presidents and other officers of the L.N.S. of 1897–98 with a membership list of the Garden City Association, 1899.

18. Howard Papers, Draft of an Autobiography, Folio 10.

19. E. Howard. "The Late Honorable Mr. Justice Neville," *Garden Cities and Town Planning* 9, no. 1 (Jan. 1919): 4–6. The article by Neville was "The Place of Cooperation in Social Economy," a Labour Association pamphlet (London, 1901).

20. Neville, "The Place of Cooperation," p. 14.

21. Ralph Neville, in the "Garden City Conference at Bournville" (London, 1901), p. 11.

22. Ralph Neville, "The Divorce of Man from Nature," *Garden Cities and Town Planning* 4, no. 34 (August 1909), p. 227.

23. Neville, "The Place of Cooperation," p. 5.

24. G. D. H. Cole, *A Century of Co-operation* (London, 1944), p. 284.

25. My own count, based on a comparison of the officers of the Labour Association in 1901 and the Garden City Association in 1902.

26. John Squire, *The Honeysuckle and the Rose* (London, 1937), p. 174.

27. See the important work by Walter R. Creese, *The Search for Environment* (New Haven, 1966), especially useful for relating the planning tradition of Bournville and Port Sunlight to the Garden City.

28. Quoted by Georges Benoît-Lévy, *La cité-jardin*, vol. II (Paris, 1911), p. 193.

29. F. L. Olmsted, "Through American Spectacles: An Expert's View of the English Garden City Schemes," *Garden Cities and Town Planning* 4, no. 33 (May 1909): 199.

30. "Garden City Conference at Bournville" (London, 1901).

31. William Ashworth, *The Genesis of Modern British Town Planning* (London, 1954).

32. G. B. Shaw, "Garden City Conference at Bournville," p. 17.

33. Howard, "The Late Hon. Mr. Justice Neville," p. 4.

34. Howard, "Garden City Conference at Bournville," p. 21.

35. Minutes of the Third Annual Meeting of the Garden City Association, December 10, 1901. The Minute Book is now in the possession of the Town and Country Planning Association, Carlton Terrace, London.

36. Ibid., July 1902.

37. Fletcher, p. 419.

38. F. M. L. Thompson, p. 105.

39. John H. Clapham, *An Economic History of Great Britain*, vol. II (Cambridge, 1961), p. 86.

40. C. B. Purdom, "At the Inception of Letchworth," *Town and Country Planning* 21, no. 113 (Sept. 1953): 426–430.

41. Ibid., p. 427.

Chapter Five

1. E. Howard, *Garden Cities of To-morrow*, ed. F. J. Osborn (Cambridge, Mass., 1965), p. 108. Hereafter, *GCT*.

2. *The Thirty-Sixth Annual Co-operative Congress* (Manchester, 1904), p. 63.

3. Ibid., pp. 65 and 83.

4. See especially Aneurin Williams, "Co-operation in Housing and Town Building," Thirty-ninth Co-operative Congress (Manchester, 1909), pp. 379–397.

5. Minutes of the Manchester Branch of the Garden City Association, April 1, 1902. Now in the possession of the Town and Country Planning Association.

6. Howard Papers, Letter of Neville to Howard, November 13, 1903. Folio 25.

7. Howard Papers, Letter of Neville to Howard, December 14, 1903. Folio 25.

8. Howard Papers, Draft of 1000 year lease dated "around 1902."

9. The details of Neville's position and the controversy that followed are in Aneurin Williams, "Land Tenure in the Garden City," Appendix A in C. B. Purdom, *The Garden City* (London, 1913).

10. E. Howard, "The Relation of the Ideal to the Practical," *The Garden City*, n.s. 2, no. 13 (Feb. 1907): 267.

11. See Barry Parker and Raymond Unwin, *The Art of Building a Home* (London, 1901), for the best record of the early career and interests of both men.

12. See Walter L. Creese, ed., *The Legacy of Raymond Unwin: A Human Pattern for Planning* (Cambridge, Mass., 1967), especially the editor's introduction.

13. Raymond Unwin, "The Beautiful in Town Building," *The Garden City*, n.s. 2, no. 13 (Feb. 1907): 267.

14. Unwin, *Town Planning in Practice* (London, 1909).

15. Herbert Read, "A Tribute to Ebenezer Howard," *Town and Country Planning* 14, no. 53 (Spring 1946): 14.

16. Raymond Unwin, "On the Building of Houses in the Garden City," Garden City Tract no. 8 (London, 1901), p. 4.

17. Unwin, "Co-operation in Building," in Parker and Unwin, *The Art of Building a Home*, p. 92.

18. Ibid., p. 92.

19. "Co-operation in Building," in Parker and Unwin, *The Art of Building a Home*, pp. 91–108. See also Raymond Unwin, *Cottage Plans and Common Sense*, Fabian Tract no. 109 (London, 1901).

20. E. Howard, "Co-operative Housekeeping," *The Garden City*, n.s. 1, no. 8 (Sept. 1906): 170.

21. Homesgarth was designed not by Unwin but by another architect associated with the Garden City movement, H. Clapham Lander. See his early advocacy of co-ops, "The Advantages of Co-operative Dwellings," Garden City Tract no. 7 (London, 1901).

22. Howard, "Co-operative Housekeeping," p. 171.

23. Aneurin Williams, "Land Tenure in the Garden City," p. 220.

24. First Garden City Ltd., *Prospectus*, 1909.

25. Charles Lee, "From a Letchworth Diary," *Town and Country Planning* 21, no. 113 (Sept. 1953): 434–442.

26. *Daily Mail* (London), June 17, 1905.

27. Lee, "Letchworth Diary," pp. 439–440.

28. Ernest Rhys, *Everyman Remembers* (London, 1931).

29. C. B. Purdom, *The Building of Satellite Towns* (London, 1949), pp. 214–238.

30. *The Garden City* 1, no. 3 (June 1905): 11.

31. Ibid., n.s. 1, no. 4 (Nov. 1907): 4.

32. Ibid., 1, no. 2 (Feb. 1904): 1.

33. Catalogue of the Cheap Cottage Exhibition at Letchworth (Letchworth, 1905).

34. The best source for Unwin's designs is his "Cottage Planning" in *Where Shall I Live?* (Letchworth, 1907), pp. 103–109.

35. Howard Papers, How the Bicycle Saved the City, Folio 10. Manuscript of an article, probably unpublished, by Howard.

Chapter Six

1. E. Howard, "How Far Have the Original Garden City Ideals Been Realized," Appendix H in C. B. Purdom, *The Garden City* (London, 1913), pp. 279–284.

2. A. K. Cairncross, "Internal Migration in Victorian England," pp. 115–143, in his *Home and Foreign Investment* (Cambridge, 1953), p. 121.

3. *The Garden City* 3, no. 5 (Dec. 1906): 3.

4. C. B. Purdom, *The Garden City After the War* (Letchworth, 1917).

5. Ibid.

6. F. J. Osborn et al., *New Towns After the War* (London, 1918).

7. Howard Papers, Town Planning *Ab Initio*, Folio 3.

8. Ibid., Letter from Howard to Henry Holiday, July 7, 1919, Folio 26.

9. E. Howard, "The Genesis of the Second Garden City," *Garden Cities and Town Planning* 9, no. 10 (Oct. 1919): 183–188. See also the revised edition of F. J. Osborn's *New Towns After the War* (London, 1942), pp. 9–11.

10. Osborn, *New Towns After the War*, rev. ed., p. 11.

11. *Garden Cities and Town Planning* 10, no. 5 (May 1920): 103.

12. W. R. Hughes, *New Towns* (London, 1919).

13. Howard Papers, The Welwyn Stores, Folio 20. A draft prospectus written by Howard, 1920.

14. Howard Papers, Early Draft of *To-morrow*, Folio 3.

15. See especially the article by W. Steele Anderson, "The Future of the City," *Town Planning Review* 14, no. 1 (Jan. 1925): 1–18.

16. Dugald MacFadyen, *Sir Ebenezer Howard and the Town Planning Movement* (Manchester, 1970), pp. 185–187.

17. C. B. Purdom, *The Building of Satellite Cities* (London, 1949), p. 40.

18. Letter of G. B. Shaw to A. C. Howard (Ebenezer's son), 25 May 1928. Howard Papers, Folio 22. Shaw, who never got his money back, said in this letter of Howard, "He was one of those heroic simpletons who do great things whilst our prominent worldlings are explaining why they are Utopian and impossible. And of course it is they who will make the money out of his work."

19. Howard Papers, Draft of an Autobiography, Folio 10.

20. Ibid., Letter of Howard to G. G. André [a spiritualist], October 18, 1926, Folio 25.

Chapter Seven

1. Howard Papers, Letter to G. G. André [a spiritualist], October 18, 1926, Folio 25.

2. F. J. Osborn, "Much Housing and No Garden Cities," *Garden Cities and Town Planning* 16, no. 8 (Oct. 1926): 194–196.

3. Raymond Unwin, "Garden Cities and Regional-Planning," *Garden Cities and Town Planning* 22, no. 1 (Jan. 1932): 7–8.

4. I base these observations on Osborn on a interview with him at his home at Welwyn Garden City, March 11, 1971; and on his extensive publications, especially *Greenbelt Cities: The British Contribution* (London, 1946).

5. *Report of Royal Commission on Distribution of Industrial Population* (London, 1940). Known as the "Barlow Report." Osborn was especially anxious to see the implementation of these findings because a previous commission had in 1935 advocated the creation of garden cities and a national planning policy but no action had followed. See the *Report of Departmental Committee on Garden Cities* (London, 1935). Known as "Marley Report."

6. *Report of Expert Committee on Compensation and Betterment* (London, 1942). Known as "Uthwatt Report."

7. New Towns Committee, *First, Second, and Final Reports* (London, 1946). As the first director general of the British Broadcasting Corporation, Reith was a great believer in quasi-governmental organizations.

8. For the recent history of the New Towns program, see Hazel Evans, ed., *New Towns: The British Experience* (New York, 1972). See also the annual reports of the Commission for the New Towns.

9. E. Howard, "Response to a Letter to the Editor," *The Garden City* 3, no. 2 (Feb. 1907): 16.

10. C. B. Purdom, *The Letchworth Achievement* (London, 1963); this corporation, though similar in structure to the new town development corporations, is wholly independent. Letchworth, therefore, does not appear in the list of New Towns.

Chapter Nine

1. Frank Lloyd Wright, *Taliesin* 1, no. 1 (Oct. 1940): 26. *Taliesin* was a journal printed privately by Wright and his students and distributed to friends of the Taliesin Fellowship. Its first issue contains what is perhaps Wright's best explication of the Broadacre City idea.

2. Ralph Waldo Emerson, "Self-Reliance," in *Emerson's Complete Works*, vol. II (Boston, 1890), p. 47. Norris Kelly Smith was the first to call attention to the importance of Emerson's concept of individualism for understanding Wright. Smith's succinct and suggestive *Frank Lloyd Wright, A Study in Architectural Content* (Englewood Cliffs, N.J., 1966) remains the most profound interpretation of the relationship between Wright's thought and his architecture.

Chapter Ten

1. Wright usually gave his birthdate as 1869, but Thomas S. Hines presents conclusive evidence that he was born in 1867. Thomas S. Hines, "Frank Lloyd Wright, the Madison Years," *Wisconsin Magazine of History* 50, no. 2 (Winter 1967): 109. The vision of Broadacre City occurs in Book Six of *An Autobiography*, published separately in mimeographed form as *Broadacre City, Book Six of An Autobiography* (Spring Green, Wis., 1943).

2. Frank Lloyd Wright, *An Autobiography*, 2d ed. (New York, 1943), pp. 3–46.

3. Ibid., p. 49.

4. Ibid., p. 10.

5. Ibid., pp. 13–14. For the significance of these gifts, see Grant Manson, "Wright in the Nursery: The Influence of Froebel Education on the Work of Frank Lloyd Wright," *The Architectural Review*, no. 113 (June 1953).

6. Wright, *An Autobiography*, p. 49.

7. Ibid., p. 51.

8. Ibid., p. 30.

9. Ibid., p. 561.

10. Ibid., p. 60.

Chapter Eleven

1. Frank Lloyd Wright, *An Autobiography*, 2d ed. (New York, 1934), pp. 67–72.

2. Louis Sullivan, *Kindergarten Chats and Other Writings*, ed. Isabella Athey (New York, 1947), p. 106.

3. Sullivan, "The Young Man in Architecture," in Athey, p. 82.

4. Ibid., p. 89.

5. Sullivan, "An Unaffected School of Modern Architecture," in Athey, p. 30.

6. These quotations are taken from the chapter *"Ceci tuera cela"* in *Notre-Dame de Paris*.

7. The Frank Lloyd Wright Foundation, which holds the original manuscript, dates the speech at 1894, based on a pencilled notation that Wright himself made at the head of the manuscript. Bruce Brooks Pfeiffer, archivist of the foundation, has kindly provided me with a copy of this document. The best edition, however, reprints a 1901 version, Edgar Kaufmann and Ben Raeburn, *Frank Lloyd Wright: Writings and Buildings* (New York, 1960), pp. 53–73. There is some internal evidence for the 1894 date. See, for example, the reference to the "Fair," presumably the Chicago World's Fair of 1893–94. I would guess the speech was delivered and revised several times.

8. Jane Addams, *Twenty Years at Hull House* (New York, 1911), pp. 235–245.

9. Frank Lloyd Wright, *A Testament* (New York, 1957), p. 23.

10. Kaufmann and Raeburn, *Wright: Writings and Buildings*, p. 61.

11. Ibid., p. 60.

12. Ibid., p. 67.

13. Alan Crawford, "Ten Letters from Frank Lloyd Wright to Charles Robert Ashbee," *Architectural History* 13 (1970): 64.

14. Kaufmann and Raeburn, *Wright: Writings and Buildings*, p. 73.

15. Henry-Russell Hitchcock, *In the Nature of Materials* (New York, 1942), p. 6.

16. Kaufmann and Raeburn, *Wright: Writings and Buildings,* pp. 92 93.

17. Wright, *An Autobiography,* p. 79.

18. Richard Sennett, *Families Against the City* (Cambridge, Mass., 1970), p. 53; see also Robert C. Twombly, "Saving the Family: Middle Class Attraction to Wright's Prairie Houses, 1901–1909," *American Quarterly* 27 (Mar. 1975): 57–72.

19. Kaufmann and Raeburn, *Wright: Writings and Buildings,* p. 69.

20. Frank Lloyd Wright, "In the Cause of Architecture," *Architectural Record* 23 no. 3 (Mar. 1908): 163.

21. Wright, *An Autobiography,* p. 162.

22. Ibid., p. 163.

Chapter Twelve

1. Wright to Ashbee, July 8, 1910, in A. Crawford, "Ten Letters from Frank Lloyd Wright to Charles Robert Ashbee," *Architectural History* 13 (1970): 67.

2. Frank Lloyd Wright, "In the Cause of Architecture" *Architectural Record* 23, no. 3 (Mar. 1908): 155. See Smith's exposition of the "cause conservative" in *Frank Lloyd Wright, A Study in Architectural Content,* pp. 7–34.

3. Wright, *An Autobiography,* 2d. ed. (New York, 1943), p. 164.

4. Ibid., p. 163.

5. Ibid., p. 168.

6. Ibid., p. 169.

7. Ibid., p. 170.

8. Robert C. Twombly, whose *Frank Lloyd Wright, An Interpretive Biography* is the best researched and most complete account of Wright's life, devotes only one paragraph to his activities during this period. Robert C. Twombly, *Frank Lloyd Wright, An Interpretive Biography* (New York, 1973), pp. 141–142.

9. Olgivanna Lloyd Wright, *Frank Lloyd Wright* (New York, 1966), pp. 212–213. In dating Wright's houses I have relied on William Allin Storrer, *The Architecture of Frank Lloyd Wright* (Cambridge, Mass., 1974).

10. Twombly, *Wright, An Interpretive Biography,* p. 143.

11. O. L. Wright, *Frank Lloyd Wright*, p. 212.

12. Wright, *An Autobiography*, p. 118.

13. *New York Times*, November 28, 1925, p. 3.

14. *New York Times*, October 22, 1926. Wright, *An Autobiography*, pp. 279–290.

15. Ibid., August 27, 1928, p. 24.

16. Ibid., June 5, 1926, p. 6.

17. Wright to W. R. Heath, n.d. (1927), W. R. Heath Papers, Library of Congress Manuscript Division.

18. Wright to Alexander Woollcott, n.d. (1927), Woollcott Papers, Houghton Library, Harvard University.

19. Wright, *An Autobiography*, p. 276.

20. This at least was Wright's own derivation for Usonia. No one has been able to find the name in Samuel Butler's work.

Chapter Thirteen

1. Frank Lloyd Wright, "In the Cause of Architecture—The Logic of the Plan," *Architectural Record*, vol. 43, no. 1 (Jan. 1928), p. 49.

2. Frank Lloyd Wright, *The Living City* (New York, 1958), p. 119.

3. Frank Lloyd Wright, *The Disappearing City* (New York, 1932), p. 26.

4. Frank Lloyd Wright, *When Democracy Builds* (Chicago, 1945), p. 28.

5. Wright, *The Disappearing City*, p. 9.

6. Wright, *When Democracy Builds*, p. 1.

7. Wright, *The Disappearing City*, p. 4.

8. Wright, *When Democracy Builds*, p. 47.

9. Wright, *The Disappearing City*, p. 38.

10. Wright, *The Living City*, p. 85.

11. *Taliesin* 1, no. 1 (Oct. 1940): 13.

12. Friedrich Schiller, *Sixth Letter on Aesthetic Education, Sämtliche Werke* (Munich, 1966).

13. Wright, *When Democracy Builds*, p. 37.

14. Wright, *The Living City*, p. 207.

15. Ibid., p. 153.

16. *Taliesin* 1, no. 1 (Oct. 1940): 6.

17. Wright, *When Democracy Builds*, p. 32.

18. Silvio Gesell, *The Natural Economic Order* (San Antonio, Tex., 1934 and 1936).

19. Wright, *When Democracy Builds*, p. 94.

Chapter Fourteen

1. Frank Lloyd Wright, *The Living City* (New York, 1958), p. 85.

2. Frank Lloyd Wright, *When Democracy Builds* (Chicago, 1945), p. 97.

3. *Taliesin* 1, no. 1 (Oct. 1940): 14.

4. Frank Lloyd Wright, *Broadacre City, Book Six of An Autobiography* (Spring Green, Wis., 1943), p. 25.

5. Frank Lloyd Wright, *Genius and the Mobocracy* (New York, 1949), p. 31.

6. Wright, *When Democracy Builds*, p. 102.

7. Frank Lloyd Wright, *An Autobiography*, 2d ed. (New York, 1943), p. 331.

8. Wright, *When Democracy Builds*, p. 67.

9. *Taliesin Square Paper*, no. 4 (June 1941).

10. *Taliesin Fellowship Prospectus*, reprinted in Wright, *An Autobiography*, pp. 390–394.

11. Olgivanna Lloyd Wright, *Frank Lloyd Wright* (New York, 1966), p. 92.

12. Ibid., p. 88.

13. Herbert Jacobs, *Frank Lloyd Wright* (New York, 1965), p. 169.

14. Wright, *When Democracy Builds*, p. 101.

15. Ibid., p. 100.

16. *Taliesin* 1, no. 1 (Oct. 1940): 17.

Chapter Fifteen

1. Frank Lloyd Wright, "Broadacre City, A New Community Plan," *Architectural Record* 77, no. 4 (Apr. 1935): 243–244.

2. *Taliesin* 1, no. 1 (Oct. 1940): 5–6.

3. Frank Lloyd Wright, in Baker Brownell and Frank Lloyd Wright, *Architecture and Modern Life* (New York, 1937), p. 275.

4. Ibid., p. 334.

5. Ibid.

6. Ibid., p. 311.

7. Ibid.

8. Frank Lloyd Wright, *The Disappearing City* (New York, 1932), p. 83.

9. Wright, in Brownell and Wright, *Architecture and Modern Life*, p. 309.

10. Frank Lloyd Wright, *Broadacre City, Book Six of An Autobiography* (Spring Green, Wis., 1943), p. 11.

11. *Taliesin* 1, no. 1 (Oct. 1940): 9.

12. Russell Means quoted in Richard Hofstadter, *The Progressive Historians* (New York, 1969), p. 91.

13. *Free America* 1, no. 5 (May 1937): 10.

14. *Free America* 1, no. 6 (June 1937): 3.

15. *Architectural Forum* 88, no. 1 (Jan. 1948): 83.

16. Ibid., p. 83.

17. *Taliesin* 1, no. 1 (Oct. 1940): 31.

18. Frank Lloyd Wright, *When Democracy Builds* (Chicago, 1945), p. 42.

19. *Taliesin Square Paper*, no. 12 (July 1948).

20. *Taliesin Square Paper*, no. 3 (June 1941).

21. *Taliesin* 1, no. 2 (Feb. 1941).

22. *Taliesin Square Paper*, no. 1 (May 15, 1941).

23. *Taliesin Square Paper*, "Letter to London" (Spring 1941).

24. *Taliesin Square Paper*, no. 6 (Oct. 1941).

25. Ibid.

26. *Taliesin Square Paper*, no. 8 (May 1945). Wright's dissatisfaction with government policy did not prevent him from circulating a petition among his supporters asking for federal support for his architectural projects. See Frank Lloyd Wright, "The New Discretion" (Jan. 1, 1943), mimeographed copy in the Oswald Garrison Villard Papers, Houghton Library, Harvard University.

27. *Taliesin Square Paper*, no. 12 (July 1948).

28. Wright, *When Democracy Builds*, p. 56.

Chapter Sixteen

1. Frank Lloyd Wright, *Genius and the Mobocracy* (New York, 1949), p. 106.

2. Ibid., p. 50.

3. Ibid., p. 33.

4. "In the Cause of Architecture, Second Paper," *Architectural Record* 25, no. 5 (May 1914): 412.

5. Wright, *Genius and the Mobocracy*, p. 30.

6. Ibid., p. 106.

7. Ibid., p. 38.

8. See Robert C. Twombly, *Frank Lloyd Wright: An Interpretive Biography* (New York, 1973), pp. 190–306 for a well-researched account of Wright's final years.

9. Frank Lloyd Wright, *The Living City* (New York, 1958), p. 59.

Chapter Seventeen

1. Frank Lloyd Wright, *The Disappearing City* (New York, 1932) pp. 3 8.

Chapter Eighteen

1. Le Corbusier, *La ville radieuse* (Boulogne-Seine, 1935), p. 9.

Chapter Nineteen

1. Le Corbusier, *Vers une architecture* (Paris, 1923), translated as *Towards a New Architecture*, trans. Frederick Etchells (New York, 1960), p. 252.

2. Karl Marx, *Capital* (New York, 1964), 1:203.

3. Le Corbusier, *Le Corbusier lui-même*, ed. Jean Petit (Geneva, 1970), pp. 27–28.

4. Maximilien Gauthier, *Le Corbusier, ou l'architecture au service de l'homme* (Paris, 1944), p. 19.

5. Paul V. Turner, "The Education of Le Corbusier" (Ph.D. diss., Harvard University, 1971), pp. 24–29. Schuré was a prominent theosophist whose work also influenced Mondrian. See Peter Gay, *Art and Act* (New York, 1976), pp. 199–200.

6. Le Corbusier, *L'art décoratif d'aujourd'hui* (Paris, 1925), pp. 198–199.

7. Le Corbusier, *Le Corbusier lui-même*, p. 28.

8. Le Corbusier, *L'art décoratif*, p. 201.

9. Le Corbusier, *Le Corbusier lui-même*, p. 36.

10. Ibid., p. 33.

11. Ibid., p. 36.

12. Ibid.

13. Ibid.

14. Ibid., p. 34.

15. Ibid.

16. Gauthier, *Le Corbusier, ou l'architecture*, p. 35.

17. Reprinted in Le Corbusier, *Un mouvement d'art à La Chaux-de-Fonds* (La Chaux-de-Fonds, 1914), p. 41.

18. Le Corbusier, *Le Corbusier lui-même*, p. 38.

19. Le Corbusier originally described this incident in his *Voyage d'Orient,* written at the time of his travels but not published until 1966. I have quoted his words from *L'art décoratif*, p. 34.

20. Charles-Édouard Jeanneret [Le Corbusier], *Étude sur le mouvement d'art décoratif en Allemagne* (La Chaux-de-Fonds, 1912), p. 74.

21. Le Corbusier, *Après le cubisme* (Paris, 1918), p. 26. This work was co-signed with Amédée Ozenfant, but this quotation was drawn from a section generally acknowledged to be by Le Corbusier alone.

22. Le Corbusier, *Le Corbusier lui-même*, p. 45.

23. Gauthier, *Le Corbusier, ou l'architecture*, p. 37.

24. Le Corbusier, *Oeuvre complète de 1910–1929*, 5th ed. (Paris, 1948), pp. 15–18.

25. Brian Brace Taylor, *Le Corbusier at Pessac* (Cambridge, Mass., 1972), pp. 4–5.

26. Ibid., p. 2.

27. Ibid., p. 3. Le Corbusier was thought to have left La Chaux-de-Fonds in the spring of 1917, but Taylor's dating, based on original documents, is almost surely correct.

Chapter Twenty

1. Le Corbusier, *Le Corbusier lui-même*, ed. Jean Petit (Geneva, 1970), p. 45.

2. Le Corbusier, *Après le cubisme* (Paris, 1918), p. 27. With Amédée Ozenfant.

3. Le Corbusier, *Towards a New Architecture*, trans. Frederick Etchells (New York, 1960), pp. 102–103.

4. Ibid., p. 202.

5. Ibid., p. 121.

6. Ibid., p. 89.

7. Ibid., p. 23.

8. Ibid., p. 251.

9. Ibid., p. 256.

10. Ibid., p. 259.

11. Ibid., p. 269.

Chapter Twenty-One

1. Le Corbusier, *Creation Is a Patient Search* (New York, 1966), p. 63.

2. Le Corbusier's sketchbooks for 1914 and 1915, now in the possession of the Fondation Le Corbusier, show sketches for a city of towers surrounded by satellite cities.

3. Le Corbusier, *Urbanisme* (Paris, 1925), p. 158. One inspiration for embarking on an ideal city may well have been the example of Tony Garnier's *Cité Industrielle*, a detailed plan for an industrial city of 35,000, a copy of which was in his library. (The plan was first exhibited in 1904 and Le Corbusier's edition is from 1917). Le Corbusier had met Garnier, who was municipal architect of Lyons, and praised his work in *Towards a New Architecture*. But the theoretical framework and the scale of the Contemporary City were very much Le Corbusier's own. For an excellent account of the *Cité Industrielle*, see Dora Wiebenson, *Tony Garnier: The Cité Industrielle* (New York, 1969).

4. Le Corbusier in *Plans*, n.s. 2, no. 5 (July 1932): 8.

5. Le Corbusier, *Urbanisme*, p. 169.

6. Sir John Summerson, *Heavenly Mansions* (London, 1949), p. 191.

7. Le Corbusier, *Urbanisme*, p. 177.

8. Ibid., p. 93.

9. Ibid., p. 283.

10. "Sixth Letter of Henri de Saint-Simon to an American," in *Social Organization, The Science of Man and Other Writings*, ed. Felix Markham (New York, 1953), p. 70.

11. See *Le redressement français: organisation et réformes,*

(Paris, 1927). See also Charles S. Maier's brilliant analysis "Between Taylorism and Technocracy: European Ideologies and the Vision of Industrial Productivity in the 1920s," *Journal of Contemporary History* 5 (1970): 27–61. Also Richard F. Kuisel, *Ernest Mercier* (Berkeley, Calif., 1967).

12. Le Corbusier, *Towards a New Architecture*, trans. Frederick Etchells (New York, 1970), p. 264.

13. *Le redressement français*, p. 3.

14. Le Corbusier, *Towards a New Architecture*, p. 41.

15. Peter Serenyi, "Le Corbusier, Fourier, and the Monastery at Ema," *Art Bulletin* 49 (Dec. 1967): 277–286.

16. Le Corbusier's library, preserved at the Fondation Le Corbusier, contains a copy of Georges Benoît-Lévy, *La cité–jardin*, 2d ed. (Paris, 1911), with Le Corbusier's extensive annotations on plans for cooperative quadrangles.

17. Le Corbusier, *Towards a New Architecture*, p. 222.

18. Marie-Geneviève Raymond, *La politique pavillonnaire* (Paris, 1966).

19. Le Corbusier, *Précisions sur un état présent de l'architecture et de l'urbanisme* (Paris, 1930), p. 217.

20. Pierre Francastel, *Art et technique* (Paris, 1960), p. 36.

21. Le Corbusier, *Précisions*, p. 217.

22. Ibid., p. 91.

23. Le Corbusier, *Urbanisme*, pp. 22–23.

Chapter Twenty-Two

1. Le Corbusier, *Urbanisme* (Paris, 1925), pp. 78–79.

2. Le Corbusier, *Oeuvre complète de 1910–1929*, 5th ed. (Paris, 1948), p. 113.

3. Ibid.

4. Ibid., p. 114.

5. Le Corbusier, *Urbanisme*, p. 55.

6. Ibid., p. 101.

7. Le Corbusier, *Le lyrisme des temps nouveaux et l'urbanisme*, appeared as an issue of *Le point* 4, no. 20 (Apr. 1939): 9.

8. Le Corbusier, *Urbanisme*, p. 263n.

9. Le Corbusier, "On demande un Colbert," in *Vers un Paris nouveau? Cahiers de la république des lettres* no. 12, n.d. [1928]: 80.

Chapter Twenty-Three

1. Le Corbusier, *Vers le Paris de l'époque machiniste*, supplement to the bulletin of the *Redressement français*, February 15, 1928, p. 13.

2. Le Corbusier, *La ville radieuse* (Boulogne-Seine, 1935), p. 249.

3. Fernand Léger, "Color in Architecture," *Le Corbusier: Architect, Painter, Writer*, ed. Stamo Papadeki (New York, 1948), p. 78.

4. "Le Corbusier, apôtre de l'architecture moderne," *Le mois* (Mar. 1934): 230–231.

5. Le Corbusier, *Le lyrisme des temps nouveaux et l'urbanisme*, appeared as issue of *Le point* 4, no. 20 (Apr. 1939): 13.

6. Le Corbusier, *Précisions sur un état présent de l'architecture et de l'urbanisme* (Paris, 1930), p. 86.

7. Maurice Besset, *Qui était Le Corbusier?* (Geneva, 1968), p. 184.

8. Le Corbusier, *Le Corbusier lui-même*, ed. Jean Petit (Geneva, 1970), p. 34.

9. Maximilien Gauthier, *Le Corbusier, ou l'architecture au service de l'homme* (Paris, 1944), p. 135.

10. Le Corbusier, *Towards a New Architecture*, trans. Frederick Etchells (New York, 1960), p. 261.

11. Le Corbusier, *Précisions*, p. 187.

12. Le Corbusier, *Vers le Paris de l'époque machiniste*, p. 13.

13. Ibid., p. 1.

14. Ibid., p. 14.

15. Le Corbusier, *La ville radieuse*, p. 129.

16. It appears that his Radiant City concept, discussed in chapter 24, of a high-rise residential district for all citizens had its origins in a plan Le Corbusier submitted for Moscow in 1930. See Le Corbusier, *La ville radieuse*, p. 46. Although Le Corbusier's disillusionment with the Soviets and their hostility toward him was evident by that time, this did not prevent him from submitting a magnificent design for the Palace of the Soviets in 1931. The plan, along with all other modern designs, was contemptuously rejected. Le Corbusier explained this turn away from modernism with the curious theory that it was not the will of the elite but a decision that was forced on them by the Russian masses who liked only academic architecture. See his *Sur les 4 routes* (Paris, 1941), p. 125, for his explanation.

17. See Georges Sorel, *Reflections on Violence* (New York, 1961).

18. Eugene Weber, *Action Française* (Stanford, Calif., 1962), p. 74.

19. Ibid., p. 75.

20. Hubert Lagardelle, *"Au delà de la démocratie,"* *Plans* 1, no. 3 (Mar. 1931): 15–23.

21. *Le nouveau siècle*, May 16, 1928.

22. Pierre Winter, "La ville moderne," ibid., p. 4.

23. Le Corbusier in *Plans*, n.s. 2, no. 5 (July 1, 1932): 8.

24. Le Corbusier, *La ville radieuse*, p. 181.

25. Ibid.

Chapter Twenty-Four

1. Le Corbusier, *La ville radieuse* (Boulogne-Seine, 1935), p. 192.

2. Ibid., title page.

3. Ibid., p. 154.

4. Ibid., p. 153.

5. Le Corbusier, *Quand les cathédrales étaient blanches* (Paris, 1937), pp. 280–281.

6. Le Corbusier, *La ville radieuse*, p. 167.

7. Ibid., p. 146.

8. Peter Serenyi, "Le Corbusier, Fourier, and the Monastery at Ema," cited footnote 15, chapter 21.

9. Charles Fourier, "An Architectural Innovation: The Street Gallery," in Jonathan Beecher and Richard Bienvenu, eds. and trans., *The Utopian Vision of Charles Fourier* (Boston, 1971), p. 243.

Chapter Twenty-Five

1. Le Corbusier, *La ville radieuse* (Boulogne-Seine, 1935) pp. 340–341.

2. Ibid., p. 93.

3. Ibid., p. 9.

4. Ibid., p. 340.

5. Le Corbusier, "Programme pour la grande industrie," *Prélude*, no. 11 (May 1934): 6.

6. Michel Crozier, "*La France, terre de commandement*," *Esprit* (Dec. 1957): 779–797.

7. *Prélude*, no. 2, February 15, 1933, p. 2.

8. Le Corbusier, "*Esprit grec, esprit roman, esprit greco-roman*," ibid., p. 2.

9. Le Corbusier, in *Stile futurista* 1, no. 2 (Aug. 1934): 13; text in French.

10. Le Corbusier, *La ville radieuse*, p. 192.

11. Le Corbusier, *Des canons, des munitions? Merci! Des logis . . . s.v.p.* (Boulogne–Seine, 1938), p. 98.

12. For Le Corbusier's concept of spontaneous theatre, see "Théâtre spontané," *La revue théâtrale* 5, no. 12 (Spring 1950): 17–22.

Chapter Twenty-Six*

1. Le Corbusier, *La ville radieuse* (Boulogne–Seine, 1935), p. 343.

2. Le Corbusier, *Des canons, des munitions? Merci! Des logis . . . s.v.p.* (Boulogne–Seine, 1938), p. 11.

3. Le Corbusier, *La ville radieuse*, p. 154.

4. Ibid., p. 228.

5. Le Corbusier to B. Bordachar, December 30, 1940, in B. Bordachar, "Le Corbusier à Bétharram, témoignage d'un prêtre qui fut son ami," *Les rameaux de notre dame* (Bétharram B.-P.), no. 67 (Aug.-Nov. 1965): 170.

6. Ibid.

7. Le Corbusier, *Le Corbusier lui-même*, ed. Jean Petit (Geneva, 1970), p. 87.

8. For du Moulin and his relations with Le Corbusier, see du Moulin's Vichy memoir, *Le temps des illusions* (Geneva, 1946). The best general study of Vichy in any language is Robert O. Paxton, *Vichy France: Old Guard and New Order, 1940–1944* (New York, 1972).

9. "Décret du 27 mai portant création d'une commission d'étude pour les questions relatives à l'habitation et la construction immobilière," *Journal officiel* 73, no. 148 (May 29, 1941): 2241. The

* Primary sources in this chapter are drawn from the "Algiers" dossier in the Fondation Le Corbusier. The numbering of the documents is as of Fall 1971.

report of this commission was not published until after Le Corbusier had fallen from favor. It appeared under the name of his associate André Boll as *Habitation moderne et urbanisme* (Paris, 1942). Le Corbusier's name was not mentioned in this work, but the style and content are recognizably his.

10. Le Corbusier, *Le Corbusier lui-même*, p. 87.

11. These ideas can be found in Le Corbusier, *La maison des hommes* (Paris, 1941); portions of text by François de Pierrefeu.

12. Ibid., pp. 30–38.

13. Le Corbusier, *Poésie sur Alger* (Paris, 1950); this work was written in 1941–1942.

14. Emery to Le Corbusier, January 25, 1941, Algiers dossier, no. 120.

15. Le Corbusier to General Maxime Weygand, June 30, 1941, Algiers dossier, no. 29.

16. Le Corbusier, "Note à l'intention de M. Dumoulin [sic] de la Barthète," July 27, 1941, Algiers dossier, no. 53.

17. Le Corbusier, "Note relative au Plan directeur," July 12, 1941, Algiers dossier, no. 30, p. 1.

18. Ibid., p. 5.

19. "Note à l'intention du Cabinet de Maréchal," quoted in Le Corbusier to Bordachar, July 15, 1941, in Bordachar, "Le Corbusier à Bétharram," p. 174.

20. Ibid.

21. Le Corbusier to du Moulin, June 21, 1941, Algiers dossier, no. 138.

22. Le Corbusier to Emery, September 15, 1941, Algiers dossier, no. 114.

23. Ménétrel to Le Corbusier, April 1, 1942, Algiers dossier, no. 435.

24. Le Corbusier to Emery, January 26, 1942, Algiers dossier, no. 4.

25. Le Corbusier to Chatel, May 6, 1942, Algiers dossier, no. 405.

26. Le Corbusier, manuscript note dated March 18, 1942, ibid., no. 281.

27. Le Corbusier, "Proposition d'un Plan directeur d'Alger et de sa Région," April 1942, Algiers dossier, unnumbered.

28. Le Corbusier to Monsieur le Gouveneur Pagès [prefect of Algiers], May 18, 1942, Algiers dossier, no. 484.

29. Le Corbusier, "Le Plan directeur sauve les valeurs historiques," in "Proposition d'un Plan directeur d'Alger."

30. Le Corbusier to Pagès, May 18, 1942, Algiers dossier, no. 483; this is a manuscript draft of a letter that appears to have never been sent.

31. Minutes of Algiers City Council, June 12, 1942, Algiers dossier, unnumbered.

32. Le Corbusier to Bordachar, n.d., in Bordachar, "Le Corbusier à Bétharram," p. 176.

33. One sign of this is that after returning to Paris he worked closely with Charles Trochu, general secretary of the ultra-rightist *Front national,* who was then president of the *conseil municipal* in German-occupied Paris. Trochu is listed as a co-editor along with Le Corbusier and Pierre Winter in an issue of *Architecture et urbanisme* (Paris, 1942) devoted to Le Corbusier's work, to which he also contributed an admiring preface, pp. 3–4. Le Corbusier was no doubt hoping that Trochu would appoint him to a "Committee for the study of housing and urbanism" in Paris similar to the one he wanted to head in Algiers. I have found no evidence, however, that any committee actually existed.

34. This phrase is scattered through his responses after World War II to those who wished him to align himself either with the United States or the Soviet Union. "I refuse to accept the dilemma," he would reply. Dossier labeled "Documents sur la paix," Fondation Le Corbusier.

Chapter Twenty-Seven

1. Le Corbusier, *Quand les cathédrales étaient blanches* (Paris, 1937), p. 54.

2. Le Corbusier, *Le Corbusier lui-même,* ed. Jean Petit (Geneva, 1970), 183.

3. On Chandigarh see Norma Evenson's excellent and authoritative *Chandigarh* (Berkeley, Calif., 1966); also Stanislaus von Moos, "Anatomie d'une ville, Chandigarh ville morte?" *Architecture d'aujourd'hui,* no. 146 (1969): 54–61.

4. The plan appears to date from the early 1940s; its essential features can be found both in André Boll, *Habitation moderne et urbanisme* (the Vichy report discussed in chapter 26) and in Le Corbusier, *Les trois établissements humains* (Boulogne-Seine, 1944). Le Corbusier began emphasizing the trans-European aspects of the linear city as his "alternative" to the Cold War. This can be found

in the documents collected in the "Documents sur la paix" dossier at the Fondation Le Corbusier.

5. Le Corbusier, *Mise au point* (Paris, 1966), pp. 12 and 14.

6. Siegfried Giedion, *Space, Time and Architecture*, 5th ed. rev., (Cambridge, Mass., 1967), p. 578.

7. Le Corbusier, *Oeuvre complète 1946–52* (Zurich, 1953), p. 190.

8. Le Corbusier, *Le lyrisme des temps nouveaux et l'urbanisme*, appeared as issue of *Le point* 4, no. 20 (Apr. 1939): 18.

Chapter Twenty-Eight

1. Lewis Mumford, "Architecture as a Home for Man," *Architectural Record* 143 (Feb. 1968): 114.

2. Lewis Mumford, "Yesterday's City of Tomorrow," *Architectural Record* 132 (Nov. 1962): 139–144.

3. Lewis Mumford, "Architecture as a Home for Man," p. 114. Mumford does, however, go on to say that "in the right-about-face that Le Corbusier made at the end of his life, he deliberately turned his back on his original mechanical cliches and slogans, and sought expression in forms that emphasized not rationality but fantasy, not Cartesian order but emotional depth. Had these two aspects of Le Corbusier's mind been equally cultivated from the beginning, I should have been proud to be counted as his admirer and advocate."

4. Madeleine Prouvé, *Victor Prouvé* (Paris, 1958), p. 53.

5. Le Corbusier, *Les maternelles vous parlent* (Paris, 1968), p. 86.

Conclusion

1. Ebenezer Howard, "Spiritual Influences Toward Social Progress," *Light* (April 30, 1910): 195.

2. Jane Jacobs, *The Death and Life of Great American Cities* (New York, 1961), p. 14.

3. Ibid., pp. 121–122.

4. Ibid., p. 195.

5. Ibid., p. 141.

6. Ibid.

7. Ibid., p. 19.

8. Ibid., p. 17.

9. Ibid., p. 413.

10. William F. Buckley, Jr., *Did You Ever See a Dream Walking?* (Indianapolis, 1970).

11. Richard Sennett, *The Uses of Disorder: Personal Identity and City Life* (New York, 1970), p. 8.

12. Ibid., p. xvii.

13. Ibid., p. 144.

14. Ibid., p. 160.

15. Paul Goldberger, "Radical Planners Now Mainstream," *New York Times* (June 13, 1976): 21.

16. *New York Times* (March 19, 1972): 32. The project was not to be completely abandoned but reconstructed as a balanced community of smaller structures.

17. Jacobs, *The Death and Life of Great American Cities*, p. 410. Jacobs attributes the phrase to another, unnamed planner, but the sentiment is her own.

18. Samuel Johnson, "Miscellaneous Thoughts and Reflections," in *Complete Works*, ed. Walter Raleigh (Oxford, 1912), p. 249; quoted in Richard Mayne, *The Recovery of Europe* (Garden City, N.Y., 1973), p. 349.

BIBLIOGRAPHY

Introduction

Any bibliography on this subject must begin with Lewis Mumford. From his early account of *The Story of Utopias* (New York, 1922) to his confident synthesis of *The Culture of Cities* (New York, 1938) to his magisterial summation of *The City in History* (New York, 1961), Mumford's work on the significance of the city (and of the plans for changing it) constitutes one of the most important chapters in twentieth-century American intellectual history. As an advocate of regional planning in the United States and an influential supporter of the world-wide New Town movement, Mumford has contributed to changing the history of cities as well as to writing it.

Three other writers who have shaped my understanding of the nineteenth-century urban context from which Howard, Wright, and Le Corbusier began are Leonardo Benevolo, *Le origini dell'urbanistica moderna* (Bari, 1963; English trans., 1967); Françoise Choay, *L'urbanisme: utopies et réalités* (Paris, 1965), an anthology built around her own original conceptualizations; and Walter L. Creese, *The Search for Environment* (New Haven, Conn., 1966). The authoritative account of the twentieth-century revolution in technology, planning, and design is Siegfried Giedion, *Space, Time and Architecture* (Cambridge, Mass., 1941).

Anyone interested in nineteenth-century society and the nineteenth-century city will want to see—even if he cannot afford to own—the magnificent two-volume *The Victorian City: Images and Realities*, ed. H. J. Dyos and Michael Wolff (London, 1973). A more modest but more accessible collection of contemporary accounts and recent scholarship is *The Urbanization of European Society in the Nineteenth Century*, ed. Andrew and Lynn Lees (Lexington, Mass., 1976) with a useful introduction and bibliographical essay.

A similarly useful collection of recent thought on utopias is Frank
E. Manuel, ed., *Utopias and Utopian Thought* (Boston, 1966).

Ashworth, William. *The Genesis of Modern British Town Planning.*
London, 1954.

Banham, Reyner. *Theory and Design in the First Machine Age.*
New York, 1960.

Beecher, Jonathan, and Richard Bienvenu, eds. *The Utopian Vision
of Charles Fourier.* Boston, 1971.

Benevolo, Leonardo. *Le origini dell'urbanistica moderna.* Bari,
1963. Trans. Judith Landry as *The Origins of Modern Town
Planning.* Cambridge, Mass., 1967.

Buber, Martin. *Paths in Utopia.* Trans. R. F. C. Hull. Boston, 1958.

Choay, Françoise. *L'urbanisme: utopies et réalités.* Paris, 1965.

————. *The Modern City: Planning in the Nineteenth Century.*
New York, 1969.

Cioran, E. M. *Histoire et utopie.* Paris, 1960.

Coleman, B. I., ed. *The Idea of the City in Nineteenth-Century
Britain.* London, 1973.

Creese, Walter L. *The Search for Environment: The Garden City
Before and After.* New Haven, Conn., 1966.

Doxiadis, C. A. "Historic Approaches to New Towns." *Ekistics* 18,
no. 108 (Nov. 1964): 346–364.

Engels, Friedrich. *Zur Wohnungsfrage,* 2d ed. Leipzig, 1887.

Feiss, Carl. "The Debt of Twentieth Century Planners to Nineteenth Century Planners." *American Journal of Economics and
Sociology* 9, no. 1 (Oct. 1949): 35–44.

Geddes, Patrick. *City Development: A Study of Parks, Gardens
and Culture Institutes.* Birmingham, 1904.

————. *Cities in Evolution.* London, 1915.

Giedion, Siegfried. *Space, Time and Architecture: The Growth of a
New Tradition.* Cambridge, Mass., 1941; 5th rev. ed., 1967.

Goodman, Percival, and Paul Goodman. *Communitas: Means of
Livelihood and Ways of Life.* Chicago, 1947.

Gropius, Walter. *Scope of Total Architecture.* New York, 1962.

Harrison, J. F. C. *Quest for the New Moral World: Robert Owen
and the Owenites in Britain and America.* New York, 1969.

Hilberseimer, Ludwig. *Groszstadt Architektur.* Stuttgart, 1927.

Kateb, George. *Utopia and Its Enemies.* New York, 1963.

Lane, Barbara Miller. *Architecture and Politics in Germany, 1918–
1945.* Cambridge, Mass., 1968.

Bibliography

Lang, S. "The Ideal City from Plato to Howard." *Architectural Review* 112 (Aug. 1952): 91–101.

Lees, Andrew. "Debates about the Big City in Germany, 1890–1914." *Societas* 5 (1975): 31–47.

Lees, Andrew, and Lynn Lees, eds. *The Urbanization of European Society in the Nineteenth Century.* Lexington, Mass., 1976.

Mann, Peter H. "Octavia Hill: An Appraisal." *Town Planning Review* 23, no. 3 (Oct. 1952): 223–237.

Mannheim, Karl. *Ideology and Utopia.* New York, 1968.

————. "Utopia." In *Encylopaedia of the Social Sciences.* New York, 1934.

Manuel, Frank E. *The New World of Henri Saint-Simon.* Cambridge, Mass., 1956.

————, ed. *Utopias and Utopian Thought.* Boston, 1966.

Mumford, Lewis. *The Story of Utopias.* New York, 1922.

————. *Technics and Civilization.* New York, 1934.

————. *The Culture of Cities.* New York, 1938.

————. *City Development.* New York, 1945.

————. *From the Ground Up.* New York, 1956.

————. *The City in History.* New York, 1961.

————. *The Highway and the City.* New York, 1963.

————. *The Urban Prospect.* New York, 1968.

————. *Architecture as a Home for Man.* New York, 1975.

Pinkney, David H. *Napoleon III and the Rebuilding of Paris.* Princeton, N.J., 1958.

Reiner, Thomas A. *The Place of the Ideal Community in Urban Planning.* Philadelphia, 1963.

————. "The Planner as Value Technician: Two Classes of Utopian Constructs and Their Impact on Planning." In *Taming Megalopolis.* Ed. H. Wentworth Eldredge. Garden City, N.Y., 1967. Pp. 232–247.

Riesman, David. "Some Observations on Community Plans and Utopia." In his *Individualism Reconsidered and Other Essays.* New York, 1954. Pp. 70–98.

Rosenau, Helen. *The Ideal City in its Architectural Evolution.* London, 1959.

Saalman, Howard. *Haussmann: Paris Transformed.* New York, 1971.

Sutcliffe, Anthony. *The Autumn of Central Paris: The Defeat of Town Planning, 1850–1970.* London, 1970.

Tunnard, Christopher. *The City of Man.* New York, 1953.

Verhaeren, Émile. *Les villes tentaculaires.* 4th ed. Paris, 1908.

Weber, Adna Ferrin. *The Growth of Cities in the Nineteenth Century.* Ithaca, N.Y., 1899.

Weber, Max. *The City.* Trans. and ed. Don Martindale and Gertrude Neuwirth. Glencoe, Ill., 1958.

Wiebenson, Dora. *Tony Garnier: The Cité Industrielle.* New York, 1969.

Ebenezer Howard and The Garden City Movement

Almost fifty years after his death, Ebenezer Howard still lacks an adequate biography. *Sir Ebenezer Howard and the Town Planning Movement,* "compiled and written by Dugald MacFadyen," as the title page puts it (Manchester, 1933, reprinted 1970), is a labor of love with many important documents, but Howard himself is often lost amid pages of gush and irrelevancies. Fortunately, an excellent edition of *Garden Cities of To morrow* is widely available, ed. Sir Frederic Osborn (Cambridge, Mass., 1965). It has an important preface by the editor and an equally important introductory essay by Lewis Mumford.

PRIMARY SOURCES

The Ebenezer Howard Papers. Hertfordshire County Archives, Hertford, England.

Minute Books and Papers of the Garden City Association. Now in the possession of the Town and Country Planning Association, London.

PUBLISHED WORKS OF EBENEZER HOWARD (in chronological order)

"Summary of E. Howard's Proposals for a Home Colony." *Nationalisation News* 3 (February 1893): 20–21.

To-morrow: a Peaceful Path to Real Reform. London, 1898.

Letter to the *Echo,* August 31, 1899.

Letter to the editor of the *Citizen,* September 30, 1899.

Interview in *Builders Journal and Architectural Record,* October 25, 1899.

Garden Cities: Manufactures and Labour. Garden City Tract no. 5. London, 1901.

Garden Cities of To-morrow. London, 1902.

Bibliography

"The Relation of the Ideal to the Practical." *Garden City* 1, no. 2 (Feb. 1905): 15–16.

"Cooperative Housekeeping." *Garden City*, n.s. 1, no. 8 (Sept. 1906): 170–171.

"The Garden City—What It Is." In *Where Shall I Live? A Guide to Letchworth*. Letchworth, 1907.

"The Progress of the Movement." *Garden Cities and Town Planning* 4 (Jan.-Feb. 1909): 166–169.

"The Land Question at Letchworth." *Garden Cities and Town Planning* 1, no. 7 (July 1909): 153–157; no. 8 (Aug. 1909): 177–184.

"Spiritual Influences Towards Social Progress." *Light* (April 30, 1910): 195–208.

"An International Project." *Garden Cities and Town Planning* 2, no. 10 (October 15, 1912): 177–184.

"How Far Have the Original Garden City Ideals Been Realized?" In Appendix H of C. B. Purdom. *The Garden City*. London, 1913.

"A New Outlet for Woman's Energy." *Garden Cities and Town Planning* 3, no. 6 (June 1913): 153–159.

"The Transit Problem and the Working Man." *Town Planning Review* 4, no. 2 (July 1913): 127–132.

"The Late Hon. Mr. Justice Neville." *Garden Cities and Town Planning* 9, no. 1 (Jan. 1919): 4–6.

"The Genesis of the Second Garden City." *Garden Cities and Town Planning* 9, no. 10 (Oct. 1919): 183–188.

"Lord Northcliffe." *Garden Cities and Town Planning* 12, no. 8 (Sept.-Oct. 1922): 141.

"The Originator of the Garden City Idea." *Garden Cities and Town Planning* 16, no. 6 (July 1926): 132–134.

SECONDARY SOURCES

Adams, Thomas. *Garden City and Agriculture*. London, 1904.

Bellamy, Edward. *Looking Backward, 2000–1887*. Boston, 1888.

Benoît-Lévy, Georges. *La cité-jardin*, 2d ed. Paris, 1911.

Brown, W. H. "Ebenezer Howard: A Modern Influence." *Garden Cities and Town Planning* 3 (Sept. 1908): 117–120.

Buder, Stanley. "Ebenezer Howard: The Genesis of a Town Planning Movement." *Journal of the American Institute of Planners* 35, no. 6 (Nov. 1969): 390–397.

Cairncross, A. K. "Internal Migration in Victorian England." In *Home and Foreign Investment*. Cambridge, 1953.

C. C. R. "The Evolution of Ebenezer Howard." *Garden Cities and Town Planning* 2, no. 3 (March 1912): 48–50.

Canty, Donald, ed. *The New City.* New York, 1969.

Chambers, Theodore G. "London's First Satellite Town: An Account of the Garden City at Welwyn." *Garden Cities and Town Planning* 10, no. 5 (May 1920): 95–99.

Clapham, John H. *An Economic History of Modern Britain.* Cambridge, 1951, Vol. 2.

Cole, G. D. H. *A Century of Cooperation.* London, 1944.

Creese, Walter L. *The Search for Environment.* New Haven, Conn., 1966.

———, ed. *The Legacy of Raymond Unwin: A Human Pattern for Planning.* Cambridge, Mass., 1967.

Deane, Phyllis, and W. A. Cole. *British Economic Growth 1688–1959.* Cambridge, 1964.

Eden, W. A. "Ebenezer Howard and the Garden City Movement." *Town Planning Review* 19, nos. 3–4 (Summer 1947): 123–143.

Evans, Hazel, ed. *New Towns: The British Experience.* New York, 1972.

Fletcher, T. W. "The Great Depression of English Agriculture." *Economic History Review* (second series) 13, no. 3 (Apr. 1961): 417–432.

Foley, Donald. "Idea and Influence: The Town and Country Planning Association." *Journal of the American Institute of Planners* 28, no. 1 (Feb. 1962): 10–17.

Garden City Association Conference at Bournville. London, 1901.

Garden City Association. *Town Planning in Theory and Practice.* London, 1907.

George, Henry. *Progress and Poverty.* In *The Complete Works of Henry George.* New York, 1911. Vol. 1.

Grey, Albert Henry George, 4th earl. *What Co-operation Will Do for the People.* London, 1898.

Harris, G. Montagu. *The Garden City Movement.* London, 1906.

Hobson, J. H., ed. *Co-operative Labour upon the Land.* London, 1895.

Hood, Alfred. "The Road to Garden City." *Co-operative News.* July 8, 1899.

Hughes, Michael, ed. *The Letters of Lewis Mumford and Frederic J. Osborn: a Transatlantic Dialogue.* Bath, 1971.

Hughes, W. R. *New Town: A Proposal in Agricultural, Industrial and Social Reconstruction.* London, 1919.

Kropotkin, Peter. *Fields, Factories and Workshops.* London, 1899.

Bibliography

Lander, H. Clapham. *The Advantages of Co-operative Dwellings.* Garden City Tract no. 7. London, 1901.

———. "Associated Homes: A Solution to the Servant Problem." *Garden Cities and Town Planning,* n.s. 1, no. 3 (Apr. 1911): 71–72.

Lawrence, Elwood P. *Henry George in the British Isles.* East Lansing, Mich., 1957.

Lee, Charles. "From a Letchworth Diary." *Town and Country Planning* 21 (Sept. 1953): 434–442.

Marshall, Alfred. "The Housing of the London Poor." *Contemporary Review* 45, no. 2 (Feb. 1884): 224–231.

Marshall, Peter. "A British Sensation." In *Edward Bellamy Abroad,* ed. Sylvia E. Bowman. New York, 1962. Pp. 86–118.

Moore, Harold E. *Agricultural Cooperation.* London, 1887.

———. *Back to the Land.* London, 1893.

———. *The Economic Aspect of the First Garden City.* London, 1903.

Morrison, Herbert. "A New London: Labour's View of the Satellite Towns." *Garden Cities and Town Planning* 10, no. 5 (May 1920): 99–102.

Mumford, Lewis. *The Culture of Cities.* New York, 1938.

———. "The Garden City Idea and Modern Planning." In *Garden Cities of To-morrow,* ed. F. J. Osborn (Cambridge, Mass., 1965), pp. 29–40.

Neville, Ralph. *The Place of Co-operation in Social Economy.* London, 1901.

———. *Co-operation and Garden Cities.* London, 1901.

———. "The Divorce of Man from Nature, the Evils of the Big Town." *Garden Cities and Town Planning,* n.s. 4 (Aug. 1909): 227–228.

———. *Papers and Addresses on Social Questions.* London, 1919.

Olmsted, Frederick Law, Jr. "Through American Spectacles: An Expert's View of the English Garden City Schemes." *Garden Cities and Town Planning,* n.s. 4 (May 1909): 198–200.

Osborn, Sir Frederic J. "Much Housing and No More Garden Cities." *Garden Cities and Town Planning* 16, no. 8 (Oct. 1926): 194–196.

———. "Shops at Welwyn Garden City." *Garden Cities and Town Planning* 20, no. 1 (Jan. 1930): 18–20.

———. *Transport, Town Development and Territorial Planning of Industry.* London, 1934.

————. *New Towns After the War*, rev. ed. London, 1942.

————. *Greenbelt Cities: The British Contribution.* London, 1946.

————. *The New Towns: The Answer to Megalopolis.* London, 1963, rev. ed. 1969. With Arnold Whittick.

————. "Sir Ebenezer Howard: The Evolution of His Ideas." *Town Planning Review* 21, no. 3 (Oct. 1950): 221–235.

Parker, Barry, and Raymond Unwin. *The Art of Building a Home.* London, 1901.

Petersen, William. "The Ideological Origins of Britain's New Towns." *Journal of the American Institute of Planners* 34, no. 3 (May 1968): 160–170.

Prospectus of the First Garden City Ltd. London, 1909.

Purdom, C. B. *The Garden City: A Study in the Development of a Modern Town.* London, 1913.

————. *The Garden City After the War.* Letchworth, 1917.

————. *The Building of Satellite Towns.* London, 1925, rev. ed. 1949.

————. "At the Inception of Letchworth." *Town and Country Planning* 21 (Sept. 1953): 426–430.

————. *The Letchworth Achievement.* London, 1963.

————, ed. *Town Theory and Practice.* London, 1921.

Read, Herbert. "Tribute to Ebenezer Howard." *Town and Country Planning* 14 (Spring 1946): 14.

Richardson, Benjamin Ward. *Hygeia, A City of Health.* London, 1876.

Schaffer, Frank. *The New Town Story.* London, 1970.

Sennett, A. R. *Garden Cities in Theory and Practice.* 2 vols. London, 1905.

Spencer, Herbert. "The New Toryism." *Contemporary Review* 45, no. 2 (Feb. 1884): 153–167.

Squire, Sir John. *The Honeysuckle and the Rose.* London, 1937.

Thompson, F. M. L. *English Landed Society in the Nineteenth Century.* London, 1963.

Unwin, Raymond. *On the Building of Houses in the Garden City.* Garden City Tract no. 7. London, 1901.

————. *Cottage Plans and Common Sense.* Fabian Tract no. 109. London, 1902.

————. "Cottage Planning." In *Where Shall I Live? A Guide to Letchworth.* Letchworth, 1907. Pp. 103–109.

————. "The Beautiful in Town Building." *Garden City*, n.s. 2 (Feb. 1907): 266–267.

Bibliography

————. *Town Planning in Practice*. London, 1909.

————. "Co-operative Architecture." *The City* 11 (Nov. 1909): 249–255.

————. "The Planning of Garden City." In Appendix B of C. B. Purdom. The Garden City. London, 1913.

————. "Garden Cities and Regional Planning." *Garden Cities and Town Planning* 22, no. 1 (Jan. 1932): 7–8.

Wallace, Alfred Russel. *Land Nationalisation*. London, 1882.

Wallace, J. Bruce. *Towards Fraternal Organisation*, 2d ed. London, 1894.

Warren, Herbert. "Finding and Purchasing the Letchworth Estates." *Garden Cities and Town Planning* 20, no. 6 (June-July 1930): 151–155.

Where Shall I Live? A Guide to Letchworth. Letchworth, 1907.

Williams, Aneurin. "Co-operation in Housing and Town Building." *Thirty-Ninth Co-operative Congress*. Manchester, 1909. Pp. 379–397.

————. "Land Tenure in Garden City." In Appendix A of C. B. Purdom. *The Garden City*. London, 1913.

Frank Lloyd Wright

Of the Wright biographies, Robert C. Twombly's *Frank Lloyd Wright: An Interpretive Biography* (New York, 1973) is by far the most reliable and the most complete. Twombly's interpretation, however, qualifies but does not supersede the profound and provocative essay by Norris Kelly Smith, *Frank Lloyd Wright: A Study in Architectural Content*. (Englewood Cliffs, N.J., 1966). Smith's thesis is decidedly one-sided: that Wright was dedicated to the "cause conservative" of preserving the traditional values of his society. But Smith advances his thesis with such learning, brilliance and originality that all subsequent students of Wright are deeply in his debt.

The most complete and reliable guide to Wright's buildings is William Allin Storrer, *The Architecture of Frank Lloyd Wright* (Cambridge, Mass., 1974). Storrer generally confines himself to cataloguing (and sometimes discovering) Wright's buildings, so there is still much to learn from Vincent Scully's *Frank Lloyd Wright* (New York, 1960) and Henry-Russell Hitchcock's classic *In the Nature of Materials: The Buildings of Frank Lloyd Wright 1887–1941* (New York, 1942).

PRIMARY SOURCES

Wright's papers and drawings are in the possession of the Frank Lloyd Wright Foundation, and, as Henry-Russell Hitchcock acknowledged in 1974, "access to the Taliesin holdings has become, as is well known, all but impossible." I am, however, indebted to the Foundation's archivist, Bruce Brooks Pfeiffer, for furnishing me with photocopies of documents relating to the text and date of Wright's "Art and Craft of the Machine" address. In addition, I was able to consult Wright letters and manuscripts in the following collections: Baker Brownell Papers, Northwestern University; Hamlin Garland Diaries, The Huntington Library; W. R. Heath Papers, The Library of Congress; Oswald Garrison Villard Papers, Houghton Library, Harvard University; Alexander Woollcott Papers, Houghton Library; Frank Lloyd Wright Collection, Avery Library, Columbia University; Frank Lloyd Wright Collection, State Historical Society of Wisconsin, Madison.

PUBLISHED WORKS OF FRANK LLOYD WRIGHT (in chronological order)

"The Architect." *The Brickbuilder* 9, no. 6 (June 1900): 124–128.
"In the Cause of Architecture." *Architectural Record* 23, no. 3 (Mar. 1908): 155–221.
Ausgeführte Bauten und Entwürfe von Frank Lloyd Wright. Berlin, 1910.
The Japanese Print: An Interpretation. Chicago, 1912.
"In the Cause of Architecture, Second Paper." *Architectural Record* 35, no. 5 (May 1914): 405–413.
Experimenting with Human Lives. Hollywood, Calif., n.d. [1923].
"In the Cause of Architecture." *Architectural Record.* "The Architect and the Machine" 61, no. 5 (May 1927): 394–396; "Standardization, The Soul of the Machine" 61, no. 6 (June 1927): 478–480; "Steel" 62, no. 2 (Aug. 1927): 163–166; "Fabrication and Imagination" 62, no. 4 (Oct. 1927): 318–321; "The New World" 62, no. 4 (Oct. 1927): 322–324; "The Logic of the Plan" 63, no. 1 (Jan. 1928): 49–57; "What 'Styles' Mean to the Architect" 63, no. 2 (Feb. 1928): 145–151; "The Meaning of Materials —Stone" 63, no. 4 (Apr. 1928): 350–356; "The Meaning of Materials—Wood" 63, no. 5 (May 1928): 481–488; "The Meaning of Materials—The Kiln" 63, no. 6 (June 1928): 555–561; "The Meaning of Materials—Glass" 64, no. 1 (July 1928): 11–16; "The Meaning of Materials—Concrete" 64, no. 3 (Aug.

1928): 99–104; "Sheet Metal and a Modern Instance" 64, no. 4 (Oct. 1928): 334–342; "The Terms" 64, no. 6 (Dec. 1928): 507–514.

"Towards a New Architecture." *World Unity* 2, no. 6 (Sept. 1928): 393–395. Review of Le Corbusier's *Vers une architecture*.

Modern Architecture, being the Kahn Lectures for 1930. Princeton, N.J., 1931.

Two Lectures on Architecture [Scammon Lectures 1930]. Chicago, 1931.

An Autobiography. New York, 1932; 2d ed. rev. 1943.

The Disappearing City. New York, 1932.

"Broadacre City: A New Community Plan." *Architectural Record* 77, no. 4 (April 1935): 243–254.

"Architecture and Life in the U.S.S.R." *Architectural Record* 82, no. 4 (Oct. 1937): 58–63.

Architecture and Modern Life. New York, 1937. With Baker Brownell.

"To the Fifty-eighth, Mr. Frank Lloyd Wright Replies." *Journal of the Royal Institute of British Architects* (third series), no. 20 (October 16, 1939): 1005–1006.

An Organic Architecture: The Architecture of Democracy. London, 1939.

The Industrial Revolution Runs Away. New York, 1969. "Publisher's note: This edition includes a facsimile of Frank Lloyd Wright's copy of the original 1932 edition of *The Disappearing City* subsequently revised in his hand and contains the new text with his revisions on facing pages." This version of Wright's basic Broadacre City book appears to date from the period 1939–1941.

Taliesin: The Taliesin Fellowship Publication 1, no. 1 (Oct. 1940).

Taliesin Square Paper: A Nonpolitical Voice from Our Democratic Minority. Published irregularly from 1941 to 1951.

Frank Lloyd Wright on Architecture: Selected Writing, 1894–1940. Ed. Frederick Gutheim. New York, 1942.

An Autobiography. Book Six: Broadacre City. Spring Green, Wisc., 1943.

When Democracy Builds. Chicago, 1945.

"Berm Houses for Cooperative Workers." *Architectural Forum* 88, no. 1 (Jan. 1948): 82–83.

Genius and the Mobocracy. New York, 1949.

The Future of Architecture. New York, 1953.

The Natural House. New York, 1954.

A Testament. New York, 1957.

The Living City. New York, 1958.

Frank Lloyd Wright: Writings and Buildings. Ed. Edgar Kaufmann and Ben Raeburn. New York, 1960.

SECONDARY SOURCES

Addams, Jane. *Twenty Years at Hull House*. New York, 1911.

————. *The Spirit of Youth and the City Streets*. New York, 1917.

Banham, P. Reyner. "Frank Lloyd Wright as Environmentalist." *Architectural Design* 37 (Apr. 1967): 174–177.

Blake, Peter. *The Master Builders*. New York, 1960. Has excellent chapters on both Wright and Le Corbusier.

Borsodi, Ralph. *This Ugly Civilization*. New York, 1929.

————. *Flight from the City*. New York, 1933.

Collins, George R. "Broadacre City: Wright's Utopia Reconsidered." In *Four Great Makers of Modern Architecture*. New York, 1961. Pp. 55–75.

Duncan, Hugh Dalziel. *Culture and Democracy: The Struggle for Form in Architecture and Society in Chicago and the Midwest during the Life and Times of Louis H. Sullivan*. Totowa, N.J., 1965.

Eaton, Leonard K. *Two Chicago Architects and Their Clients: Frank Lloyd Wright and Howard Van Doren Shaw*. Cambridge, Mass., 1969.

Gannett, William C. *The House Beautiful*. River Forest, Ill., 1897.

Gesell, Silvio. *The Natural Economic Order*. Trans. from the 6th German ed. by Phillip Pye. San Antonio, Tex., 1934 and 1936.

Goodman, Paul, and Percival Goodman. "Frank Lloyd Wright on Architecture." *Kenyon Review* 4, no. 1 (Winter 1942): 7–28.

Griswold, A. Whitney. *Farming and Democracy*. New York, 1948.

Hines, Thomas S. "Frank Lloyd Wright: The Madison Years." *Wisconsin Magazine of History* 50, no. 2 (Winter 1967): 109–119.

Hitchcock, Henry-Russell. *In the Nature of Materials: The Buildings of Frank Lloyd Wright, 1887–1941*. New York, 1942.

Hugo, Victor. *Notre-Dame de Paris*. First published Paris, 1831. The chapter to which Wright refers, "Ceci tuera cela," although forming part of the original manuscript, was not published until the October 1832 edition.

Jacobs, Herbert. *Frank Lloyd Wright: America's Greatest Architect*. New York, 1965.

Bibliography

Manson, Grant C. *Frank Lloyd Wright to 1910: the First Golden Age*. New York, 1958.

March, Lionel. "Imperial City of the Boundless West." *The Listener* (April 30, 1970): 581–584.

Schapiro, Meyer. "Architect's Utopia." *Partisan Review* 4, no. 4 (Mar. 1938): 42–47.

Scully, Vincent, Jr. *Frank Lloyd Wright*. New York, 1960.

Sennett, Richard. *Families Against the City, 1872–1890*. Cambridge, Mass., 1970.

Smith, Norris Kelly. *Frank Lloyd Wright: A Study in Architectural Content*. Englewood Cliffs, N.J., 1966.

Starr, Ellen Gates. "Arts and Labour." In *Hull House Maps and Papers*. New York, 1895. Pp. 165–182.

Storrer, William Allin. *The Architecture of Frank Lloyd Wright*. Cambridge, Mass., 1974.

Sullivan, Louis H. *Kindergarten Chats and Other Writings*. Ed. Isabella Athey. New York, 1947.

Twombly, Robert C. *Frank Lloyd Wright: An Interpretive Biography*. New York, 1973.

————. "Saving the Family: Middle Class Attraction to Wright's Prairie Houses, 1901–1909." *American Quarterly* 27 (Mar. 1975): 57–72.

White, Morton and Lucia. *The Intellectual Versus the City: from Thomas Jefferson to Frank Lloyd Wright*. Cambridge, Mass., 1962.

Wright, John Lloyd. *My Father Who Is On Earth*. New York, 1946.

Wright, Olgivanna Lloyd. *Our House*. New York, 1959.

————. *The Shining Brow*. New York, 1960.

————. *Frank Lloyd Wright: His Life—His Work—His Words*. New York, 1966.

Le Corbusier

Since 1944 when Maximilien Gauthier published *Le Corbusier— ou l'architecture au service de l'homme* (written with the assistance of its subject) Le Corbusier has not lacked biographies. Perhaps the best so far is Stanislaus von Moos, *Le Corbusier: Elemente einer Synthese* (Frauenfeld, 1968; French trans., 1971; English translation forthcoming from MIT Press). It may be supplemented with the invaluable collection of primary sources that Le Corbusier and Jean Petit began to assemble shortly before the former's death and which Petit completed and published as *Le Corbusier lui-même* (Geneva, 1970).

The Open Hand: Essays on Le Corbusier, ed. Russell Walden (Cambridge Mass., 1977), is an important collection of some of the best recent work. *Le Corbusier in Perspective*, ed. Peter Serenyi (Englewood Cliffs, N.J., 1975) brings together some of the "classic" articles on Le Corbusier and also contains a very useful bibliography.

PRIMARY SOURCES

Le Corbusier Papers. La Fondation Le Corbusier, Paris.

PUBLISHED WORKS OF LE CORBUSIER (in chronological order)

Étude sur le mouvement d'art décoratif en Allemagne. La Chaux-de Fonds, 1912.

Un mouvement d'art à la Chaux-de-Fonds. La Chaux-de-Fonds, 1914. Co-signed by Charles Eplattenier, Leon Perrin, and Georges Aubert; the style, however, is recognizably Le Corbusier's.

Après le cubisme. Paris, 1918. With Amédée Ozenfant.

Vers une architecture. Paris, 1923.

Urbanisme. Paris, 1925.

L'art décoratif d'aujourd'hui. Paris, 1925.

Vers le Paris de l'époque machiniste. Supplement to the bulletin of the *Redressement français*, February 15, 1928.

Pour bâtir: Standardiser et Tayloriser. Supplement to the bulletin of the *Redressement français*, May 1, 1928.

"Réflexions à propos de la loi Loucheur." *La revue des vivants* 2, no. 8 (Aug. 1928): 239–245.

"On demande un Colbert." In *Vers un Paris nouveau, Cahiers de la république des lettres*, no. 12, n.d. [1928]: 79–89.

Requête addressé par MM. Le Corbusier et Pierre Jeanneret à M. le président et MM. les membres du conseil de la Société des Nations. Paris, 1928; rev. ed. 1931. With Pierre Jeanneret. Le Corbusier's complaints after losing the League of Nations competition.

Une maison—un palais. Paris, 1928.

Précisions sur un état présent de l'architecture et de l'urbanisme. Paris, 1930.

Oeuvre complète 1910–1929. Zurich, 1930. With Pierre Jeanneret.

Bibliography

"Esprit grec—esprit latin—esprit greco-latin." *Prélude*, no. 2, February 15, 1933, p. 2.

Croisade, ou le crépuscule des académies. Paris, 1933.

"Programme pour la grande industrie." *Prélude*, no. 11, May 1934, pp. 6–7.

[Untitled article] *Stile futurista* 1, no. 2 (Aug. 1934): 13.

Aircraft. London, 1935.

Oeuvre complète 1929–1934. Zurich, 1935. With Pierre Jeanneret.

La ville radieuse. Boulogne (Seine), 1935.

Quand les cathédrales étaient blanches. Paris, 1937.

Des canons, des munitions? Merci! Des logis . . . s.v.p. Boulogne (Seine), 1938.

Le lyrisme des temps nouveaux et l'urbanisme, appeared as an issue of *Le point* 4, no. 20 (Apr. 1939).

Oeuvre complète 1934–1938. Zurich, 1939.

"Architecture et la guerre." *Gazette Dunlop*, no. 232 (May 1940): 10–13.

La maison des hommes. Paris, 1941. With François de Pierrefeu.

Sur les 4 routes. Paris, 1941.

"Il faut réconsiderer l'hexagone français." In *Architecture et urbanisme*. Ed. Le Corbusier, Charles Trochu, Dr. Pierre Winter, and Paul Boulard. Paris, 1942. Pp. 5–28.

Les constructions "murondins." Paris, 1942.

Les trois établissements humains. Boulogne-Seine, 1944.

"Y-a-t-il une crise de l'art français?" In *La crise français*. Paris, 1945. Pp. 185–192.

"Visions et projets." *Pages françaises*, no. 11 (Mar. 1946): 120–124.

Manière de penser l'urbanisme. Paris, 1946.

Oeuvre complète 1938–1946. Zurich, 1946.

New World of Space. New York, 1948.

"Théâtre spontané." *La revue théâtrale* 5, no. 12 (Spring 1950): 17–22.

"L'appel de Stockholm." *L'observateur* (July 6, 1950): 23–24.

Le modular. Boulogne-Seine, 1950.

Poésie sur Alger. Paris, 1950.

Oeuvre complète 1946–1952. Zurich, 1953.

Modular 2. Paris, 1954.

"L'urbanisme est une clef." In *Forces vives*, no. 5–7 (1955).

Oeuvre complète 1952–1957. Zurich, 1957.

Le Corbusier (l'atelier de la recherche patiente). Paris, 1960.

Oeuvre complète 1957–1965. Zurich, 1965.

Mise au point. Paris, 1966.

Voyage d'Orient. Paris, 1966.

Les maternelles vous parlent. Paris, 1968.

Le Corbusier lui-même. Ed. Jean Petit. Geneva, 1970.

SECONDARY SOURCES

Benoît-Lévy, Georges. "A French Garden Hamlet." *Town Planning Review* 7, nos. 3 and 4 (Apr. 1918): 251–252. Describes Le Corbusier's plans for a garden hamlet in Normandy.

Besset, Maurice. *Qui était Le Corbusier?* Geneva, 1968.

Boll, André. *Habitation moderne et urbanisme.* Paris, 1942.

Bordachar, B. "Le Corbusier a Bétharram, Témoignage d'un prêtre qui fut son ami," *Les rameaux de Notre Dame* (Bétharram B.-P.), no. 67 (Aug.-Nov. 1965): 156–178; no. 68 (Feb. 1966): 246–270; no. 69 (May 1966): 314–348.

Boudon, Philippe. *Pessac de Le Corbusier.* Paris, 1969.

Choay, Françoise. *Le Corbusier.* New York, 1960.

Daria, Sophie. *Le Corbusier: sociologue de l'urbanisme.* Paris, 1964.

Du Moulin de Labarthète, Henry. *Le temps des illusions.* Geneva, 1946.

Evenson, Norma. *Chandigarh.* Berkeley, Calif., 1966.

———. *Le Corbusier: The Machine and the Grand Design.* New York, 1969.

Frampton, Kenneth. "The City of Dialectic." *Architectural Design* 39 (Oct. 1969): 541–546.

Francastel, Pierre. *Art et technique.* Paris, 1956.

Gauthier, Maximilien. *Le Corbusier—ou l'architecture au service de l'homme.* Paris, 1944.

Gropius, Walter. "Gropius on Le Corbusier." *Connection* (Winter 1966): 19–21.

Jencks, Charles. *Le Corbusier and the Tragic View of Architecture.* London, 1973.

Kuisel, Richard F. *Ernest Mercier; French Technocrat.* Berkeley, Calif., 1967.

Lagardelle, Hubert. "Au delà de la démocratie." *Plans* 1, no. 3 (Mar. 1931): 15–23.

Lamour, Philippe. *Entretiens sous la Tour Eiffel.* Paris, 1929.

Maier, Charles S. "Between Taylorism and Technocracy: European Ideologies and the Vision of Industrial Productivity in the 1920s." *Journal of Contemporary History* 5 (1970): 27–61.

Mumford, Lewis. "Yesterday's City of Tomorrow." *Architectural Record* 132, no. 5. (Nov. 1962): 139–144.

Bibliography

————. "Architecture as a Home for Man." *Architectural Record* 143, no. 2 (Feb. 1968): 113–116.

Ozenfant, Amédée. *Mémoires*. Paris, 1968.

Papadaki, Stamo, ed. *Le Corbusier: Architect, Painter, Writer*. New York, 1948.

Paxton, Robert O. *Vichy France: Old Guard and New Order, 1940–1944*. New York, 1972.

Prouvé, Madeleine. *Victor Prouvé*. Paris, 1958.

Prouvé, Victor. *L'art et l'industrie*. Nancy, 1907.

Raymond, Marie-Geneviève. *La politique pavillonnaire*. Paris, 1966.

Le Redressement francais: organisation et réformes. Paris, 1927.

Serenyi, Peter. "Le Corbusier, Fourier, and the Monastery at Ema." *Art Bulletin* 49, no. 4 (Dec. 1967): 277–286.

————, ed. *Le Corbusier in Perspective*. Englewood Cliffs, N.J., 1975.

Sert, José Luis. "Sert on Le Corbusier." *Connection* (Winter 1966): 23–25.

Taylor, Brian Brace. *Le Corbusier at Pessac*. Cambridge, Mass., 1972.

Turner, Paul Venable. "The Education of Le Corbusier." Ph.D. dissertation, Harvard University, 1971.

————. "The Beginnings of Le Corbusier's Education, 1902–07." *Art Bulletin* 53, no. 4 (June 1971): 214–224.

Vidler, Anthony. "The Idea of Unity and Le Corbusier's Urban Form." *Architects' Year Book* 15 (1968): 225–237.

Von Moos, Stanislaus. *Le Corbusier: Elemente einer Synthese*. Frauenfeld, 1968.

————. "Anatomie d'une ville, Chandigarh ville morte?" *L'architecture d'aujourd'hui*, no. 146 (1969): 54–61.

Walden, Russell, ed. *The Open Hand: Essays on Le Corbusier*. Cambridge, Mass., 1977.

Weber, Eugen. *Action Française*. Stanford, Calif., 1962.

Winter, Pierre. "La ville moderne." *Le nouveau siècle* (May 16, 1926): 4.

Conclusion

Burchell, Robert W., and David Listokin, eds. *Future Land Use: Energy, Environmental and Legal Constraints*. New Brunswick, N.J., 1975. An important collection of articles, mostly pessimistic, about the future of the American environment.

Goldberger, Paul. "Radical Planners Now Mainstream." *New York Times* (June 13, 1976): 21. The "radicals" referred to in the title are Jane Jacobs and her supporters.

Goodman, Robert. *After the Planners.* New York, 1971. An outspoken critique of professional planners.

Jacobs, Jane. *The Death and Life of Great American Cities.* New York, 1961.

———. *The Economy of Cities.* New York, 1969.

Sennett, Richard. *The Uses of Disorder: Personal Identity and City Life.* New York, 1970.

INDEX